GEORGE V's
CHILDREN

ALSO BY JOHN VAN DER KISTE

GEORGE V's
CHILDREN

JOHN VAN DER KISTE

The
History
Press

First published in 1991
This edition first published in 2003 by Sutton Publishing Limited

Reprinted in 2013, 2019

The History Press
97 St George's Place
Cheltenham, Gloucestershire, GL50 3QB
www.thehistorypress.co.uk

British Library Cataloguing in Publication Data
A catalogue record for this book is available from the British Library

ISBN 978 0 7509 3468 8

Typeset in 10/12pt Photina.
Typesetting and origination by
Sutton Publishing Limited.
Printed and bound by
TJ International Ltd, Padstow, Cornwall

Contents

Foreword

Writing a biography of King George V's children as a family presents problems not encountered in so doing with the lives of the children of his father and grandmother. Even more than half a century after the crisis precipitated by the abdication of King Edward VIII, thereafter Duke of Windsor, feelings still run high in the royal family. It is therefore too early for definitive judgements about an issue which divided family and country, and which still provokes forceful argument to this day. As Hugo Vickers so rightly noted in a review of a rather sensational account of the Duke's tenure as Governor of the Bahamas during the Second World War, Michael Pye's *The King over the Water*, the Duke and Duchess of Windsor 'seem never to be treated fairly. They inspire either undue loyalty or violent abuse.'[1]

Of the ever-increasing titles about the Duke and Duchess which have poured off the printing presses since the former's death in 1972, most have been criticized on the grounds of varying degrees of sycophancy or unreasoned hostility towards their subject. Not until 1990, with the publication of Philip Ziegler's masterly *King Edward VIII: the official biography*, written with full access to the Royal Archives, Windsor, were readers presented with a fully balanced portrait. Despite the restricted sources available to her at the time, Frances Donaldson's Edward VIII, published in 1974, was a perceptive and admirably balanced account, although the King's most ardent defenders felt its tone to be uniformly unfavourable and unflattering.

Of those titles that appeared in the interim, it is best left to the reader to judge on their respective validity – or lack of it. Perhaps the only really essential ones are Michael Thornton's exhaustively-researched and penetrating *Royal feud: The Queen Mother and the Duchess of Windsor* (1985), which is in effect partly a biography of the Duke, notwithstanding the emphasis in the sub-title; J. Bryan III and Charles V. Murphy's *The Windsor story* (1979); and Michael Bloch's works, notably *The Duke of Windsor's war* (1986), and *The secret file of the Duke of Windsor* (1988), both written very much from the Duke and Duchess's view, with full access to their files in Paris.

The Duke published his memoirs, *A King's Story*, in 1951. They are discussed in Chapter 11 of the present work.

King George VI has likewise attracted several biographers. The 800-page official life by Sir John W. Wheeler-Bennett, published in 1958, made extensive use of his diaries and letters, but was understandably circumspect on the abdication. That the Duke of Windsor was sent a proof copy of the book, but found nothing in the text to which he could object, says much about the author's caution. Sarah Bradford's biography, thirty-one years later, for which she had access to archive sources not available to writers of other interim studies (among them Denis Judd, Christopher Warwick, and Patrick Howarth), was less constrained in her retelling of the episode, and her portrait of the Duke of Windsor is not a flattering one.

Even if the abdication had not been such a traumatic episode in the history of the British monarchy, it would have been surprising if the biographies of both Kings, the two eldest children of King George V and Queen Mary, had not heavily outnumbered those of their younger brothers and sisters. For the three who lived to maturity, the literature can almost be counted on the fingers of one hand. Princess Mary, Countess of Harewood and Princess Royal, has yet to find a biographer, apart from M.C. Carey, who published his *Princess Mary* the same year as she was married. She is, however, also represented by brief chapters in two collected biographies of all the Princesses Royal, by Geoffrey Wakeford and Helen Cathcart respectively.

Prince Henry, Duke of Gloucester, is the subject of what reviewer Richard Usborne called 'a dutiful life history of a dutiful English royal prince whose widow and son are still alive',[2] by Noble Frankland, published in 1980. The Duchess published her memoirs in 1983. To quote another review, it is 'a gentle, unpretentious volume that is delightful to read but gives away no secrets.'

To the youngest son of King George V to reach maturity, George, Duke of Kent, more than a whiff of scandal was attached during his bachelor days, and Christopher Warwick's *George and Marina* (1988), and Audrey Whiting's *The Kents* (1985) are both the soul of discretion on the subject of a Prince whose children are still only in middle age.

Not for many years, therefore, will all papers be made available to the biographer and reader who will be content with nothing less than a total warts-and-all portrait of the family. Meanwhile, I hope this will serve as a suitably objective account of the lives of two Kings, of whom one was arguably the most controversial ever to occupy the British throne and the other destined to be head of state in what has been called the country's finest and her darkest hours, their brothers, and their sister. Anecdotes abound on the foibles, fancies and follies of this family of six, some of which may be discredited in time, others not. In attempting to distinguish between fact and fantasy, hagiography and demonology, I hope this account treads a fine line between 'undue loyalty and violent abuse'.

I am grateful to the Hon. David Astor for permission to quote material from the correspondence between his mother, Lady Astor, MP, and members of the royal family, which is published here for the first time, and to the staff, Reading University, Department of Archives and Manuscripts, for access.

I am indebted to the following copyright holders for permission to quote from published works: William Collins Ltd (*King Edward VIII*, by Philip Ziegler); Macmillan & Co. (*King George VI*, by John W. Wheeler-Bennett); and George Weidenfeld & Nicolson (*Prince Henry, Duke of Gloucester*, by Noble Frankland).

My thanks for constant help, encouragement and advice

during the writing of this book are due to my parents, Wing Commander Guy and Nancy Van der Kiste; Theo Aronson; Steven Jackson, of the Commemorative Collectors Society; Joyce Kilvington; Shirley Stapley, and John Wimbles.

John Van der Kiste
2003

Prologue

Three British sovereigns married in England during the reign of Queen Victoria. The Queen's own wedding, to a prince from Saxe-Coburg Gotha who was desperately homesick, little-known and not much liked in his adopted country, took place on a cold, wet February morning in 1840. That of their eldest son and heir, Albert Edward, Prince of Wales, in March 1863, was overshadowed by her long mourning for her husband, who had died fifteen months earlier but might have just passed away the previous week, judging by the gloom which still enveloped the court of Windsor. Only her grandson's wedding, on a brilliantly sunny day in July 1893, was free of shadows. At the time, the lady-in-waiting of the bride's mother called it 'the greatest success ever seen or heard of! not a hitch from first to last.'[1]

Prince George Frederick Ernest Albert was born on 3 June 1865 at Marlborough House, the London residence of his parents the Prince and Princess of Wales. He was their second child, an elder brother Prince Albert Victor Christian Edward having entered the world on 8 January 1864.

Throughout childhood the boys, who so differed in character, were devoted to each other. Though seventeen months younger, George was stronger and more high-spirited. Amusing, inquisitive and hot-tempered, from nursery days he showed himself a born leader. Inclined to be shy, he had an easy-going manner, and was naturally neat and well-organized.

Eddy took much more after their mother. He was taller, more diffident, lethargic, and lacked his brother's healthy complexion. His mother's favourite, she treated him with greater sympathy than their father, who was impatient with the boy's apathetic manner – an impatience which became more evident as the boy approached maturity. Eddy had been

1

born two months prematurely, and to some it seemed that he had never really recovered from this unfortunate start in life. Along with his mother's charm of manner, he had also inherited her premature deafness, or what she would call her 'beastly ears', and an apparent inability to learn anything in the schoolroom. A melancholy, wistful-looking child, he always smiled or laughed with something of the delicacy of his mother's manner, rather than the heartiness of his father or brother. George, others considered, was much more like his father at a similar age.

In 1877, both princes entered the Royal Navy. It had always been the intention that Prince George should enter the service and Eddy the army. But Eddy was strangely dependent on his brother. Their tutor, John Dalton, advised that the stimulus of Prince George's company was vital to induce the strangely lethargic Albert Victor to work at all. They entered as naval cadets on board HMS *Britannia* at Dartmouth for a period of training which lasted two years. In 1879 they joined HMS *Bacchante* which, with a few interruptions, was to be their home for the next three years as they cruised around the world.

On their return in 1882, it was apparent that life on board ship had helped them to mature a little, but by comparison with their public school contemporaries, they were still woefully ill-educated. George had largely made up for this deficiency by a steady application in the practical aspects of seamanship and navigation, but his spelling and grammar were very poor. Meanwhile the apparently ineducable Eddy was still as listless and vacant in conversation as with the written word. Worse, he was tending to drink heavily, and to enjoy disappearing, while in port, to frequent the underworld with the wilder element of his fellow midshipmen. They were despatched to Lausanne, Switzerland, for six months to learn French, but with little success.

None the less George remained in the navy, where he continued to make good progress. Eddy was enrolled as a student at Trinity College, but after rumours of his immoral behaviour there, he was taken away from Cambridge and joined the army. Gazetted as Lieutenant in the 10th Hussars, he was no better as a soldier. He never mastered the theory and practice of arms, or elementary drill movements on the parade ground. In turn he thought the commanding officers were lunatics, and he resented the rigours of military discipline.

By the time he reached the age of twenty-one in January 1885, Prince Albert Victor did not give the impression of a promising King in the making. Not all the prince's shortcomings could be blamed on his upbringing, his mother's possessiveness, and the lax moral example of his father. His deafness had been apparent since infancy, but as the Princess of Wales was so sensitive about this hereditary handicap, nobody ever broached the subject with her, and so nothing was done to treat him for a physical condition which might have been cured or alleviated if attended to in time. Yet her realization that he suffered from 'beastly ears' as much as she did increased the protectiveness she felt towards her firstborn. So did his slowness, inability to learn, and evident lack of character, all negative qualities which irritated his father. He had a piercing, high-pitched voice which others found unpleasant, and an easy-going nature which bordered on imbecility. It was possible that he also suffered from porphyria, an ailment in which a chemical imbalance in the blood causes symptoms such as bulging eyes and manic depression, and which had been mistakenly diagnosed as insanity in the case of his great-great-grandfather King George III.

Whatever Eddy's problems, the elder generation were impatient for him to settle down. It was rumoured that he was involved in the 'Jack the Ripper' murders in Whitechapel in 1888, and in a homosexual brothel in Cleveland Street which was raided the following year. Whatever the truth, or lack of it, in these matters, it was clear that his dissipated lifestyle was undermining his never very strong constitution. By the time Queen Victoria created him Duke of Clarence and Avondale in May 1890, he was becoming a major worry to the senior royal family.

Efforts were made to interest him in two of his German

cousins with regard to marriage, but Princess Alix of Hesse turned him down, and he never showed any enthusiasm for Princess Margaret of Prussia. Instead he perversely fell in love with such ineligible ladies as Princess Helene d'Orleans, daughter of the pretender to the French throne, and with Lady Sibyl St Clair Erskine. Helene was a Roman Catholic, and the question of her marriage raised grave constitutional implications; and Lady Sibyl was already on the point of engagement to another suitor.

By summer 1891, the 'Eddy problem' could not be deferred any longer. Nothing would be gained by keeping him in the army. The three alternatives chosen by the family were either a tour of the more remote British colonies; a series of visits to different European countries, where it was hoped he would gain a sound knowledge of continental languages and political personalities of the day; or an arranged marriage with some suitable princess who would be the making of him.

It was convenient that such a princess was available.

Princess Victoria Mary of Teck, known in the family as May, was the eldest child of the Duke and Duchess of Teck. She was already closely related; the Duchess of Teck was a younger sister of Queen Victoria's cousin, the Duke of Cambridge. Born on 26 May 1867, May had three younger brothers. The family had been brought up at White Lodge, Richmond, until heavy debts necessitated a temporary move to Florence, where they could live more economically. Being close counterparts of the Prince of Wales's children, they had been playmates and companions from childhood.

May was intelligent, well-educated, efficiently-minded and attractive, with a strong sense of duty. Although shy and lacking in self-confidence, she had matured quickly, as if to compensate for the shorcomings of her kind-hearted but grossly extravagant mother and her ailing father, whose mental state had been disturbed by a mild stroke in middle age. In 1891 she and her parents were invited to stay at Sandringham for six days, and also spent some time with the Prince of Wales's eldest daughter and her husband, the

Duke and Duchess of Fife. Although the plans being made were still a closely-guarded secret, May suspected from her own parents' suppressed excitement what was afoot. Later that year, she and her brothers were commanded to visit Her Majesty at Balmoral, on what was obviously in the nature of an inspection by the Queen as to the suitability of Princess May to marry the young heir presumptive.

It was taken for granted that Eddy would do as he was told. Among his many faults, disobedience was mercifully not one of them. He would shortly be invited as one of the guests to Luton Hoo, the Bedfordshire home of the Danish minister and his family. Princess May would also be there. He must show her particular attention and be on his best behaviour at all times, but should wait until the new year before proposing. She and her family would be invited to Sandringham for his twenty-eighth birthday celebrations, and he was to ask for her hand there and then – and not before. Eddy solemnly agreed, but his enthusiasm ran away with him and he proposed during his stay at Luton Hoo.

Needless to say, May knew that he was going to propose, and there had never been any question in her mind of turning him down. She had been brought up to venerate the throne, and knew that with the right guidance from her future parents-in-law and from Queen Victoria, she would be prepared perfectly well for the destiny that such a marriage would bring her. Moreover, she had felt keenly the humiliation of being forced to live abroad, almost in exile, because of her mother's spendthrift ways. That 'poor May', the temporary exile, should become May the future Queen Consort, was a reversal of fortune which seemed almost too good to be true.

Childhood memories of the simple-minded cousin who had teased and bullied her counted for little. She had the example of her mother before her in making the most out of marriage to a weak-willed and unstable husband. How much she knew of Eddy's vices, and the scandals surrounding his private life, is open to question. Their parents had tried to keep as much as possible from her ears, and although she was intelligent, she had led a sheltered life. It can therefore be assumed that she had little idea of what she was letting herself in for, that evening of 3 December 1891, when Prince Albert Victor, Duke of Clarence, took her by the hand from a crowded ballroom and into an adjoining boudoir which had been carefully left deserted for them.

After a cheerful Christmas, May and her parents joined the party at Sandringham in the first week of January. However the gathering was subdued, for an epidemic of influenza was taking its toll. Eddy's sister Princess Victoria and two of the equerries had taken to their beds with the virus, and several of the others were suffering from heavy colds. Eddy had caught a chill after attending a funeral, and on 8 January, his birthday, he came downstairs in a dressing gown to receive his presents. But he felt so wretched that he was ordered straight back to bed. The following day, he developed inflammation of the lungs, and despite the attention of one doctor after another and the devoted nursing of his distraught mother, nothing could be done to save him.

Eddy had never been particularly robust, and influenza dealt the final blow to a frame already weakened by drink, cigarettes, gout and probably venereal disease as well. On the morning of 14 January, he died.

Still weak after a serious attack of typhoid two months earlier, Prince George was as stunned as his parents by his brother's death. Not only had he been devoted to him, but now he was second in line to the throne which he had never expected to inherit. He was well aware of his shortcomings in temperament and education; a slight lisp and knock-knees had further undermined his self-confidence. It was recognized that changes had to be made to prepare him for the future. Accordingly he was given his own accommodation, a suite of apartments in St James's Palace, and the 'Bachelors Cottage' in the grounds of Sandringham. In May 1892 he was created Duke of York, Earl of Inverness and Baron Killarney.

Most important of all, earnest consideration was given to the weighty matter of finding a Duchess of York. The succession had to be safeguarded; it was clear that the Prince of Wales's children did not enjoy the robust health of their uncles and aunts, and twice Prince George had been in danger of premature death – once from shipwreck, and once from typhoid. Next in succession was the eldest of his three sisters, Louise, Duchess of Fife. She was a shy, listless woman of indifferent health and very little character, married to a rich, boorish Scots aristocrat with a pronounced taste for the bottle. The prospect of Queen Louie was not an entertaining one.

Like his brother, Prince George had already twice lost his heart; firstly, to Julie Stonor, orphaned daughter of one of his mother's ladies-in-waiting, but ineligible as she was a Roman Catholic and a commoner; and secondly to his cousin Princess Marie of Edinburgh. Marie's mother, however, born a Russian Grand Duchess, so disliked her English in-laws that she vowed no daughter of hers would marry an English prince. In order to forestall the possibility, she quickly arranged a betrothal between Marie and Crown Prince Ferdinand of Roumania.

Yet those who had already predicted who would be Duchess of York did not have to wait long to be proved right.

As shocked relatives had gathered to Sandringham in mourning, the Duke of Teck embarrassed everyone by wandering around muttering to himself, 'It must be a Tsarevich'. He was alluding to Tsarevich Nicholas, who had died of tuberculosis in 1865 shortly after becoming betrothed to the Princess of Wales's younger sister Dagmar. Nicholas's dying wish had been for her to marry his eldest surviving brother Alexander, which she did the following year. This arranged marriage had proved very happy, and Alexander (now Tsar Alexander III) had defied Romanov tradition by remaining faithful to his wife. Before long, the Duke of Teck's prophetic words were echoed by others. After a respectful interval, why should Princess May, who in the Prince of Wales's words had 'virtually become a widow before she is a wife', not become betrothed to the late fiancé's brother?

A quick engagement between George and May would be an insult to Eddy's memory, at least as far as his parents were concerned, but at length common sense prevailed over sentimental considerations. May had all the attributes needed for an excellent Queen consort-in-waiting, and, the Prince of Wales warned his son, Queen Victoria was 'in a terrible fuss about your marrying.'

In the spring of 1893, George went to stay with the Duke and Duchess of Fife at Sheen Lodge, and May was invited to tea. 'Now, Georgie,' the Duchess suggested brightly after they had eaten, don't you think you ought to take May into the garden to look at the frogs in the pond?' Dutifully he led her into the picturesque gardens, and, away from the inquisitive onlookers, made his proposal to her. She accepted.

They were married on 6 July, in the Chapel Royal, Windsor. By some error of ceremonial planning, Queen Victoria was not the last of the royal family to arrive at the wedding, as protocol and tradition demanded, but the first. Amused rather than annoyed, she enjoyed watching the guests assemble, and smiled to herself as she sensed their mild panic when they realized the mistake. The Duke wore the uniform of a Captian in the Royal Navy, to which rank he had recently been promoted; the bride was dressed in white silk with a train of silver and white brocade.

Their honeymoon was spent rather unimaginatively at York Cottage, Sandringham, which was to be their home for the next seventeen years.

By nature the Duke and Duchess of York were shy, undemonstrative individuals. They found it difficult to express or show what they really felt for each other. Though it was very much an arranged marriage, both partners were to prove well-matched. Yet their mutual reserve distressed them, to the point where they had to apologize between themselves (by letter) during the honeymoon period for being so undemonstrative. 'The more I feel, the less I say, I am so sorry but I can't help it,' May wrote on one occasion, prompting an answer from George that he was eternally grateful that they understood each other so well, making it unnecessary for him to say how much he loved her, 'although I may appear shy and cold.'

Soon, jokes were being cracked in London society about how successful the couple would be in providing the nation with more heirs to the throne. As it was, any fears that may have been entertained on that score were groundless. By Christmas, it was known that the Duchess was expecting a child.

1

'A regiment, not a family'

On the evening of 23 June 1894, at White Lodge, the Duchess of York gave birth to a son.

'At 10.0 a sweet little boy was born,' the Duke noted in his diary. 'Somehow I imagine,' the prince recalled some fifty years later, 'this was the last time my father was ever inspired to apply to me that precise appellation.'[1] Queen Victoria made a special visit to Richmond to see her great-grandson, whom she pronounced 'a very fine strong boy, a pretty child'.

'You rejoice as I do, indeed,' she wrote to the Empress Frederick, 'and as the whole nation does, to the most wonderful degree, at the birth of dear Georgie's boy. It is a great pleasure and satisfaction . . . it is true that it has never happened in this country that there should be three direct heirs as well as the sovereign alive.'[2] The Prince of Wales was host that evening at a ball in the Fishing Temple at Virginia Water, Windsor Great Park. On being told the news, he stopped the orchestra for a moment so he could proudly announce the birth, and propose a toast to the young prince.

The Duke and Duchess of York had wanted to call their first son Edward, in memory of Eddy. They had reckoned without Queen Victoria, who intended his first name to be Albert, after his great-grandfather. As a compromise, Albert became the second name of seven with which he was christened on 16 July – Edward Albert Christian George Andrew Patrick David. Although always known to the public as Prince Edward, *en famille* he would be called David.*

---

* For convenience, he will be referred to as Edward throughout this book, although quotations from family papers referring to him as David will be left as originally written.

Prince Edward of York had entered the world during midsummer and Ascot Week, when society was *en fete*. For the next occupant of the nursery at York House, the omens were less propitious. The second son of the Duke and Duchess of York had the misfortune to be born on 14 December 1895, eighteen months later. It was the double black-edged anniversary of the Prince Consort's death in 1861 and that of Princess Alice, the first of his and Queen Victoria's children to pass away, in 1878. 'Darling May was safely confined of a son at 3.30 this morning both doing well,' the Duke telegraphed in some trepidation to his grandmother. The Prince of Wales had to admit that 'Grandmama was rather distressed', but he himself trusted that the young prince's birth would 'break the spell' of the unlucky date. He advised his son that it would be tactful to invite the Queen to be the baby's godmother, and to call him Albert. 'It is a great pleasure to me that he is to be called Albert, but in fact, he could hardly have been called by any other name,'[3] the Queen commented to her eldest daughter. To the family, he would always be 'Bertie'.

The two elder York children suffered from two handicaps in their earliest years – firstly, undemonstrative and not particularly understanding parents; secondly, a most unsuitable nanny.

As parents, the Duke and Duchess of York were much more strict than their own had been. The Duke was by nature less tolerant and less easy-going than his father, while the Duchess was curiously unmaternal. Her earnest, seriousminded character was at odds with the informal and carefree upbringing meted out by her mother and mother-in-law, and she was determined that her own children would be treated differently. Yet, according to some, the future King George V's reputation for paternal strictness verging on bullying has been exaggerated over the years. It was never denied that the boys enjoyed many a rough-and-tumble, riotous games of golf with scant regard for the rules, and boisterous cycle rides around the Sandringham estate. A few years later, they were not too afraid of their father to play occasional practical jokes on him.

Perhaps the fairest verdict on the Duke and Duchess

as parents was that of the latter's lady-in-waiting Mabell, Countess of Airlie. She praised them for conscientious devotion to their children's upbringing, but thought that neither had any understanding of a child's mind. For George, who lacked imagination, it was never too soon to try and inculcate the highest standards of behaviour and principle in them. Moreover, he was given to 'chaffing' them, but his bark was worse than his bite. 'Where have you been?' he would ask his sons. 'Cutting up the paths with your bicycles, I suppose.' Such rebukes probably sounded less severe in everyday speech than the written word suggests.

Much has been made of King George V's comments that he was always frightened of his father, and that it was only right that his sons should be frightened of him. His remarks have been handed down from speaker to speaker, and doubtless distorted in the retelling. None the less the King was never afraid of his father, whose outbursts of rage in front of courtiers could be terrifying, but who was never anything less than a devoted father, particularly to his second son. In their letters, King Edward frequently admitted that they were more like brothers than father and son.[4]

All the same, Alexander Hardinge, later a private royal secretary, was less inclined to give him the benefit of the doubt. It was a mystery, he was once moved to remark, why King George, in other respects such a kind man, was 'such a brute to his children'.

In the case of Edward and Albert, problems were compounded by a sadistic and incompetent nurse. She showed a marked preference for the elder of her charges, and in order to demonstrate the superiority of her power over him to that of his parents, she would twist and pinch Edward's arm before bringing him into the drawing room each evening just before he said goodnight to his parents. He bawled and screamed at them to much that they would impatiently order her to take him away at once.

Apparently she never liked Bertie. In her rather warped fashion, she seemed to resent the arrival of another infant who might compete with his elder brother for everyone else's attention. She neglected him in the nursery, and gave him his bottle when taking him out each morning and afternoon in his pram, an unsprung vehicle which made for extremely rough rides around the paths of Sandringham. When he was ready to begin eating soft foodstuffs, she would snatch the bowl away from him at meals, telling the shocked under-nurse Charlotte ('Lalla') Bill, that he had had quite enough for one day. Such treatment resulted in chronic stomach trouble, and perhaps laid the foundations for the gastric complaint which afflicted him throughout life.

At length, Miss Bill could stand this mentally unbalanced woman's treatment of her infant charges no longer. Although fearful that if she spoke out, the senior nurse would vent her anger on the children, especially Albert, Miss Bill told the housekeeper all. On investigation, it was established that the half-crazed woman had not had a day off for three years, and that she was unable to have children herself and had been deserted by her husband, and in short was suffering from frustrated and warped maternal instincts. However, she had trained as a children's nursemaid before marriage, and as a result of working for the Duke and Duchess of Newcastle, she obtained a good reference which led to her being employed in the York nursery. When the truth came out, early in 1897, she was dismissed at once and her place taken by the more understanding Miss Bill, who sought to alleviate the mental damage already inflicted on the two small boys.

On 25 April 1897 May gave birth to her third child and only daughter. It was suggested by her grandfather and great-grandmother that she might be named 'Diamond', as she was born in the latter's Diamond Jubilee year, but wiser counsels prevailed. The parents pointed out tactfully that in later life she would not relish carrying the year of her birth forever. Instead she was named Victoria Alexandra Alice Mary, and known in the family as Mary, to distinguish her from her mother.

Now that Miss Bill presided over the nursery, peace and

contentment reigned for a while. The Duchess of York was allowed a brief respite from childbearing, and her three elder children, born within a space of less than three years, formed a tightly-knit group. Edward was a high-spirited child, and as the eldest was a natural leader in nursery games. Mary was something of a tomboy, and as the only girl she was much petted and spoilt. In particular her disciplinarian father treated her more leniently than the others, although she was easily embarrassed and his teasing sometimes made her blush to a deep shade of red.

As the middle child, Albert was at a disadvantage. By nature shy, nervous and affectionate, easily frightened and more prone to tears than the others, he compared unfavourably with both. It was significant that Queen Victoria noted in her journal, after a visit from 'the dear little York children' in May 1898, that 'David is a delightful child, so intelligent, nice and friendly. The baby is a sweet pretty little thing.'[5] There was no reference to Albert.

On 31 March 1900 May gave birth to a third son, christened Henry. 'I think I have done my duty & may now *stop*,' she wrote to her Aunt Augusta, 'as having babies is highly distasteful to me tho' when once they are there they are very nice! The children are so pleased with the baby who they think flew in at my window & had to have hs wings cut off!'[6] This explanation of the baby's arrival at York House came from the Duke, in response to what he called 'some very funny questions'[7] from Prince Edward. The six-year-old boy's sleep was disturbed for weeks afterwards, he later claimed, by the nightmare vision of his baby brother's bleeding wings.

At the time Britain was embroiled in the second Boer war, and Lord Roberts and the German Emperor William were invited to act as the baby's godparents. They were appropriate choices, for this prince would be the only one to pursue a military career.

He was also the last of the family whom his great-grandmother was to see. Among the last photographs taken of the ageing Queen is one showing her on the lawn outside Osborne House that summer, apparently holding Prince Henry on her lap, while the three others stand or sit beside her. By this time, she was so frail and so afraid of dropping her baby great-grandson that Miss Bill concealed herself behind the chair and supported her arm until the photographer's exposure was completed.

When they were small, the Duke of York saw little of his children. Most of his indoor leisure time was spent reading *The Times*, writing up his game book, looking after his guns, or working on his stamp collection in the library, a forbidding room furnished with a large desk and well-worn leather sofa, its most conspicuous item being a closet with a glass door containing his prized shotguns.

A conventional Victorian father, the Duke considered his children primarily his wife's responsibility. When at home the Duchess used to rest in her boudoir before dinner, and she set an hour of this time aside for her family. At 6.30 p.m. each evening they were brought in from the nursery or schoolroom, and as they sat on wooden chairs beside her on the sofa, she would read and talk to them. The years she had spent abroad as a young woman, her eldest son recalled, had 'mellowed her outlook; and reading and observation had equipped her with a prodigious knowledge of Royal history.'[8] Members of the household of those days would paint a cosy picture of the atmosphere at York Cottage, the children gathered round a lamp-lit table playing some educational card game, usually one with the counties of England.

The Duchess was inclined to treat them as young adults. When they behaved well, she accepted it as quite normal. When they did not, she was surprised. With some astonishment, she noted on one occasion that Edward was 'jumpy' yesterday morning, however he got quieter after being out, what a curious child he is.'[9] It seems far more curious in retrospect that she should have been startled at the restless energy of a child not yet aged two, only fidgeting because he wanted to go outside and play in the fresh air. Just as odd was another comment she made on him at the same age; one evening at tea he was in 'a charming frame of mind'. She really believed, she wrote, 'he begins to like me at last, he is most civil to me.'[10]

The children were much happier when at home with her, and their father was not present. When they were small, his teasing or 'chaffing' questions were a regular cause of embarrassment. Although their mother always backed him up where parental discipline was concerned, she never shrank from taking their side whenever she thought he was being too harsh with them. Though not in awe of her husband, she accepted the prevailing nineteenth-century view that the father was head of the family; his word was therefore law. All the same, when he overstepped the bounds beyond fairness, she did not hesitate to speak out.

The boys were terrified in the presence of Queen Victoria, though whether it was she who struck fear into their hearts, or the formidable Indian servants who waited upon her, nobody knew. But when left to sit with her they would burst into tears, much to her distress and that of their parents. Crossly she would ask the Duke and Duchess of York 'what she had done wrong now'.

In January 1901 Queen Victoria died and King Edward VII ascended the throne. Among the first decisions made concerning his family was one regarding a tour to be made of the British Empire by the Duke and Duchess of York. Shortly before the late Queen's last illness, plans were made for them to visit Australia to open the first parliament of the new federation. The King was reluctant to see them go, being unwilling to have the life of his only surviving son 'unnecessarily endangered for any political purpose', but his ministers insisted. The heir and his wife therefore set sail in March from Portsmouth for Australia.

During their eight-month absence, the children were at last allowed a prolonged respite from their parents' strict upbringing. King Edward and Queen Alexandra had spoiled their own children when they were small, and were even more indulgent with what the Queen called 'the Georgiepets'. The

King eagerly allowed them to race pats of butter down the seams of his trousers, taking bets on whose would win. One day at lunch, he persistently told Edward not to interrupt him while he was talking. Having finished what he wanted to say, he turned to the boy to ask what he wanted. Triumphantly, the lad told Grandpapa that there had been a slug on his lettuce. Now it was too late to warn him as he had eaten it.

Though Edward's cheerful habit of answering back and his precocious charm made him a favourite, the King went out of his way to pay attention and write short, grandfatherly letters to Albert. As a second child himself who had been overshadowed at the same age by a lively, intelligent elder sister, he must have appreciated that his second grandson found it difficult to compete with the winning ways of his brother, and found the inevitable comparisons frustrating.

Lessons were cheerfully disregarded. Many an afternoon the King and Queen were too engrossed in turning up at York House, to play with the children or read them the latest letter from Mama and Papa, to allow their unfortunate governess Mlle Bricka to interfere. She was dismissed with a wave of the regal hand, and on one family visit to Sandringham she was left behind fuming, in London, 'lest she should spoil the fun'. An angry letter of protest was dispatched overseas to the Duchess of York, who replied in tones of similar annoyance to Queen Alexandra. Needless to say, May could have spared herself the effort, for all the effect it had.

On 1 November, the Duke and Duchess returned, landing at Portsmouth. With a twinkle in his eye, King Edward had told the youngsters that their parents would return with black skins after their exposure to the tropical heat, and they were relieved to see Mama and Papa tanned but still recognizable.

It was a relatively undisciplined, cheerful group of children who greeted their parents on their return home. Four-year-old Mary, the apple of their eye, could be forgiven, and Harry, not yet two, was likewise considered too young to be ready for anything in the way of 'character moulding'. However Edward and Albert, it was decided, had reached an age when they could no longer be controlled by feminine supervision. Their days in the nursery under the indulgent eye of Miss Bill were almost over.

On New Year's Day, 1902, they were told that they would now be in the care of Frederick Finch, formerly nursery footman. He was to be a kind of male nursemaid, who heard their prayers every morning and evening, who tucked them up in bed, and when necessary smacked them. Fortunately he was neither a bully nor an excessive disciplinarian; the boys liked and respected him, treated him as a trusted confidant as they became older, and he went on to serve Edward as valet and steward until his retirement in 1935.

The boys' education was an even more pressing matter. For this the Prince of Wales* chose Henry Hansell, a former Eton schoolmaster and lately tutor to Prince Arthur of Connaught. Hansell, who in Prince Edward's words 'combined a mild scholarship with a muscular Christianity, accentuated by tweeds and an ever-present pipe'[11] appealed particularly to the Prince of Wales as he was the son of a Norfolk country gentleman, and a keen yachtsman. A bachelor, he was considered something of a bore by his contemporaries, but he had the sound conviction that boys should grow up in an environment with others of their age. When his suggestion that the princes should go to preparatory school was vetoed, he attempted to create a schoolroom atmosphere in one room at York Cottage. A classroom was fitted with two standard desks, a blackboard and bookshelves. Here, from 7.30 to 8.15 a.m., the boys would do their preparation before breakfast, and from 9.00 to 1.00 p.m. and between tea and supper they attended to their lessons. Sometimes informal and immature football matches would be organized by Hansell, the princes joining in with boys from the village school. It was an artificial atmosphere far removed from the ideal school conditions which he tried to create, but it is difficult to see what alternative he had.

---

* The Duke and Duchess of York were created Prince and Princess of Wales on 9 November, the King's sixtieth birthday.

Hansell had no sense of humour, and took his duties very seriously. The reports which he wrote on his charges for the parents were almost as ponderous as, albeit less verbose than, Baron Stockmar's pedantic comments half a century earlier on the reluctant pupil now reigning as King Edward VII. Unfavourable reports, on being read by the Prince of Wales, would lead to a summons for Prince Edward or Prince Albert for a dressing down. Nothing struck so much fear into their hearts as the ominous verbal message from Hansell that 'Your father wishes to see you in the library.'

Around the age of seven Albert developed the stammer which, like chronic stomach disorders, was to plague him throughout his life. It was the result of chiding and repression, and being naturally left-handed but forced to use the right. Being slower and by nature less articulate than his brother, and more sensitive, he suffered the more from his father's regular admonitions. Less able to answer for himself, he found himself increasingly cut off not only from his parents, but also from his brother and sister.

Even though they were often unhappy in the schoolroom, it would be an overstatement to suggest that the young princes had a miserable childhood. There were relaxed evenings at York Cottage and at Marlborough House, given to the Prince of Wales as a London residence when the King and Queen moved into Buckingham Palace. Of an evening their mother would sit at the piano and lead them in singing nursery rhymes and childrens' songs. In the country they learned to ride, and in London Mr Hansell took them around the sights of the city, including the zoo, racing at White City, and cricket at Lord's.

In June 1902 they had their first taste of royal pageantry, watching preparations for their grandfather's Coronation at Westminster Abbey. They shared in the nation's disappointment and general anxiety, when the ceremony was postponed due to the King's sudden appendicitis, and in the excitement on 9 August when a slimmer, impatient but otherwise more relaxed King Ewdard VII was crowned. Before leaving Buckingham Palace for the Abbey that morning, the monarch greeted his grandchildren, gazing at him in his robes with awe. 'Good morning children, am I not a funny-looking old man?' From the royal box in the Abbey, dressed in their Balmoral-costume, they watched under the supervision of Hansell and Finch.

Of all their childhood haunts, summer holidays in Scotland were those most eagerly anticipated by the children. At Abergeldie, near Balmoral, they cast off all restraint. There were no lessons in the schoolroom, but instead the joys of exploring rugged scenery around Deeside, and the rural pursuits of salmon fishing, grouse shooting and deer stalking. They were thrilled to be told that the castle tower was haunted by the ghost of a woman who had been burned as a witch in medieval times, and they revelled in cycle rides around the hills while Finch ran after them, shouting warnings which could hardly be heard. In particular Albert took to the Highland atmosphere so beloved by his great-grandmother, and he was the only one of the Prince of Wales's children to retain an abiding affection for Balmoral to the end of his days.

By the time of the Coronation, the Princess of Wales was pregnant again. Christmas was spent quietly at Sandringham, with a new infant in the cradle – a fourth son, named George after his father, born on 20 December. 'I shall soon have a regiment, not a family,' the latter remarked. Though his use of the phrase was meant as a joke, perhaps he betrayed more than he meant to in referring to his children as 'a regiment', as if they were not so much a family group, more a crowd of little soldiers to be kept firmly in order.

The youngest child, a fifth son, was born on 12 July 1905. It was ironic that the sixth and last child of Queen Alexandra had also been a boy named John, who lived for only twenty-four hours. The sixth and last baby of the next Prince of Wales, another Prince John, was likewise never to reach maturity.

He was an affectionate and mischievous little boy, nicknamed 'The Imp' as he was always getting up to pranks, such as putting glue on door handles and pins on chairs. Once he got hold of his sister Mary's paintbox, made himslef up to look like a Red Indian and rushed whooping into the dining room where his parents were holding a dinner party. Another time when he saw his father return from stalking and watched him bend over Mary to greet her affectionately, he remarked loudly, 'She kissed Papa, *ugly* old man.'[12] When his mother told him one morning that she thought he told her he had promised to be good during Lent, he replied with a grin, 'and so I did, mother – but you never told me when I promised that Lent was going to be so long.'[13]

Apart from David, the rest of the children suffered from another handicap, knock-knees. Albert was the worst afflicted. When he was eight Sir Francis Laking, the Prince of Wales's physician-in-ordinary, devised splints to straighten the boy's legs. For a while he had to wear them part of the day and night, and though they were painful he seemed to accept them as a necessary evil. With dogged determination he wrote to his mother in February 1904 that he was sitting in an armchair, with his legs in the new splints; 'I have got an invalid table, which is splendid for reading but rather awkward for writing at present. I expect I shall get used to it.'[14] At first Mr Hanell found that in the schoolroom the splints caused his pupil such agony that concentration was severely impaired, but at length they proved so successful that Laking advised they need only be worn at night.

When Princess Mary was five years old, Miss Bill was put in charge of Prince Henry. Else Korsukawitz, a plump, good-tempered, cheerful German, was chosen to look after her, and Mlle José Dussau was appointed her tutor. According to Edward, Mademoiselle had 'a sharp and agile tongue', and was not above reporting on the boys' lapses of behaviour as well. In her eyes petty misdemeanours were crimes, duly reported in detail to their parents. Those dreaded summons to the library became more frequent.

There was nothing of the rebel about Mary, who accepted discipline and relished conformity. The threat to her brothers of

'I'll tell Mama', though rarely carried out, acted as a powerful deterrent. She inherited a passion for riding, in Hyde Park when in town, in Windsor Great Park when the court was in residence at the castle, but above all in the open countryside around Sandringham.

Mary's history lessons were brought to life by visits to the Tower and Hampton Court, and geography was taught with large-scale models. She also studied French and German, and great emphasis in her case was placed on deportment. A keen botanist, she made and developed a collection of plants and seaweed indigenous to the Sandringham area. Enthusiastic about her lessons, she was the best-educated of the family. 'What a pity it's not Mary,' her eldest brother was once reported to have said when reminded of his destiny; 'she is far cleverer than I am.'[15]

Lunch at 1.00 p.m. was taken with Miss Bill, Finch, and one of the tutors, then sewing and painting for an hour. She became proficient with the needle, taking great delight in making clothes at first for her dolls, and later for her mother's various charitable guilds. Following this were outdoor activities – usually riding on her own, or cycling with her brothers, and sometimes an improvised game of cricket under the watchful eye of Hansell. She also learnt to enjoy lawn tennis, angling and swimming.

At the age of six, she was given her first donkey, called Ben, on whom she doted. The rest of the family saw that she had the makings of a first-class horsewoman. Albert later remarked that 'My sister was a horse until she came out'; while Edward admiringly commented that 'her yellow curls concealed a fearlessness that commanded our respect.'[16]

As the only girl in the family, she became quite a tomboy, enjoying boys' adventures stories by Ballantyne, Rider Haggard and Robert Louis Stevenson, and sharing in most of her brother' activities. This did not stop her from 'wielding a sweet tyranny over our lives', they noted, with the formidable Mademoiselle ever supporting her.

Herbert Asquith remarked on her 'shy, girlish charm which

leaves one with an impression of nervous pleasure and fatherly respect.'[17] Shy in public, in private she was the least inhibited of them all. Though she held her father in some awe, she found him less intimidating than her brothers did. He was less strict with her, and for her there were no dreaded summons to the library. She grew up very like her mother in personality, and inherited her rather low-pitched voice. Dame Nellie Melba thought she might have developed into a mezzo-soprano of concert standard, but for the restraints imposed on her by royal blood. Her brothers refused to recognize her talents. When she took singing lessons at Frogmore, they lurked beneath the music-room window, making noises imitating the midnight serenades of a lovesick tomcat.

She also became an accomplished pianist, though her father's indulgence did not extend to her regular practice of playing scales within earshot. She therefore had to use the piano at the 'big house', Sandringham, where her increasingly deaf grandmother was not disturbed at all. As a young woman Queen Alexandra had enjoyed music herself, though, and she would have been the last to discourage such talent in her grandchildren.

The Coronation of King Haakon and Queen Maud (the Prince of Wales's youngest sister) of Norway in 1906 gave Princess Mary her first trip abroad, as she accompanied her parents. The Princess of Wales wrote to Aunt Augusta with some amusement of the King's son, Crown Prince Olav; 'he has fallen in love with my Mary who is rather shy & blushes at his advances, she is happy as the day is long at being with us here & we actually took her to the Coronation & she behaved quite beautifully thro' the long service.'[18] 'Little Olav' was not quite three years old at the time.

Yet Mary also suffered in childhood from isolation from others of her own age. For perhaps weeks at a time, she saw no girls at all; the only women with whom she came into contact were her tutors and female members of her staff. Else was her closest friend and personal confidante, and she would talk to her as a sister.

As the two elder boys approached their teens, Edward was becoming too old for such confined educational instruction, and Albert began to resent his elder brother's superiority. In January 1907, Hansell reported how the presence of one acted as 'a sort of "red rag" to the other.'[19] That spring Edward was enrolled as a cadet at the Royal Naval College, Osborne. He was succeeded in the schoolroom by Henry, now aged seven. Albert was grandly appointed head boy, and Hansell reported that he gave 'promise of taking a serious and sensible view of his responsibilities.'

It had been decided that Albert would follow his brother to Osborne. He was poor at mathematics, and solving elementary problems often brought him close to despair. 'You really must give up losing your temper when you make a mistake in a sum,' his father admonished. Through perseverance on the part of the boy and his tutors, he managed to grasp the subject well enough to appear before the examining board in November 1908, and despite his nerves and stammer almost getting the better of him, he was accepted. A month later he took the written examination, and was judged to have done very well in English, history and French. His results in the dreaded mathematics and geography were better than expected, and he had passed 'most creditably'.

Prince Albert, it was noted, was a 'bad starter', but his perseverance stood him in good stead. 'He was one of those who need the spur of actual challenge to evoke their finest effort.'[20]

When Edward and Albert were sent to naval college, they were the first generation of the royal family to be sent to school alone. The Prince of Wales had wanted them to attend naval college rather than public school, as he himself had been to one. It was typical of his lack of imagination that what had been good enough for him was good enough for his boys. The Princess of Wales would certainly not have agreed. She never ceased to bemoan the inferior education of a husband who had not the slightest vestige of artistic appreciation, had a barely rudimentary knowledge of British or European history, and found foreign languages a closed book.

On Edward's arrival, he was faced with numerous difficulties. Not having been to school before, unlike the rest of his peers, he was embarrassed by questions about his parents and home life, and at having to answer 'just Edward' when asked for his name and 'Edward who?' At first he was bullied by the other boys; once his head was thrust though a window, the sash was let down on his neck, and he was left to reflect on the fate of Charles I and the treatment that English people gave to disobedient Kings, until someone heard his cries for help. Another time, a bottle of red ink was poured down his hair and neck and over his shirt, but bravely he washed, changed and accepted his punishment for being late at evening prayers, rather than make it evident to the authorities what had happened. His willingness to take the rough-and-tumble made him popular, and he was nicknamed 'Sardine', a diminutive of W(h)ales.

He was in his last term when Prince Albert was enrolled at the college, and etiquette forbade him to be seen in the company of a new boy, even his own brother. They found a way round this when Edward arranged for them to meet on the far side of a playing field from time to time, so that Bertie could tell him about any particular problems he had and on which he needed friendly brotherly advice.

Albert's problems were similar to those which had been faced by his elder brother. He had never been to school, or sat in a class of more than three; he had led a sheltered family life, albeit one ruled over by a stern disciplinarian of a father; and he was very homesick. Even worse, he was abnormally shy, and had never played a serious game of football or cricket; and his stammer made him an easy target for teasing. With dogged perseverance, reluctant to make a fuss, in his first letter home to his mother he wrote that he had 'quite settled down here now'.[21] Although he took longer to settle down, as his father realized he would, his efforts did not pass unheeded. The college captain said that he showed 'the grit and "never say I'm beaten" spirit which is strong in him – it's a grand trait in anybody's character.'[22]

He tried very hard at games, revealed a sense of fun and mischief, a complete lack of 'side', and was seen as the kind of boy who would never let a friend down. Though shyness made it difficult for him to get to know others well, with the small circle of friends he did make, he was completely at ease, and the dreaded stutter temporarily vanished.

Whenever practicable, the authorities tried to honour the request of the heir to the throne to treat both princes as they would any other boys, though it was not always possible. The end of the summer term 1909 was enlivened by preparations for a state visit of Tsar Nicholas II, who was to arrive at Spithead in the imperial yacht *Standart* on 2 August 1909.

The Russian imperial family's arrival was heralded by a flotilla of twenty-four battleships, sixteen armoured cruisers and forty-eight destroyers. Edward, Albert and Mary were to act as companions for the Grand Duchess and the Tsarevich. While staying with his parents at Barton Manor, Albert caught a cold and subsequently developed whooping-cough. As a result he had to be kept in quarantine until after the imperial guests had departed. The risk of the Tsarevich, a haemophiliac, catching the infection and rupturing a blood vessel from prolonged bouts of coughing was too great, and it was left to Edward to show 'Uncle Nicky' around Osborne, and to Mary to be a playmate to the Grand Duchesses, of whom Tatiana was her exact contemporary in age.

Prince Henry was fortunate to escape the presssures to which his elder brothers were subjected. Not only was there little likelihood of him ever succeeding to the throne, but persistent ill-health in infancy gave him some advantage. He was sickly and undersized, and suffered from knock-knees and weakness in the legs, and perpetual colds. After he took to his bed with influenza in February 1909, his father admonished Hansell for having taken him out earlier that week in the bitter cold at Sandringham. The tutor had to 'remember that he is rather fragile & must be treated differently to his two elder brothers who are more robust.'[23] The weather in Norfolk was particularly cold at that time of year, and, continued the concerned father,

'I fear he is not very strong, & will require a lot of watching.' Henry was also prone to his family's uncontrollable temper, manifested in outbursts of crying one moment and fits of giggling the next. His parents might have found it hard to believe that he would overcome these initial handicaps and grow up to be the tallest of their children in adult life, and also one of only two to live beyond the age of seventy.

Henry was due to follow the same course as his elder brothers, remaining in Hansell's York Cottage schoolroom until the age of twelve or so, and then go to Royal Naval College. However, because of his delicate health, notably an attack of influenza which affected the base of one lung, it was decided that he could not be subjected to the rigours of college. Sir Francis Laking offered his residence at Broadstairs as a suitable place for the young Prince to convalesce. The Prince of Wales's nurse, Sister Edith Ward, was sent there to look after him and to continue his education.

They arrived there in February 1910 and, as part of his education, she ensured that Prince Henry wrote to his parents regularly, and kept a daily diary as a spelling and writing exercise. In its pages he dutifully recorded such activities as the pleasures of the sands, of fossil and shell hunting; the electric tram to Ramsgate, walks on the eastern esplanade and the pier at Margate, and French lessons taken by Mlle de Lisle from Folkestone.

A fortnight after this regime began, the Prince of Wales expressed his gratitude to Sister Edith for speaking to him seriously 'about the sudden fits of crying, for tho' I feel he sometimes cannot help it, yet he ought gently to be cured of this tiresome nervous habit.'[24] The Prince thought that his son's readiness to cry could be attributed to 'nerves', and would naturally disappear 'as he gets stronger'.

Henry's adviser on his fossil hunts was Mr A.J. Richardson, headmaster of the local preparatory school, and a friend of Hansell. Eighteen months earlier, Hansell had been in touch with him with a view to enrolling the Prince at St Peter's Court. Having failed to persuade the Prince and Princess of Wales to send the two elder boys to school, he hoped to convince them that the third might do so instead. The father was writing to his son that he 'must learn to behave like a boy & not like a little child';[25] and the effect was more likely to be achieved if the boy went to school rather than remain under the tutelage of a nurse.

On 2 May 1910, Hansell summoned Richardson to Marlborough House, and they had a long talk. Sister Edith had already agreed that the boy should be given a 'careful trial' of school life as a day pupil, while continuing to live under her supervision at York Gate House.

Before this could be done, though, Prince Henry and his brothers would all be one step closer to the throne, and their father would be His Majesty the King.

2

Children of the King

By the spring of 1910, the moment that the family had long dreaded was imminent.

King Edward VII's zest for life was gradually diminishing. He returned from his customary annual sojourn in Biarritz on 27 April, suffering from one of the coughing fits to which persistent bronchial attacks had made him a martyr. He was also deeply worried by the constitutional crisis provoked by the threat of a clash between the Commons and the Lords over a controversial budget introduced by the Chancellor of the Exchequer, David Lloyd George, the previous year. The English weather was unusually cold for the time of year, and at Sandringham the King spent too long out in the garden during a bitterly cold wind. Suffering from sleepless nights, wheezing and coughing by day, and losing his gargantuan appetite, he insisted crossly to his family and household that he would carry on working regardless. On 5 May Queen Alexandra and their unmarried daughter, Princess Victoria, summoned home urgently from their Mediterranean cruise, returned to London.

Edward and Albert were preparing for another term at college, when their father sent for them. Trying to suppress his anxiety, he told them that he had informed the captains at college that his sons were to stay with him for the present; 'Grandpapa' was very ill, and the end might not be far off.[1]

Two days later, on the morning of 7 May, the boys awoke in their room at Marlborough House overlooking The Mall at Buckingham Palace. Albert was the first to look out of the window, and he told his brother that the Royal Standard was at half-mast. As they were dressing, Finch came to tell them that their father wished to see them downstairs.

His face grey with fatigue, their father – now addressing them for the first time as King George V – informed them that their grandfather was dead. Edward replied that they already knew, as they had seen the Standard at half mast. At first he did not seem to hear, as he described to them the deathbed scene; then he broke off suddenly. 'What did you say about the Standard?' he asked sharply. When they repeated it, he frowned and muttered, 'But that's all wrong. The King is dead. Long live the King!'[2] An equerry was promptly sent to hoist the Standard again.

Two days later, Edward and Albert stood at the salute at Marlborough House to see their father proclaimed King in Friary Court, St James's, opposite.

King Edward's funeral took place at Windsor on 20 May, a sweltering day with men and women fainting in the hushed crowds. For England it proved to be the last defiant display of European royal and imperial power at its zenith. Apart from King George V, his eldest cousin, the German Emperor William, and Ferdinand, Tsar of Bulgaria, six other crowned heads, plus representatives from all other reigning continental dynasties, attended the ceremony. Princes Edward and Albert and Princess Mary rode in one of the state coaches with their mother, now Queen Mary.

For all the children except the youngest, their father's accession to the throne meant greater changes. The family moved from Frogmore into the grandeur of the royal apartments at Windsor Castle; in Scotland the move was from Abergeldie to Balmoral; and in London, instead of Marlborough House, they took up residence in Buckingham Palace. Of their old homes, only York Cottage remained theirs. Queen Alexandra could not bear to leave the 'Big House', which had been her home ever since she had come to England to marry the then Prince of Wales in 1863, and King George did not have the heart to ask 'Motherdear' to move. Consequently she lived there till her death fifteen years later.

With his father's accession, Prince Edward automatically became Duke of Cornwall, inheriting large estates and properties in the south west of England and at Kennington in London. During his grandfather's reign, his sole income at college had been one shilling pocket money a week; now it amounted to millions. After his grandfather's funeral, the new Duke of Cornwall returned to Dartmouth, where he was still just given the pocket money of a naval cadet. However he was conscious of a subtle change in the attitude of his fellow cadets towards him.

In June, the King had a long conversation with Lord Esher about his eldest son, whom he intended to create Prince of Wales on his sixteenth birthday, three weeks later. Esher noted that he did not wish the prince 'to lose any chance of improving his mind and realizes that the boy is young for his years. He would like to postpone his entry into public life for some years, but I told him I did not think he would manage to do this beyond the time when the boy was "royally" of age. The boy is a mere child now, much of which is due to the limitations of his tutor, a man, however, in whom the King reposes great confidence.'[3]

The father's confidence in Hansell was not shared by the son. If he had ever harboured strong views about anything, Prince Edward recalled years later, he was careful to conceal them. It was impossible for him to remember 'anything brilliant or original' that he ever said; 'looking back over those peculiarly ineffectual years under him, I am appalled to discover how little I really learned.'[4]

On 23 June the King carried out his intention and conferred the title of Prince of Wales on his eldest son.

The King and Queen maintained royal tradition by spending a few weeks at Balmoral in the summer. Among their guests that year was Lloyd George, and he wrote his wife a charming account of family life there. When the cigars were brought after lunch, he noted, the children began a game of blowing out the lighter. 'Then the Queen and the rest of us all joined in and the noise was deafening until the little Princess (Mary) set her lamp on fire. We thought then it was time to stop.'[5]

'Cadet Prince Albert' was also due to go from Osborne to Dartmouth in due course, if he could achieve the right academic grade. However, like his father and grandfather, he was not a natural student. At the end of each term he was rarely far from bottom of his class. 'I am sure the boy has determination and grit in him,' Captain Christian wrote, 'but he finds it difficult to apply it to work, tho' with games it comes out strongly.' Disappointed by suggestions that the boy did not appear to take his work seriously, the King rebuked him sternly; 'unless you now put your shoulder to the wheel & really try & do your best to work hard, you will have no chance of passing any of your examinations.'[6] In spite of making a greater effort to concentrate, his final position at the end of term, December 1910, was a lowly sixty-eighth out of sixty-eight. His tutor, Watt, regretted there was no denying that 'P.A. has gone a mucker,' but in mitigation added that he was at the least stable part of his development; 'I expect another year will produce a great change in him.'[7]

Though delayed slightly by his father's accession, Prince Henry became the first son of a British monarch to go to school. After his first three days as a day boy at St Peter's Court, he told his father that he liked it, and on Hansell's advice he was sent there as an ordinary boarder, so that he would be subject to proper discipline like any other boy of his age. Naturally it turned out to be not quite so simple as that; for the school, authorities and the other boys, it was quite a novelty to have a Prince in their midst. They did not know how to address him; 'Prince Henry' seemed rather cumbersome. Christian names were not then in common usage at prep schools, and although the reigning house was at that time the house of Saxe-Coburg Gotha, it was debatable as to whether members of the royal family should use that as a surname. In addition there was difficulty, albeit less so than in a later age, of protecting the Prince from journalists and photographers.

Prince Henry's academic progress was slow, but he had started late in the term. He had also pleased his father and tutor by his good behaviour; their greatest fear had been that he would regularly lose his temper if provoked by the other boys, but his report at the end of the first term from Mr Richardson remarked that he had apparently never done so; 'He has been very easy to manage & I think wishes to do the right thing'.[8] In the Christmas term, he began to play football. Academically he was not so bright, although good at mathematics, and at the end of term he won the form arithmetic prize.

In January 1911, despite coming bottom of his form, Prince Albert went on to the second stage of his naval education, when he joined Prince Edward (now in his final term) at Dartmouth Royal Naval College. The following month there was a severe epidemic of measles and mumps at Dartmouth. Two cadets died, and although the princes were kept isolated in the commandant's house for a time, they did not escape the virus, and were ill enough for bulletins to be issued to the press. Despite a reassuring statement in *The Lancet* that the princes were 'at the age of least danger', there was the unspoken but much-feared risk of the complication of orchitis. A complaint that can impair procreative capacity, it would have been serious for the heir to the throne, and a definite risk in adolescent and adult males, leaving some degree of infertility in one patient in ten. That the Prince of Wales had numerous affairs before his marriage but never fathered any children, and that it was rumoured that there was something 'wrong with his gland',[9] as it was put politely, suggests that the epidemic may have left him sterile. His belief that he was incapable of fathering a child may have had some degree of influence on his private life.

At St Peter's Court there was also an outbreak of mumps in the spring, but here it was less serious. Prince Henry was confined to bed with the illness in the third week of May, but with perfect timing recovered fully for the following month's festivities.

The Coronation of King George V took place at Westminster Abbey on 22 June. Prince Edward had been invested with the Order of the Garter so that at the ceremony he could wear the robes of this ancient order of chivalry. As he had not yet attained his majority, he was not entitled to wear a peer's robes; but as he took precedence over the peers of the realm, it was thought appropriate that he should have some suitably distinctive attire.

From the King's own account of the Coronation in his diary, there was one really moving moment. His description of most of the day's events is quite matter-of-fact until mentioning the presence of the Queen, and their eldest son: 'I nearly broke down when dear David came to do homage to me, as it reminded me so much of when I did the same thing to beloved Papa, he did it so well.'[10]

Kneeling before his father, he recited the oath: 'I, Edward, Prince of Wales, do become your liege man of life and limb and of earthly worship; and faith and truth I will bear unto you, to live and die against all manner of folks. So help me God.'

John was not quite six years old, and his parents thought him too young to attend the ceremony. Not wanting to be left out, he went to see one of the boy messengers at Buckingham Palace and suggested they both slip out together to join the crowds in the Mall. They would have done so if watchful staff had not stopped them before they could reach the Palace gates. All the other children, sat watching from the royal gallery, Albert in naval cadet uniform, Mary in a robe of state, Henry and George in Highland dress. On their way to the Abbey, riding in a coach in the Prince of Wales's procession, they all behaved impeccably. But on their journey back to Buckingham Palace afterwards, the youngsters soon became bored. The diarist Lord Crawford noted that 'a rough-and-tumble took place in full view of the delighted spectators in Whitehall.' Princess Mary's 'sincere but ineffectual' attempts to pacify Henry and George had no effect, and her coronet was nearly knocked off.

Three weeks later the scene of pageantry shifted to Caernarvon Castle. There had been no ceremony of investiture for a Prince of Wales since that of the future King Charles I in 1616, the issue of Letters Patent of Creation and Introduction into the House of Lords being considered sufficient. Ironically it was David Lloyd George, the self-styled enemy of inherited privilege, whose idea it was to transform the ceremony into a Welsh pageant.

It was held at Caernavon Castle, within the ruined battlements, on 14 July 1911. The seventeen-year-old Prince wore white satin breeches and a mantle and surcoat of purple velvet edged with ermine. On first sight of what he called this 'fantastic' costume, there ensued a 'family blow-up'. Whereas there had at least been a 'condoning historical precedent' for wearing the Garter dress and robe, he pointed out, what would his navy friends say if they saw him in this 'preposterous rig'? Soothingly, the Queen told him that they would understand that as a Prince he was 'obliged to do certain things that may seem a little silly.'[11]

So on a sweltering summer day he donned his costume, the Home Secretary, Winston Churchill, proclaimed his titles, and he was formally invested by his father as Prince of Wales. The King placed a coronet cap on his head as a token of principality, the gold verge of government into his hand, and the ring of responsibility on to his middle finger. Leading him by the hand through an archway to one of the towers of the battlements, he presented him to the people of Wales, and the Prince spoke some carefully-rehearsed sentences in Welsh.

That night, the King noted in his diary that 'the dear boy did it all remarkably well and looked so nice'.[12] But the unwilling Prince himself had thus made the painful discovery that he 'recoiled from anything that tended to set me up as a person requiring homage'.[13] To him, the ceremony had made a mockery of the intentions of his father and Hansell, to give him a strict and unaffected upbringing. All he wanted was to be treated exactly like any other boy of his age.

In 1912, Queen Mary started making plans for her daughter's future, in attempting to have her betrothed to Prince Ernest Augustus of Hanover, heir to the Duke of Brunswick and the only descendant in the male line of King George III. 'He will have a great future,' Queen Mary wrote, 'and could be in England a lot.'[14] In the event it came to nothing, and in the following year the Prince married Princess Victoria Louise, only daughter of the German Emperor.

Queen Maud of Norway was deeply attached to her childhood haunts at Sandringham, and she came to stay regularly at Appleton, a house on the estate given to her as a wedding present. Her son, Prince Olav, an only child, had been born there in July 1903. He accompanied her on her regular visits, and was always a ready playmate for his young cousins, particularly Henry, George and the delicate John. The four played at soldiers with miniature forts, cannon and lead soldiers. The King took a keen interest in these games, but imposed one rule of his own; the 'armies' were not to be named after any existing countries, so the battles had to be between different planets, such as Earth and Mars.

The boys also dressed up in cocked hats, made wooden swords, and drilled each other. After visiting a military tournament, George introduced some variations of his own and made them 'break step' when crossing a bridge. Afterwards he explained that this was in case the masonry should become dislodged by the rhythm of their marching feet. At other times they played cowboys and Indians, a traditional version with Buffalo Bill as the hero.

In the summer term of 1912, two Princes went back to St Peter's Court, when George accompanied Henry. George was not only the least shy of the brothers, he was also the most talented and intellectually gifted; academically, musically and culturally he outshone them all, and this gave him a common bond with his mother. Though nearly three years younger than Henry, he quickly rivalled the elder boy's performance in class at school. Henry's progress at schoolwork was rarely more than satisfactory, but he enjoyed sports and became an enthusiastic cricketer. In one match he took three wickets and scored sixty runs not out. The King was unimpressed; 'the bowling couldn't have been very famous.'[15] However, his soccer and squash rackets found more favour with his father the following term, both being 'capital games'. This time it was the Queen's turn to complain, 'all you write about is your everlasting football of which I am heartily sick.'[16]

Henry finished at St Peter's Court at the end of the summer

term 1913 and then went on to Eton, where he was put in the same house as Prince Leopold, later King of the Belgians. Apart from being met by a royal brougham at Slough on arriving for his first day, he was treated without undue privilege. One minor modification, however, was made to his curriculum. The King requested that he should not be taught Latin, but French and German instead, as both modern languages would be of more practical value to a prince of the royal house than a classical one. As a sovereign, he never ceased to regret the linguistic deficiencies in his own education.

Prince Henry's masters wrote on his reports that he was 'thoroughly cheerful modest & obedient', and threw himself into the life of the place 'most pleasantly' & willingly'. Several of the other boys asked for photographs of him, as they had done of his elder brother at college. Whereas they had been given unlimited supplies of prints, Henry was not granted this privilege. The Queen told him to order some more, warning him that they cost one shilling each.

At the age of eighteen the Prince of Wales was sent to Oxford. Although his father had no time for what he called 'intellectuals', he agreed with Hansell's suggestion that the heir to the throne would profit from spending a year on languages, history and political economy. The Prince complained angrily that it would be a waste of his time, but he was mollified by an assurance that he would spend his vacations on educational trips to France and Germany to learn the languages.

During the autumn and winter of 1911, while the King and Queen were away in India for the Coronation Durbar, he had stayed at Sandringham. At around this time the close bond between Edward and George began to develop. 'We became more than brothers – we became close friends,' Edward noted. Later they would discover similar tastes in music and night life, and for a time George would be the only member of his family to whom Edward could unburden himself in complete trust and confidence.

As the eldest brother, Edward found it natural to adopt a protective attitude towards his brothers and sister. It was only to be expected that he should be patronizing at times towards George, eight years his junior. George needed exercise, he decided, but 'got stitches all the time . . . he is too fat for running',[17] he complained in June 1912. The Prince of Wales was obsessed with a fear of becoming fat, and his self-imposed standards of punishing exercise and dieting often alarmed his parents.

While they had been at Oxford and Dartmouth, Edward was fiercely protective towards Albert; soon, they too became close allies and companions. Over Christmas 1912, at York Cottage, he decided it was 'hard work keeping 3 wild brothers in order; well I should say two, as my 2nd brother helps me.' The following autumn, he remarked that Bertie was 'a delightful creature and we have so many interests in common.'[18]

In the spring of 1912, travelling incognito, the Prince of Wales went to Paris to stay with the Marquis of Breteuil, a friend of King Edward VII. Although rather short of stature and slight of build, he made a favourable impression. After being introduced to French society, he stayed there five months with Hansell and Escoffer, his French tutor. The writer Compton Mackenzie drew comparisons between him and his Francophile grandfather, anybody who might have remembered the latter as a young prince of twenty, if they were still alive, 'would have recognised the same shyness, the same hint of sadness, and the same charm of feerie.'[19] The sadness, Mackenzie suggested, could be attributed to the decision to cut short his naval career and send him to Oxford. If this was the case, he had judged the Prince correctly. The prospect of Oxford, 'an awful situation', weighed heavily on him; 'and I only wish I was back quietly in the only service – the navy.'[20]

At Balmoral, after his return to England, in September 1912, Lord Esher found him 'a most captivating, strange, intelligent boy, with a remarkable vocabulary. He is sad – with the sadness of the world's burdens.' Another resemblance to King Edward VII was soon self-evident. The Prince Consort had often complained that his eldest son was only interested in his clothes. Now another Prince of Wales developed an interest in his attire which to others seemed little short of obsessive.

His taste, which some thought rather vulgar, tended towards informal clothes with bright colours and large patterns. It found little favour with the conservatively-minded King. When the Prince of Wales visited his father, he was expected to wear a morning coat, and when dining with him he was required to wear a tail coat with white tie and the Star of the Garter. It was only natural that at Oxford he should favour more informal and casual wear, such as sports coats and flannel trousers with turns-ups or plus-fours.

Although he was lonely at first when he went to Oxford, once he had settled down he soon made friends. Despite never having yet shown much interest in riding, he developed an enthusiasm for hunting with the South Oxfordshire Hounds and playing polo. Though he never made a first-class horseman, he was physically courageous as a rider, not to say foolhardy.

In the Easter and summer vacations of 1913 he went to Germany to improve his knowledge of the tongue. Many of those he stayed with were related in some way, such as the Grand Duke of Mecklenburg-Strelitz and his mother, Queen Mary's 'Aunt Augusta', and his father's cousins, the German Emperor William and his younger brother Prince Henry of Prussia, and Charles, Duke of Saxe-Coburg. Their hospitality was unstinting, and in the course of this time the Prince developed a lifelong admiration for Germany.

At Dartmouth, Prince Albert persevered with his cadet training, and his growing confidence emerged in several minor escapades which led to the punishment book. Few of the cadets left college without having taken part in any 'skylarking', and Albert once helped to drive a flock of sheep into a Saturday night dance after the lights had been cut off.

In January 1913 he joined the cruiser *Cumberland*. He worked hard and willingly at the less pleasant aspects of life aboard ship such as coaling, but he was a poor sailor in rough weather. On a tour of duty overseas, which formed his final stage of cadet training, he had his first experience of public enthusiasm for the representatives of monarchy. In Jamaica he was hard put to make his speeches for the crowds' excitement, and he persuaded another cadet of similar physique to stand in for him, smiling and waving, at engagements where he was not required to speak. Still quite shy, he was unimpressed by 'the Americans who had no manners at all and tried to take photographs all the time'. At formal functions, such as nightly balls, he was reluctant to ask the girls for a dance. Nevertheless the experience matured him considerably, and on his return home the King was delighted to see how much he had grown in confidence.

Prince Albert became a midshipman in September 1913, serving on board the battleship HMS *Collingwood*. Letters home suggested that he enjoyed the training and was glad to be able to serve his country, although he never grew to love the sea as his father had done. During the naval manoeuvres of early 1914 around the Mediterranean, he continued to travel. In Alexandria, he was presented by Lord Kitchener to the Khedive of Egypt, and he visited the pyramids. At Athens, he met King Constantine, with whom he condoled on the assassination of his father, King George, the previous March.

1914 was an unsettling year. There were tensions at home, notably industrial and suffragette agitation, and demands for Irish home rule. In Europe there was an attempt on the life of King Victor Emmanuel of Italy; manoeuvres of the French and Italian fleets took place nearby in the Mediterranean while the German fleet continued to grow apace. On 28 June came the catalyst that plunged the continent into war – the assassination of the Austrian heir, Archduke Francis Ferdinand, and his wife, Sophie, at Sarajevo.

Even at Eton, Prince Henry was aware of the unsettling times in which they lived. In May, Queen Mary wrote to him describing how she had seen the police arresting suffragettes trying to get past the gates at Buckingham Palace. Next month, information came from Scotland Yard that a suffragette plan was being hatched in Liverpool to 'molest' Prince Henry at Eton, and a policeman was posted to keep a discreet eye on him at school just in case.

Meanwhile, the Prince of Wales had at last persuaded his parents that he had had enough of Oxford – or at least the university. By December 1913 he was 'absolutely fed up with the place and it has got on my nerves.'[21] In June 1914 he went to the summer camp of the Oxford Battalion of the Officers' Training Corps. The following month, he was attached to the 1st Life Guards for a while because the King wished him to learn to ride better. Every morning for two hours he paraded in the riding school with the recruits.

However much this may have bored him, it left him free to experience for the first time the delights of the London social season. He showed an uninhibited zest for night life, with dinner parties and balls very much a priority. On 10 July, he noted in his diary that he had had no more than eight hours' sleep in the past seventy-two.

Society life where he had some measure of freedom suited him well, but he hated the drudgery and formality of court functions. He had attended his first court in March 1914, and found it 'mighty poor fun', standing round while 'hundreds of women went by, each one plainer than the last.' Two months later, a state visit by King Christian X and Queen Alexandrine of Denmark came in for criticism: 'What rot & a waste of time, money & energy all these State visits are.'[22]

Despite this youthful sense of rebellion, he shared to some extent his parents' apprehension at the course of events abroad. On 31 July, he noted, 'I was reading newspapers all night, & Papa received news of Belgium's mobilization. All this is too ghastly & that we should be on the brink of war is almost incredible. I am very depressed.'[23]

3

'This trying time'

Though he enjoyed the rounds of society life, the Prince of Wales was eager to play his full part in the patriotic effort. It was incomprehensible to him that he should be kept at home, depressed and miserable and, as he wrote to Bertie in the navy, playing no more part in the war than Harry and George, 'two irresponsible kids who run about playing inane games in the passage.' He was 'as good as heartbroken to think I am totally devoid of any job whatsoever and have not the faintest chance of being able to serve my country.'[1]

On being instructed by the King to wait in London until suitable employment was found for him, he wrote to his father of his distress at not being allowed to serve his country, and begged for a commission in the Grenadier Guards. The King granted this request without hesitation. But when the Prince found himself transferred to the 3rd Battalion, stationed at barracks in London with no immediate prospect of being sent overseas to fight, he called at the War Office and demanded to see Kitchener, Minister for War, pleading to be allowed to go to France. 'What does it matter if I am killed?' he asked. 'I have four brothers.'[2] Kitchener replied sternly that the government could not risk capture of the heir to the throne by the enemy. However his persistence paid off, and in November he was attached to the staff of Field-Marshal Sir John French, Commander-in-Chief of the British Expeditionary Force. Yet he was firmly kept away from the trenches and employed most of the time with harmless paperwork, and carrying dispatches. Whenever he managed to have himself transferred to divisional headquarters close to the fighting, he was promplty removed from the remotest chance of shellfire.

King George and Queen Mary were proud of their son. They looked forward to his dutiful, affectionate letters about the campaign in France, and read them out with pride to the family, later showing them to his ministers. But the Prince was disgusted at being awarded the French *Legion d'honneur*. Having never served in the trenches, he said, he felt he did not deserve such a decoration at all. There were many gallant, yet undecorated officers far more worthy than he, who had been kept protected from the dangers of enemy fire. King George, with his monarchical affection for the accoutrements and decorations on military uniform, was offended at this apparently subversive attitude of his heir.

No such irritation disturbed the bonds between King George and his second son. Of all the princes, none had been closer to the scene of action when war was declared than Prince Albert. 'Please God it may soon be over,' the King wrote in his diary on 6 August,' and that he will protect dear Bertie's life.' The Prince had been on board during the test mobilization of 15 July when the Fleet passed before the King in the royal yacht at Spithead. Now, for the first time since the Duke of Clarence (later King William IV) had been present at the battle of Cape St Vincent, a prince in direct line to the throne was likely to see active service.

Initially it was not gunfire, but ill-health, that would endanger his life. Gastric illness, diagnosed as appendicitis, attacked him at sea at the end of August and he was brought back to hospital at Aberdeen, a hazardous journey by sea in dense fog, through mined waters and at risk from enemy submarines. Although a considerate patient, he was sorry to miss the action of the Heligoland Bight in which three German cruisers were sunk, and the indecisive battle of Dogger Bank. From his sickbed he commiserated with his father, who 'must be very tired after all this trying time with so much work to do, and so many people to see, and never getting a rest.'[3] Later he returned to Sandringham to convalesce, but suffered a further bout of ill-health in

November and Sir Frederick Treves, the King's physician, advised that he should not return to sea. Instead he was posted to undertake shore duty at the Admiralty.

The other children were too young to serve in any active capacity, though Prince Henry helped to make comforts for the troops. When he was invited for an outing to Camberley to see German prisoners-of-war, the King vetoed this as being in bad taste; think, he told his son, 'if you were a prisoner for people to come and stare at you as if you were a wild beast.'[4]

With the outbreak of war came vilification of all things, and all people German, the most noted casualty being Prince Louis of Battenburg, First Sea Lord. Blamed for reverses at sea by jealous colleagues at the Admiralty, he was hounded into resigning his post. Another victim was Mary's German maid Else Korsukawitz. Though her devotion to the family had never been in doubt, it was with a heavy heart that Queen Mary told her she would have to leave and return to Germany, or else risk internment as an alien. Sadly Else packed her bags.

More lonely than ever after being deprived of her company, Princess Mary longed to do something for the war effort. She found it in helping to organize a fund to ensure that each soldier serving in France at Christmas 1914 received a small brass tin containing cigarettes, tobacco and chocolate. The tin was embossed with her silhouette in a garlanded circle, the names of the Allies, and *Impericum Britannicum* around the edges, plus a Christmas card and her portrait. For the Indian troops in France, sweets were sent instead.

Despite her innate shyness and a dread of public speaking. Mary grew greatly in confidence as a result of her public appearances at home. She was her mother's assistant in helping to make handbags for hospitals and comforts for men at the Front. Queen Mary found hospital-visiting an ordeal, lacking the ability to make pleasant small-talk, and having her daughter – who found it no less of an ordeal at first – to help was invaluable.

All this proved a much-needed distraction from the tedium of life at Buckingham Palace. Though she bravely maintained in letters to the Prince of Wales that he need not feel sorry for her, he regularly begged their mother to allow Mary more friends of her own age, and give her a chance to get out and about. Patient as she was, Mary could not help admitting to him on occasion that she disliked 'those rather silent dinners you know so well, when Papa will read the paper.'[5]

Mary gave her mother unstinting support during the war. One day General Haig and Lord Kitchener watched her as she stood chatting with a draft of soldiers about to leave for Flanders. 'There's a little soldier,' remarked Kitchener, 'whose example has done more than anything to rally the women of England to the colours.'[6]

She applied herself to activities such as Girl Guides, Women's Land Army, Needlework Guild, and the Red Cross. She also worked in a canteen at a munitions factory in Hayes, and joined the Voluntary Aid Detachment. In August 1918 she was made Colonel-in-Chief of the Royal Scots Regiment.

Four months earlier, as a twenty-first birthday present, she had asked for permission to work as a probationer at Great Ormond Street Children's Hospital. The family were amused but most impressed that she had not asked for jewellery instead, and her wish was readily granted. As her appeal to tour allied hospitals behind the battle lines during the war had fallen on deaf ears, she could hardly be denied this request. To save petrol she travelled from palace to hospital in a one-horse brougham, but in all other resepcts she took pains to behave and be treated as an ordinary student nurse.

She soon earned the respect of the medical and nursing staffs for the skill and tenderness with which she mothered ailing babies. Once a sister stepped in to prevent her from emptying a chamber pot, but on being given a warning 'Windsor look' quickly thought better of it. After two years of such work, she was made President of the hospital. To mark the occasion, she presented a portrait of herself in VAD dress.

The Prince of Wales never ceased to try to get into the trenches. In September 1915 his hopes were fulfilled when he was appointed to the staff of Major-General Lord Cavan, in command of the Guards Division. His life was put in jeopardy when they came under enemy fire at the trenches and the Prince's chauffeur was shot dead. When Sir John French heard of the heir to the throne's narrow escape, he issued orders for the Prince to be transferred, but the latter persuaded him to rescind the order. Though the senior commanders and the King deplored his recklessness, his personal courage was never in doubt. A bad shelling, his regimental officers said with admiration, would always produce the Prince of Wales.

That same year Prince Albert returned to duty on Scapa flow, patrolling for submarines, until gastric trouble struck him down again. The lengthy recuperation period on board hospital-ship bored and depressed him, and Admiral Colville, commander of the First Battle Squadron, suggested a complete change and rest for him at Abergeldie. Amid the happy memories of his childhood and the fresh Highland air his condition improved, but on his return to Sandringham in October he was still pronounced medically unfit for duty. Anxiety, after hearing of a serious accident to the King in France that month when his horse reared and fell on top of him, delayed Prince Albert's recovery. The Naval Medical Board could not sanction him rejoining the ship, and he was granted three months' sick leave, during which time he was attached to the Admiralty for 'light duty'.

In January 1916 he was allowed to visit the Prince of Wales for four days at the headquarters of the Guards' Division at La Gorgue. He watched a bombardment of the enemy position by British artillery and later the German retaliation, seeing several houses shelled by the Germans, with women and children running out by the back door. 'That makes one think of the horrors of war', he wrote, 'and those people are shelled every day.'[7]

Though he rarely complained, Albert was just as critical of life at Buckingham Palace as his rebellious elder brother. He found it an 'awful prison', and their parents had 'funny ideas about us, thinking we are still boys at school or something of that sort, instead of what we are.'[8]

Back in England, Prince Albert was entrusted with certain ceremonial functions, such as opening a rifle range in the cellars of the Palace of Westminster in March, and in April he was delegated by the King to welcome Alexander, Crown Prince of Serbia, on a visit to England. He acquitted himself well speaking in French to his guest, though it was 'pretty stiff time with him, as he can't talk English.'[9]

His heart, though, was not in public functions, and he was impatient to get back to *Collingwood*. In May 1916, he passed his examinations as an acting sub-lieutenant, and the doctors passed him fit for return to active service.

He was just in time to see action at the indecisive battle of Jutland, in which his ship was heavily attacked by light torpedo craft. For most of the conflict he was in no real danger from enemy fire, but he was exhilarated at being so close to the heart of the battle. While on top of the turret, 'I never felt any fear of shells or anything else,' he wrote to the Prince of Wales. 'It seems curious but all sense of danger and everything else goes except the one longing of dealing death in every possible way to the enemy.'[10]

By July he thought he had made a full recovery, but a month later he was attacked by acute pain once more. The doctors diagnosed a duodenal ulcer, perhaps the long-term result of his nanny's ill-treatment of him in infancy. Another period of rest and medical treatment intervened, and he was transferred again to shore duties.

On 14 December 1916 his twenty-first birthday was celebrated at Buckingham Palace, and he was invested with the Order of the Garter. Deeply touched at this honour, he still longed to get back to sea. In May 1917 he reported for duty again, this time on board the battleship *Malaya* as an acting lieutenant. A further recurrence of gastric trouble put an end to this, and the operation which had so long seemed inevitable took place on 29 November 1917.

At St Peter's Court, Prince George proved himself a natural scholar. His reports were so good that it seemed he might have a bright academic future ahead of him. The King and Queen decided to pay a special visit to the school, and when the King complimented the headmaster Mr Richardson on their son's results, he was told that Prince George applied himself diligently to every subject, and it was a joy to teach such a child.

It was thus with great disappointment and frustration that Prince George learnt, shortly before his fourteenth birthday, that he was to be entered for the Royal Naval College at Osborne, followed by Dartmouth. Queen Mary knew that the services would be no career for a boy of his artistic and scholastic bent, and pleaded with the King, but in vain. Initially Prince George did well; unlike his elder brothers at the same age, George was a good mixer, but his bitterness and lack of interest in service life showed up when he began to do badly in class. The monotonous naval training gave him no outlet for his creative interests. Moreover he was a bad sailor, and suffered from seasickness and insomnia. The prospect of the final training cruise in foreign waters horrified him.

By this time John's ill-health was increasingly evident. From the age of four he had been suffering from occasional seizures. Epilepsy was diagnosed, and his parents were concerned, lest he might suffer a fit in public. His attacks were becoming ever more frequent, and in 1916 they decided to give him his own 'establishment', a cottage at Wood Farm, on the Sandringham estate. For some time the belief has persisted that he was brain-damaged, and his heartless mother and father not only deliberately excluded him from family photographs but also shut him away, as he was such an embarrassment to them. He needed constant care and attention, away from the public gaze, which would have been difficult otherwise. Lalla Bill had become very fond of him, and she was the obvious choice of person to continue to care for his health. In addition to acting as his guardian, she kept him company while he tended his flowers and took him on nature rambles around the estate. An area of the garden was set aside for him, marked with a plaque, 'Prince John's Garden', and the gardeners employed at 'the big house' sometimes came to help him tend it. He became very interested in flowers, and sent his father bunches of snowdrops, lilies or other blooms which he had picked specially, accompanied by a short letter. Indoors he enjoyed reading, playing with a pedal car and ride-on train. He was not completely isolated from the war-torn world around him. He could hardly contain his excitement when a 'real live soldier' came to visit one day, or when he watched zeppelins in the skies over the Norfolk countryside.

Outwardly he still looked quite healthy, and he continued to grow strong and tall. A male orderly was ready to help restrain him whenever the attacks became violent. Allegations that he was neglected by the family are untrue; on the contrary, Queen Mary and the others came to visit him from time to time, when their other duties allowed.

Apart from Lalla and the orderly, his main companions were Lalla's niece, who came to help him feed the chickens he was allowed to keep, and Winifred Thomas, the niece of Thomas Stratton, a groom at Sandringham. About three years younger than John, she suffered from asthma, and everyone decided she might be a suitable companion for him. On her first visit to Wood Farm they became friendly, and after that she used to be taken to play with him on a regular basis. When he was ill, she sat beside his bed while Lalla read to them. Thomas Haverly, a coachman who had worked at Windsor Castle, was chosen as John's special driver. He took the boy for outings in the countryside and to the sea, as well as to Sandringham itself whenever the family were there.

Once it was clear that Prince Albert could no longer continue to serve in the navy, he joined the Royal Naval Air Service, shortly to be amalgamated into the Royal Air Force, a unified air service independent of the navy. Prince George had entered the navy as a cadet at Dartmouth, and the King thought it fitting that one of his sons should be identified with the new service. Albert received his appointment to the RNAS squadron HMS *Daedalus* at Cranwell, Lincolnshire, and reported there a month later. He was asked to take charge of the boys' squadron, and he found the relaxed attitude of some of the officers disturbing. Having much of the punctiliousness of his father and grandfather about correct uniform and proper drill, he reacted by becoming something of a martinet. A land-based post suited him, added to which was the relief at knowing that his medical problems were seemingly behind him. He learned to drive a car, and soon experienced his first flight, 'a curious sensation, and one which takes a lot of getting used to,' he told Queen Mary. Although he felt he enjoyed it on the whole, he admitted he would not like flying as a pastime – 'I would much sooner be on the ground!! It feels safer!!'[11]

In October 1918, Albert and his equerry Louis Greig were flown across the Channel to RAF headquarters at Autigny, and the Prince was able to see both day-time and night-time operations. By now, however, war was drawing to a close. The German spring offensive had been contained by the Allies, and with American troops arriving on the Western Front, the balance was tilted against the Central Powers. By early autumn the tide was visibly turning against Germany.

Barely a fortnight after Albert had arrived in France came the news for which a war-weary continent had waited so long. At the eleventh hour of the eleventh day of the eleventh month, a ceasefire was declared. 'The great day has come & we have won the war,' King George wrote to his son. 'It has been a long time coming, but I was sure if we stuck to it, we should win & it is a great victory over one of the most perfect military machines ever created.'[12]

After the war, the Independent Air Force was disbanded and Prince Albert was transferred to the staff of Major-General John Salmond, Commanding Officer of the Royal Air Force on the Western Front. He was chosen as the official British representative during King Albert of the Belgians' triumphal march back into Brussels on 22 November, and it was the first occasion on which King George had entrusted his son with representing him on an official matter of state. The Prince of Wales was still in France, and both Princes accompanied their father on a two-week visit touring French battlefields, war cemeteries and devastated areas. Princess Mary also travelled to France a few days after the Armistice, to visit members of the VAD and other women engaged in war work.

Questions now arose as to how the Princes should be employed in the intermediate stage between the Armistice and peace. The King was determined that nobody should be given grounds for criticism of any members of his family on account of their premature return to civilian life. There had already been ill-informed and malicious comment during the winter of 1917 as to Prince Albert's prolonged periods of sick leave. The King decided that both Princes should remain in France until the spring.

They were therefore away from home when the first sad, but not unexpected, break occurred in the family circle. On the afternoon of 18 January 1919, John suffered another violent epilectic attack. Afterwards he went to sleep and never woke up, Lalla Bill holding his hand as he passed away. Resigned but heartbroken, she telephoned Queen Mary at Sandringham. The Queen noted this merciful release from suffering in her diary: 'he just slept quietly into his heavenly home, no pain, no struggle, just peace for the poor little troubled spirit which had been a great anxiety to us for many years.'[13] On 21 January he was buried in the graveyard at Sandringham Church, next to Prince Alexander John who had lived but one day in 1871.

The Prince of Wales wrote an unnecesarily tactless letter to his mother about his brother's death, but when he learned how distressed she had been, he followed it up with a more sympathetic message. To Freda Dudley Ward, wife of a Liberal Member of Parliament and in the process of becoming his main confidante and mistress, he wrote on 20 January:

> He's been practically shut up for the last 2 years anyhow, so no-one has ever seen him except the family & then only once or twice a year & his death is the greatest relief

imaginable & what we've always silently prayed for; but to be plunged into mourning for this is the limit just as the war is over which cuts parties etc. right out!!. . .[14]

Though he would never have expressed himself in such blunt or self-centred terms, let alone concurred with his eldest son's allegations of virtual neglect, the King also privately thought John's death a relief and a blessing in disguise.

The one who missed him most was Queen Alexandra. Having spent so much of her adult life under the shadows of deafness and rheumatism, she had a particular sympathy for invalids and the handicapped, and her widowhood had been lonely. Her grandson's condition made him very special to her, and since he could never fully grow up, he appealed to her maternal possessiveness. Whenever she was at Sandringham she would send for the 'dear and precious little boy' to have tea with her and play games, listen to music, or do jigsaw puzzles. 'Now our two darling Johnnies lie side by side,'[15] she wrote to her daughter-in-law. To Queen Mary, it seemed ironic that her two eldest sons had not been far from the front line of battle during wartime, yet had been saved; while another should have been taken this way in peacetime.

Edward and Albert were on the point of returning to England for the funeral when they received a telegram from the King, asking them not ot come. Although nobody ever explained why, it was thought that the King and Queen wished their youngest son's obsequies to be kept as private as possible, and to have his two eldest sons leave France and travel back to England specially would make it too much of a public occasion. Grieg was particularly disgusted at what seemed an insensitive decision. The death of John brought the brothers closer together for a while, though Grieg felt that Albert was beginning to find Edward increasingly unreliable. To the equerry, the heir to the throne was a shallow playboy, 'interested only in himself'.[16] Like King George V, perhaps he was among the first to see that Prince Edward would make a far less promising King than his younger brother.

Great Britain had emerged victorious from the war, but peace brought many problems for the royal family. 'The end of the war seems to have brought great unrest behind it,' wrote the Queen, 'it seems such a pity that as all classes had worked so well during the war, it is not possible now to work for the reconstruction of the world.'[17]

They had ample knowledge during the previous two years that republicanism was not far blow the surface in Britain. In April 1917, H.G. Wells had written to *The Times* asserting that the moment had come for the British people to rid themselves of 'the ancient trappings of throne and sceptre'. The rise of the Bolsheviks in Russia and the brutal murder of the Tsar and his family at Ekaterinburg in July 1918 had tarnished the image of revolution and alienated more moderate opinion, but as Lord Cromer noted in August 1918, the position of the monarchy was less stable now than at the outbreak of war, and that 'in the critical times with which the Country is now faced no stone should be left unturned in the endeavour to consolidate the position of the Crown.'[18] The general election campaign of November 1918 was marked by scenes such as a Labour Party meeting in which the Transport Workers Union secretary, Bob Williams, announced to cheers that he hoped to see the red flag flying over Buckingham Palace.

Nine days later, King George and the Prince of Wales rode at a review of ex-servicemen in Hyde Park, and despite their initially enthusiastic reception, a group of them suddenly displayed hitherto-concealed banners with slogans voicing discontent as they thronged around the startled King. The police extricated him without harm, but he was visibly shaken. With his eldest son, he rode back to the Palace in silence. After dismounting, he remarked to the Prince of Wales, 'Those men were in a funny temper,'[19] and shaking his head, as if to rid himself of an unpleasant memory, he stode indoors.

4

*'You will find me ever
ready to help'*

In 1919 Princes Albert and Henry went to study at Cambridge. Instead of sharing to the full the life of their fellow under-graduates at Trinity College, they had to live in a separate house, as a result of their father's obsession with the likelihood of finding themselves in bad company if they lived in college.

Henry thought there was not much chance of getting to know many of the undegraduates, though he had an advantage over his brother in that he had already met a number who had been with him at Eton. However they both knew their cousin, Lord Louis Mountbatten, who was three months younger than Henry; he helped by asking them to tea to meet people 'any day'. Recreational hours were spent punting on the Cam and tearing around the countryside on motor bikes.

On the evening of 27 November, they witnessed the installation of Mr Balfour as Chancellor, and the granting of honorary degrees to several admirals and generals who had served with distinction in the war. Afterwards the Princes dined in Trinity where the new Chancellor and honorary graduates were present. 'Hundreds of people had been asked to see the visitors,' Prince Henry wrote to Queen Mary, 'but as far as I could make out nearly everybody wanted to be introduced to Bertie and myself which resulted in us having to talk to masses of people we did not know and had never heard of before.'[1] They came down from Cambridge at the end of the summer term in 1920, and Henry was then commissioned into the King's Royal Rifle Corps.

Neither made any lasting friends from their days at Cambridge, though in particular Albert learnt much from his tutors, the historian J.R.M. Butler, and the economist Dennis Robertson, both of whom managed to enliven the dullest courses.

In King George V's birthday honours on 3 June 1920, Prince Albert was granted the titles which had been conferred upon his father in 1892 – Duke of York, Earl of Inverness and Baron Killarney. He was deeply touched, and thanking his father, said he was 'very proud to bear the name that you did for many years, and I hope I shall live up to it in every way'.

In his reply, the King found a way to express the genuine affection he felt for his son but could never do so verbally: 'I hope you will always look upon me as yr. best friend & always tell me everything & you will find me ever ready to help you & give you good advice.'[2] Though it must have been difficult for Prince Albert to regard his gruff martinet of a father as his best friend, the King was beginning to soften his attitude a little. Already he was starting to see in his second son those basic qualities of character and strength of purpose which so mirrored his own.

At the same time he was beginning to have doubts about his eldest son. The Prince of Wales had been at a dance in London in February 1918 at the home of Maud Kerr-Smiley, sister of Ernest Simpson – a name which would soon feature prominently in the Prince's destiny – when an air raid warning sounded. Freda Dudley Ward, wife of a Liberal Member of Parliament, was walking across Belgrave Square, and Maud invited her to come and take shelter in the basement. The Prince of Wales started chatting to her, both got on extremely well, and they danced together for the rest of the evening.

The Dudley Wards had been married for five years and had two daughters, but husband and wife were drifting apart and by this time they were leading largely separate lives. From this chance acquaintance, an all-consuming friendship soon developed. By 1921 the Prince was writing to 'Fredie' at least once a day whenever they were separated. She conducted the affair with such discretion that her husband never objected, and the Prince's friends and staff liked and respected her. Lord Esher, to whom she was connected by marriage, found nothing objectionable in their relatinship, and was quick to draw comparisons between her and Mrs Alice Keppel, the last of King Edward VII's mistress. She was a good influence on him, making him smoke and drink less, and shaking him out of his increasing moods of depression. Her valiant attempts to broaden his limited intellectual horizons were less successful, though. 'Who is this woman Bront?' he asked her when she gave him a copy of *Wuthering Heights*. Yet for a while she was the only person who could tell him home truths without incurring his displeasure or forfeiting his confidence. In many of his letters he poured out his desolation and loneliness, acknowledging at the same time that his self-pity was 'a most degrading thing.'

For the first eighteen months or so of their relationship, as far as can be gleaned from their surviving correspondence, both cared passionately for each other. After this, Freda, recognizing with concern that his dependence on her could only spell sadness and misery for him if not for her as well, tried to put their relationship on a more platonic basis. For a time he was inconsolable, but he had no choice but to accept the fact that she was devoted to, but no longer madly in love with him. 'We are indeed a hunted and pathetic little couple,' he wrote to her in August 1922, 'but nobody can stop us loving each other.'[3]

Prince Albert and Princess Mary both recognized what she meant to him, and sympathized with him whenever there was a gap in the correspondence on her side. The King thought she was totally unsuitable as a companion for his eldest son, though the day would come when he appreciated that her influence had been basically good for him. Queen Mary also disapproved, though she held her tongue on the subject. It disturbed her, though, that Mrs Dudley Ward had made such a difference to the mother-son relationship. It was curious, the King told his wife, that David no longer confided in his mother, 'I suppose he only does so to her.'[4]

Though signs of revolutionary sentiment in the country after 1918 had soon abated, it was seen by the King and his advisers that the monarchy must be responsive to changing times if it was to survive in an age which had seen several continental dynasties toppled or tottering. Prompted by Lloyd George and others, the King soon found a suitable role for his eldest son. Despite Queen Mary's preference for keeping him in England, where he would 'learn how to govern', the Prince of Wales was sent on a series of tours throughout the Empire, ostensibly to thank the peoples abroad for their contributions to the war effort, and also to show the future King's face to his father's subjects. The Prince entered into the idea with great enthusiasm, telling Lady Airlie that while he did not intend to marry for a long time, at his age he no longer wished to live under the same roof as his parents; 'I must be free to lead my own life.'

The Prince's first major tour was of Canada and the United States between August and November 1919. During those three months, he visited several major cities, attended official functions, luncheon and dinner parties, and made speeches. 'One's head almost reels at the amount you are doing,' Queen Mary wrote to him in September, adding that she felt angry at the amount of handshaking and autograph writing he was 'compelled to face,' and that it hardly seemed dignified for him to give his left hand as the right one was swollen.[5]

At Winnipeg he bestowed decorations on returned soldiers or on their next of kin, a ceremony which moved *The Times* correspondent to remark that 'for him and for the Empire this gift of human sympathy and kindliness is a very great and valuable possession.' At Washington he visited President Wilson, who was ill and received him sitting up in bed; he visited the Red Cross headquarters and a hospital where he talked to war veterans. In New York he attended a gala at the Metropolitan Opera House, reviewed troops and cadets, decorated American soldiers, and attended balls and dinners.

Though often hard to please, the King was delighted by his son's efforts. He readily offered his 'warmest congratulations on the splendid success of your tour, which is due in a great measure to your own personality & the wonderful way in which you have played up.'[6]

Yet the personal success had been achieved at no little cost. Admiral Sir Lionel Halsey, who had accompanied the Prince as an equerry on the tour, knew that his young charge was working far too hard. At visits to the hospitals, the Prince made an effort to talk to almost every bedridden soldier, 'and his sympathy with them is so genuine that of course he finds it extremely hard to go on for any length of time.'[7] Such efforts, repeated over and over again, brought on exhaustion and an obstinate refusal to find solace – not resting or going to bed at a sensible hour, but staying up too late, talking, smoking and drinking too much. Before the tour was over he had brought himself dangerously close to collapse.

By the time he returned to England he was exhausted by his efforts, and horrified to hear that he was going to be sent off again shortly on a tour of Australia and New Zealand. Three weeks of this precious interval at home, he had been told, would be spent with his parents at Sandringham, from where he wrote to his private secretary, Godfrey Thomas, on Christmas Day 1919. 'A sort of hopelessly lost feeling has come over me and I think I'm going kind of mad!! . . . How I loathe my job now and all this press "puffed" empty "succes". I feel I'm through with it and long and long to die.'[8] It was not the first letter of this kind that Thomas had received, but this one struck him as worryingly unbalanced. A firm commonsense reply, telling him to look after his health, let off steam occasionally and be 'cross and irritable instead of pathetic', and above all 'give it a chance', did the trick.

Even so, as he set sail on board HMS *Renown* from Portsmouth that March to begin his tour of the Antipodes, he was in a gloomy frame of mind. Having his cousin Lord Louis Mountbatten to accompany him as his aide provided him with some company and a kindred soul in whom to confide. But by the end of the summer, after visiting over two hundred different places in the Australian continent and having travelled nearly forty-six thousand miles in the process, he was again physically and mentally prostrated. His letters to Freda were filled with weary references to 'desperate little parties' which he was obliged to attend, and 'boring and irritating stunts' in which he was expected to take part. 'What a hopeless mess the whole world is in just now & each day I long more & more to chuck this job & be out of it & free for YOU'[9] he wrote to her from New Zealand on 28 April 1920. By mid-July he was on the verge of a breakdown. He rambled off the point in speeches and eventually lost his voice, and even those who did not know him well found him morose and uncommunicative. His staff were so alarmed that they insisted on the itinerary for the rest of the tour being postponed by a week, so as to give him a chance to rest.

As *Renown* sailed home that autumn, according to Mountbatten, the Prince would 'shut himself in his cabin for days, alone, face drawn, eyes brooding.' Initially the King was unsympathetic to reports of his son's exhaustion, but Halsey informed his sovereign bluntly that the Prince was 'only a human being and not a machine', and could not continue at such a pitch indefinitely. At length the King was persuaded that he was overworked, and agreed to postpone his tour of India, scheduled for the autumn, for a year. In turn, once he came back to England his son was to lead 'a strictly normal life,' resting, eating and sleeping properly.

At home, an active royal patron of industrial welfare schemes was needed. In 1919 it was proposed that one of the princes should become President of the Boys' Welfare Association, an organization through which industry itself might be responsible for the development of the growing movement for the betterment of working conditions, setting up of works' committees, provision of health centres and canteens in factories, and of proper facilities for maximum of enjoyment in the workers' free time. Prince Albert, it was felt, would be the best person for this post, and he agreed, 'providing there's no damned red carpet about it.'

He was determined to make more of his duties than mere

paternalism. When he visited factories, he did so in working hours, and demanded to see the shop floor as it really was. There must be no special preparations on his behalf. He went down coal mines, climbed scaffolding, and sat at the controls of buses and tramcars. When courteously advised on one occasion that the soapworks factory on his itinerary had a glue department with an overpowering stench, he answered firmly that if the place was good enough for the people who worked there, it was good enough for him.

In time, the press dubbed him 'the Industrial Prince', and his brothers called him 'the Foreman'. When one of the ministers, brought up some question of industrial relations, the King said with a chuckle, 'Oh, that's my second son's department.'

To an extent, the effect was only cosmetic. The twenties were a time of industrial unrest on a major scale. Factory conditions and wages were not improved overnight. None the less, his interest in industrial matters was consistent over the years, and helped him to develop the human touch. He had inherited the royal memory for faces and names, many of which he remembered in his later years.

At the same time, he looked for a more personal involvement. He believed that the gulf between the working and upper classes was the greatest threat to the fabric of society. In 1921 he attended a football match between boys from Briton Ferry Steelworks and Westminster School, and afterwards he was inspired by the organizer, philanthropist Sir Alexander Grant, to reflect o the possibility of a meeting ground where the boys could get together properly. From discussions with others evolved his idea of boys' camps, held initially at a wartime aerodrome at New Romsey, Kent.

The first one, held in 1921, was a modest success. With two boys, aged between seventeen and nineteen, from each of a hundred public schools, and a hundred firms, a volunteer staff, and the Duke of York himself as host, what had begun as an experiment in which nobody else had much faith gradually took off. Competitive games for the boys were organized, in which the Duke happily joined, dressed in the standard camp kit of identical shirts and shorts. In 1930 the camp was transferred from Romsey, where privacy had been eroded by day-trippers and cameramen, to Southwold in Suffolk.

One of the great changes wrought by the war was the difficulty of finding marital partners for any of the King's children from the houses which had ruled or reigned over the German states before 1918. In retrospect it had been fortunate that Princess Mary's future had not been as Princess Ernest Augustus of Hanover. Yet newspapers, particularly in other European countries, were ever ready to speculate on the liklihood of royal brides, even sometimes announcing fictitious betrothals. In February 1919 the Prince of Wales was angered by the French press's totally unfounded announcement of his engagement to the eldest daughter of the King and Queen of Italy. He asked the Embassy to insist on immediate retraction; 'it naturally infuriates me, particularly as the girl has a face like a bottom!!'[10]

With his protective instincts, the Prince of Wales felt nothing but sympathy for the sister whom he thought was being kept as an old maid, by a possessive father. Devoted as he was to his mother, he temporarily fell out with her at one stage after asking her to talk to his father about the subject of a marriage for Princess Mary. Believing that she had done nothing about it, he was 'so annoyed with her that I haven't been near her for over a week.' To Lady Airlie, he expressed his anxiety over Mary's unhappiness, lamenting that if only she would confide in him a little more he might be able to do something, but she was too unselfish. She was still the same girl who, when smaller, had often declined the chance of a game of tennis with her brothers because she still had her French lessons to do, or had not read *The Times* that day. While staying at Sandringham over Christmas 1919, he was depressed at his family's being into 'this pompous secluded & monotonous groove'. Mary was the one for whom he felt the most sorry, as he explained in a letter to Freda on Boxing Day; her life was 'the greatest tragedy of all . . . though it's not her fault as it's the way she's been brought up & she's quite happy & not to be pitied as far as she is concerned!!'[11]

In October 1921 Princess Mary went to the Grand National, and a few days later she attended a house party at Chatsworth, where she was the guest of honour. At both, she was seen continually in the company of Henry, Viscount Lascelles.

Lascelles was the eldest son of the 5th Earl of Harewood. He was fourteen years her senior, and lacked charm and good looks – behind his back he was known as 'that dismal bloodhound' – but he had a large personal fortune, inherited from an eccentric great-uncle, and similar interests to the King and Queen – namely shooting, and a connoisseur's eye for fine paintings and antiques. His war record was impeccable. While serving in France as second-in-command of the 3rd Battalion Grenadiers – during which time he had met the Prince of Wales – he was wounded three times by enemy fire and gassed; he later received the DSO and *Croix de Guerre* for his bravery. A common passion for horses and hunting united them, and when Henry was invited to Balmoral and later to Sandringham, it was evident that an annoucement would soon be expected. In November the King officially gave his consent to their engagement.

The Prince of Wales was in India when he heard the news. With his 'inordinate dislike for weddings,' it was no great disappointment for him to miss the occasion, but he thought it marvellous that 'that poor girl is going to be free and let out of Buckhouse prison.' Lascelles was 'too old for her and not attractive,' but 'I hope to God he'll make her happy, as she does deserve that if anyone does.'[12]

The wedding, the first great state occasion since peace was declared, took place at Westminster Abbey on 28 February 1922. Mary's wedding veil of Honiton lace had been worn by her mother and her grandmother, the Duchess of Teck, and some of the lace had belonged to Catherine of Aragon.

As the family had predicted, Mary left 'a terrible blank behind her'. 'Things will be very different here now that Mary has left and Mama will miss her too terribly,' the Duke of York wrote sadly to the Prince of Wales. He hoped that their sister's wedding might jolt the King and Queen into society a little more, 'I feel that they can't possibly stay in & dine together every night of their lives . . . & I don't see what they are going to do othewise, except ask people here or go out themselves.'[13]

One of the bridegroom's relations had offered the young couple the Villa Medici at Fiesole, outside Florence, for the honeymoon. Queen Mary, remembering her sojourn there as a young woman, drew up an itinerary of places for her daughter and son-in-law to visit. In due course the Princess wrote her mother long descriptions of art galleries and historic beauty spots.

The presence of British royalty in their midst was a cause of no little excitement to the 'British colony' in Florence. One woman among them who had plenty of money but as yet few friends saw a way to take revenge on those whom she believed to be cold-shouldering her. She sent round invitations to those with whom she was not on visiting terms, inviting them to dine one night at her villa and have the honour of meeting Her Royal Highness the Princess Mary, Viscountess Lady Lascelles. The guests arrived in their evening best, were served cocktails, and only after drinking them were they told that an official engagement had suddenly prevented Her Royal Highness from attending. Despite their disappointment, the guests availed themselves of a sumptuous meal. Not for some time did they realize that the whole affair had been a hoax.

On their return home, squire and Princess based themselves in the West Riding of Yorkshire, living at the family home, Harewood House, and at Goldsborough Hall on the Harewood estate, given to them as a wedding present. They also had a London home, Chesterfield House in Mayfair, and paid regular visits to the Lascelles' Irish seat, Portumna Castle, County Galway, but it was on their Yorkshire estates that Mary felt most at home. She enjoyed her life of virtual seclusion in the countryside, doing the rounds of race meetings and agricultural shows. Within two and a half years of marriage she gave birth to two sons, George, born on 7 February 1923, and Gerald, born on 21 August the following year.

Both sons recalled their mother as very kind but a rather detached figure. Among the family, George observed in his memoirs, 'we did not talk of love and affection and what we meant to each other, but rather – and even about that not easily – of duty and behaviour and what we ought to do.'[14]

Although she was a King's daughter and lived in a proud country house, the Princess was a thrifty soul, and was said to stuff her Chippendale furniture with every scrap of used wrapping paper and string. Profoundly superstitious, she would bow to a magpie three times to ward off bad luck; and if she saw a piebald horse, she would remain silent until she had seen a dog afterwards.

Her shy temperament and poor health were regarded as signs of unhappiness, and rumour had it that despite their shared interests in horses and racing, the marriage was not a success. Indeed, as the people came to know more and more of the autocratic Lascelles, they wondered what she had ever seen in him. When a film production unit made a short movie of the Bramham Moor Hunt, of which he was Master, he ordered cuts to be made, and even then he would never allow it to be trade-shown unless Home Office officials were present. Even the family came to regard him with scant enthusiasm. 'I get commoner and commoner,' the Prince of Wales once remarked, 'while Lascelles gets more and more royal.'

For the Duke of York, wedding bells would soon ring. At the RAF ball in 1920 he had met a girl whom he vaguely remembered sitting next to at a children's party in 1905 – Lady Elizabeth Bowes-Lyon. In due course she became a close friend of Princess Mary, and a bridesmaid at the wedding.

King George and Queen Mary could not help noticing how the Duke was always talking about her. Though the Queen stoutly maintained that parents should never meddle in their children's love affairs, she was curious to find out more. On a visit to Balmoral, she drove over to the Bowes-Lyons home, Glamis Castle. As Lady Strathmore was unwell, her daughter Elizabeth acted as host. She made a favourable impression on Queen Mary, whose first reaction was that this young woman would make an ideal wife for the Prince of Wales. After being told by Lady Airlie that Edward, with his uncomfortable penchant for married women, was not quite ready to settle down just yet and that her second son was passionately fond of Elizabeth, she changed her mind.

'You'll be a lucky fellow if she accepts you,' King George warned him gruffly, intending to prepare his son for disappointment if he should be rejected. Lady Airlie thought Elizabeth was uncertain about her feelings, and afraid of the public life which would lie ahead of a King's daughter-in-law. Lady Strathmore was sorry for the persistent suitor who sometimes seemed in despair at his lack of success; she liked him very much and realized that he was 'a man who will be made or marred by his wife.' It was a comment that could have applied equally to all the princes.

In the first week of 1923, the press announced that the Prince of Wales was soon to be betrothed, and that the next Queen of England was the daughter of a well-known Scottish peer, and a close friend of Princess Mary. In all details, save one, they were correct; she was not destined to be Prince Edward's bride. A few days later, the Duke of York went to stay with the Strathmores at their Hertfordshire home, St Paul's Walden Bury. He proposed and Elizabeth, reconciled to a royal future, accepted him . News of the engagement was received with delight by the family, though diarist Henry 'Chips' Channon suggested that the London clubs were in gloom as there was not a man in England who did not envy him.

The wedding took place on 26 April, at Westminster Abbey. There had not been such a ceremony there for a prince of the royal house since that of King Richard II to Anne of Bohemia in 1383. Elizabeth looked charming in a deceptively simple medieval-styled chiffon moire dress embroidered with silver thread and pearls, and sleeves of Nottingham lace, while the groom wore RAF full dress uniform. Among the guests were thirty boys from factories, chosen through the Industrial Welfare Society. A request by the BBC to broadcast the service was refused by the Chapter of the Abbey, against the Dean's advice, on the grounds that it might be listened to in public houses by gentlemen with their hats on.

King George V, who had told Queen Mary the previous summer how he dreaded the idea of having daughters-in-law, was captivated by the Duchess of York. If he needed to remonstrate with her, he did so gently. Mildly disturbed by her willingness to cooperate with journalists, he sent word through an equerry to request that she should grant no more interviews. Yet he accepted her habitual unpunctuality, much as he deprecated it in others. When his son and daughter-in-law arrived two minutes late for dinner one evening and she apologized, he astonished everyone by telling her genially that the rest of them must have sat down two minutes too early. To a courtier who remarked privately that the Duchess was sometimes unpunctual, he defended her with a smile by saying that if she was never late, she would be perfect, 'and how horrible that would be!'

Representation on various missions abroad increased the Duke's confidence. In 1922 he had represented the King as 'Koom' or chief sponsor at the wedding of the daughter of Queen Marie of Roumania, Marie, to Alexander, King of Yugoslavia, and again in October 1923 to stand as godfather to their first child, and as 'Koom' at the wedding of the King's brother Prince Paul to Princess Olga of Greece. Closer to home, the Duke and Duchess paid a visit in 1924 to Northern Ireland, where he was impressed with Unionist loyalty shown him as the sovereign's representative, even in the poorer parts of Belfast. Wounds left by the Irish civil war and partition between the Catholic republic and Protestant Ulster had far from healed.

Yet the stammer, that still made speaking in public an ordeal, continued to undermine the now happily married Duke's confidence. As President of the British Empire Exhibition in 1925, he was called upon to speak. The Prince of Wales had done so admirably the year before; this time, noted the King tersely, 'Bertie got through alright but there were some rather long pauses.'

At length he was persuaded to consult Lionel Logue, an Australian speech therapist based in London. When the Duke walked through his door, Logue saw 'a slim quiet man, with tired eyes and all the outward symptoms of the man upon whom habitual speech defect had begun to set the sign.'[15] By teaching him the techniques of breathing rhythm and that it was his responsibility to carry out the discipline, Logue effected a considerable improvement. The Duke's impediment was never completely cured; when tired or anxious, it would manifest itself again, but he managed to master his difficulties to the extent that speaking in public was no longer the nightmare it had been before.

The Yorks' first married home was White Lodge, Richmond Park, Queen Mary's childhood home. Large, expensive to maintain, it was too close to the public gaze. The Duchess preferred the idea of a London home, and at length they moved into a house in Piccadilly. They led a modest, quiet life, in stark contrast to that of the Prince of Wales and his 'smart' set. A friend of the latter found them rather prim and proper; the Duchess's vocation 'was to look after him and be a good wife.'[16] Regarding night clubs and the social round with indifference, they preferred to lead a quiet domestic life, staying with friends in the country while he went hunting and shooting, and she went fishing. The Duke of York, it was noted, was becoming increasingly like his father, while the Prince of Wales was more like their grandfather – the difference, though, being that at least the future King Edward VII was married early in adult life and had two sons to safeguard the succession.

On 21 April 1926, the Duchess gave birth to their first child, whom they named Elizabeth Alexandra Mary, names in honour of the baby's mother, of Queen Alexandra (who had died five months previously), and of her grandmother. A hesitant enquiry as to whether the name Victoria still had to be used for all the late Queen's female descendants met with a kindly word from the King, who said he hardly thought it necessary by now. The King adored his granddaughter; while her Lascelles cousins found him explosive and rather frightening, she had no fear of him whatsoever.

In January 1927, the Duke and Duchess visited New Zealand and Australia, the main purpose of their visit being to open the new Parliament House, Canberra. The Duke was as nervous as the Australian Prime Minister, Stanley Bruce, about his ability to cope with several weeks of public speaking. Fortunately Logue's techniques had given him confidence and he acquitted himself well, particularly as the Duchess was struck down with tonsilitis on their arrival in South Island, New Zealand, and he had to undertake several functions on his own. They arrived home at Portsmouth in June, to an instruction by the King that they would not embrace at the station before so many people, 'and when you kiss Mama take your hat off.'

On 20 December 1923, his twenty-first birthday, Prince George was appointed a Knight of the Garter. He was glad to be home on leave for Christmas, and his mother in particular was always happy to have him near her. He was the only one of her children to share her interest in historical pictures, antiques and *objets d'art*; and the only one in whom she could confide easily.

His self-confidence and tact helped him to avoid the confrontations with his father that his elder brothers seemed almost invariably to provoke. He was difficult to intimidate, and had a disarming way of answering 'Papa' back with the right mixture of firmness and charm. Being more articulate, he found it easier to argue his way out of difficult situations. Moreover, as the youngest of four brothers, the royal inheritance weighed on him least heavily of all. As a son who had little chance of succeeding to the throne, his parents never felt the need to apply the same pressure on him during his upbringing as they had on the others.

Yet he too chafed under parental tyranny. While abroad on one occasion, he wrote to the Prince of Wales, saying he intended to stand up to the King when he got home, as he was determined he would 'have no more being told off without answering back. I'm sure it's the only way . . . as he's so impossible.'[17]

As a bachelor, the closest bond George ever formed was with the Prince of Wales. The differences in their characters complemented each other. Geroge sympathized with Edward's restlessness, while the latter realized how unhappy his younger brother was at sea, and regularly tried to urge the King to give him additional leave from naval duties in order to prepare himself for a more active role in public life. In 1927 George accompanied Edward on a short official visit to Spain. Edward had already undertaken several arduous tours on his own, to Australia, New Zealand, India, Japan, and the United States. He enjoyed having his brother's lively and stimulating company as much as George benefited from the break in naval routine. When they returned from Spain, the family immediately noticed how fit, bronzed and happy Prince George looked.

Prince George was popular in the navy; he was pleasant, easy going, and never tried to avoid unpopular duties. In addition he had a prankish sense of humour. On a visit to China some press photographers, hearing that a representative of British royalty was somewhere nearby, met him as he was about to board his ship and asked if he had seen the King of England. Without hesitation he gestured behind him towards the ship's doctor, a heavily-built man being carried in a sedan chair. Later he had the satisfaction of seeing the doctor's picture in a newspaper with a caption saying he was 'the English King'.

Yet he never really enjoyed life at sea, and had one narrow escape from death. When the battleship *Queen Elizabeth*, on which he was serving, had a drifter *Blue Sky* attached to her, young midshipmen were sent aboard as an exercise to improve their skills in seamanship. George asked to be allowed to board the drifter as well, but the captain refused him permission. It was just as well, for *Blue Sky* ran into fierce weather, foundered and sank with the loss of all hands. The Prince was so upset that he asked to be transferred to another ship.

None the less there were rewards to be gained from life in the navy. When George served as a lieutenant with the Mediterranean and Atlantic Fleets and the China Squadron, and on the South African and West Indies Stations, he was able to see for himself some of the greatest ports in the world. During shore leave, he was able to wander around in places as varied and as far apart as Shanghai and Rio de Janeiro. Without detectives or equerries, he saw for himself the red light districts and perimeters of shanty towns.

Not only in foreign ports did he see suffering and hardship at first hand. During short spells as duty officer on ships docked in some of the hard-hit British ports like Liverpool and Portsmouth, he became well aware that men who had fought for their country during the Great War were finding it desperately hard to get work.

Yet George was determined to leave the navy. The King envied his youngest surviving son; he had thoroughly enjoyed his own years at sea and regretted that his brother Eddy's death had cut short his service career, and in his unimaginative way could not understand why any son of his should not want to stay in the navy. An appeal to the King himself fell on deaf ears. Wanting to go into the Civil Service or the Foreign Office instead, he discussed his problem with Lady Airlie. She wisely told him that there was nothing to be gained by arguing with his father, but to take what opportunities he could while at sea to study for the civil service exams, do them and let the King see the results. Accordingly, on his last voyage he devoted all his spare time studying in his cramped cabin.

But by this time, Prince George's chronic stomach problems while at sea could no longer be ignored. A medical examination suggested that if he was forced to continue in the navy, his health and digestive trouble would be gravely impaired. In 1929 he was promoted to Commander and officially discharged from the service, to his tremendous relief.

In character the third son, Prince Henry, was very different from George. When fully grown he was the tallest of the brothers, and although an imposing-looking figure in military uniform he was the least good-looking. With his receding forehead and neat military moustache, he had inherited the Hanoverian looks – and the Hanoverian contempt for the fine arts. At a performance of *Tosca*, he watched with boredom as Maria Callas plunged over the battlements. Then his distinctive high-pitched voice rang round the opera house: 'Well if she's really dead, we can all go home.'[18]

Though she appreciated his steadfast qualities, Queen Mary had to admit in private that 'poor Harry' was inclined to be slow and somewhat boring. His detractors found him stodgy and remarked on his 'whinnying laugh'. As a young man, he found life at home with the family as tedious as his brothers generally did. The routine and formality of court life irked him, and he was always happier in a military environment, outside in the fresh air, or relaxing with friends in less formal surroundings. Resenting his father's disciplinarian attitude as much as his siblings did, and having no common ground with his mother's artistic interests, the oppressive atmosphere left him feeling like a fish out of water.

To others, his lack of 'side' could be endearing. Diana Cooper was a fellow guest at Belvoir Castle in the winter of 1919. She wrote to her husband that the Prince was 'not half bad' and a great deal better than his brother Albert. He arrived 'sans equerry, sans clothes, sans valet, sans everything', and she was 'favourably impressed with him.' After dinner, she went on, the guests played Blind Man's Buff for two hours, 'and the young ladies' dresses were torn and liberties were taken with the King's son – a fine success.' He amused them all with his story of a dove which had entered the mausoleum at Frogmore one January day as the royal family were kneeling to pray on the anniversary of Queen Victoria's death. When two of her daughters piously murmured that the dove was 'dear Mama's spirit', their sister Louise, Duchess of Argyll, indignantly retorted that 'dear Mama's spirit would never have ruined Beatrice's hat.'[19]

From an early age, Prince Henry had been determined to make the army his career, and it had been decided that after passing out of Sandhurst and leaving Cambridge he would join the King's Royal Rifle Corps. At Sandhurst he had been a promising recruit, and his Commandant informed the King that he only needed a little encouragement 'to overcome a certain diffidence as to his powers in order to develop into a really good officer.' By the time he finished at university in June 1920, the commanding officer of the 2nd Battalion told Lord Stamfordham that the unit had just been briefed for Ireland, and the latter advised against having one of His Majesty's sons stationed there at that time, not as a matter of personal risk to the Prince, but because it was inexpedient to put him in a position where he would be deployed against Irish forces. As a result, the King gave permission for him to go to Aldershot and be attached to the 13th Hussars. He joined his regiment in July 1920, and the following year joined the 10th Royal Hussars, the regiment which he would always regard as his own.

Although a conscientious and dedicated soldier, his colleagues found him as slow and sleepy as the family did at home. When attached to the Household Brigade, he was known behind his back as 'Uncle Pineapple', as his bearskin nodded like a pineapple topknot when he fell asleep without falling off his horse during rehearsals for trooping the colour.

By the 1920s, it was later understood, a career in the army had lost some of its pre-war glamour. *The Times* commented that 'it was dismissed as an irrelevance among those intellectual circles which were beginning to shape the thinking of that wild decade. Such thinking, together with the Duke's absorption in his profession, made him a decidedly less familiar personality to the public than were his brothers and sister.'[20]

However, he enjoyed shooting, point to point riding, and similar sporting activities, and he was a fearless horseman. Although never very good at polo he played with great enthusiasm, and his hunting and shooting prowess won his father's approval.

In January 1923, he had some enjoyable hunting with the Prince of Wales. He had noticed with concern how his elder brother was behaving in a spoilt fashion, objecting 'to being told what he had done wrong when he has made a mistake. It is so funny or rather – sad that he does object to being told the truth considering how keen he is.'[21]

The family encouraged him in these outdoor activities, for like the rest of his brothers he was inclined to drink too much. Although less attached to him than to his elder brothers, the Prince of Wales was probably responsible for suggesting to their parents that Harry should undertake more missions abroad. In his role as unofficial protector to his siblings, looking after their interests with an understanding of which their increasingly cantankerous father was less capable, he believed that the more Prince Henry was given to do – as long as he was not subjected to impossible demands and overwork – the less time he would have to brood and thus turn to the bottle to alleviate his boredom.

In November 1926, he was chosen to represent the King at the wedding of Crown Prince Leopold of the Belgians to Princess Astrid of Sweden, in Stockholm. As the princes had known each other well at Eton, he was an obvious choice. While he was away the King was informed by the British Minister in Warsaw, Sir William Max-Muller, of an extraordinary plan concerning his third son's future. Apparently Marshal Pilsudski, Prime Minister of Poland, was about to proclaim himself King. As he had no son to succeed him, he proposed to safeguard his new dynasty by marrying his eight-year-old daughter to Prince Henry. King George was dumbfounded at the idea, but did not take it seriously. Neither did his son; and the Marshal's monarchical and marital plans likewise came to nothing.

In March 1928 the King created Henry Duke of Gloucester, Earl of Ulster and Baron Culloden. There had not been a Duke of Gloucester since the death in 1834 of Prince William Frederick, Duke of Edinburgh and Gloucester, and nephew of King George III.

An expedition to Africa was to have unfortunate consequences. In September 1928 he and the Prince of Wales left England to go and shoot big game, and planned to spend Christmas with the Earl of Athlone, Governor- General of South Africa. At Nairobi, where the brothers parted for a while, he was entertained by various people including the Markham family. Mansfield Markham, a coal magnate, had been married for less than a year. His wife Beryl had a passion for flying, and later became the first woman to cross that Atlantic east-west solo.

Aviation, it soon turned out, was not her only passion. On her first meeting with the Duke of Gloucester, she set her cap at him, and soon it was alleged that he was completely besotted with her. They went on safari for a while, riding and shooting together, and she found him refreshingly unspoiled by privilege, good-humoured and excellent company. In November the brothers were recalled to England by the King's illness, and shortly before the end of the month Beryl, now six months pregnant, sailed back as well in order to avoid having her confinement in Kenya. The Duke met her on her return, and arranged for her to stay at a corner suite at the Grosvenor Hotel, close to Buckingham Palace. This was to be her London home for the next five years.

In February she gave birth to a son, Gervase, a sickly baby who was not expected to live for long though he eventually recovered. As devoted to her as ever, the Duke was 'said to be very attentive and attending on [Beryl] day and night', until their friends in Kenya were wondering whether 'the child could be reckoned to have royal blood'. Though it should have been clear to them that the baby was conceived long before his mother had met the Duke, the latter's obvious devotion to her was bound to result in scandal. Henry was said to be living openly with Beryl, hosting parties with her in her suite, and drinking too much. His mother took grave exception to this clandestine affair, remonstrating with him for bringing the royal family into disrepute, and the Prince of Wales was said to be 'delighted that for once Queen Mary's blue-eyed boy was in trouble instead of himself.'[22]

5

'Now all the children are married except David'

Since his injury in France in October 1915 King George V's health had never been good, and in November 1928 he took to his bed with what was at first regarded as a severe cold. Scepticaemia was diagnosed, his condition deteriorated, and on 1 December an ominous bulletin from Buckingham Palace announced 'a decline in the strength of the heart'. The Prince of Wales, on tour in East Africa, was warned of the family's anxiety, and prepared to return home. Wryly the Duke of York wrote to his brother, mentioning that he had heard rumours from the East End of London 'that the reason of your rushing home is that in the event of anything happening to Papa I am going to bag the Throne in your absence!!!! Just like the Middle Ages . . .'[1]

This levity masked feelings of deep concern, for the King was gravely ill. The Duke of York met his brother at Victoria station on his return home, telling him that he would find their father's appearance greatly changed; and that he was about to undergo an operation. The Duke was just as concerned about Queen Mary, whom he feared would have a breakdown if the worst happened . 'She is really far too reserved; she keeps too much locked up inside of her.'[2]

According to Stanley Baldwin, on his arrival at Buckingham Palace, the Prince of Wales ignored orders not to go near his father, who was apparently close to death. Taking no notice, he marched into the bedroom where the King had lain barely conscious for the past week. The invalid opened half an eye, looked up at him, and muttered, 'Damn you, what the devil are you doing here?' From that moment he began to recover rapidly. It makes a good story, though like several of Baldwin's other anecdotes, it was probably embroidered in the retelling.

The Prince's own account, written some two decades later and also perhaps distorted by memory, was rather different. He said that he was greeted with relief by Queen Mary, who told him that Papa kept asking where he was, and she took him straight to the sickroom. Although weak, he recognized his son instantly and mumbled something about how he hoped he had had good sport in Africa. Lady Mount Stephen, a close friend of Queen Mary, was told by him that he found his father 'a little, shrunken old man with a white beard,' and the shock was so great that he cried. The illness brought them together to the extent that the Prince said that he now felt for the first time he really had a father.[3]

Over Christmas, the King's condition showed some improvement, but convalescence took several months. Although a national service of thanksgiving for his recovery was held at St Paul's Cathedral in July 1929, not for another two months did the doctors feel confident enough to announce that he was really better. In fact he never enjoyed good health again. His nurse, Sister Catherine Black, remained close at hand, and the family found him ever more irascible and older than his years. 'George, don't you love your children?' his cousin and sister-in-law Alice, Countess of Athlone asked him one day. 'Of course I do,' he snapped. 'Then why don't you show it!' she retorted.

Though the Queen inwardly chafed on occasions at the quarterdeck manner he displayed towards their sons, she still accepted his word as law. 'I have always to remember,' she remarked to a friend, 'that their Father is also their King.'[4]

While recovering, he derived much pleasure from the company of his granddaughter Elizabeth. On Christmas Eve she was allowed to stay up and hear carols with him, and when she heard the line 'Glad tidings of great joy I bring to you and all mankind,' she ran across the room excitedly to hug him, saying, 'I know who Old Man Kind is!'

At Craigwell House, Bognor, a sandpit was dug for her in the corner of the garden. Queen Mary noted in her diary how delighted the King was to see her, while she played in the garden making sandpies with the child. When the King made his first public appearance to the crowd on the seafront, it was his granddaughter who stood beside him as he waved to the crowds.

At Christmas 1929 he gave her a pony of her own, and he was delighted to see how well she could ride. When she came to stay at Windsor the King and Queen were very indulgent with her, allowing her to sweep the food off his plate to feed a dog on the floor, and going down on his hands and knees to help her search for her hair-slide.

By this time the Duchess of York was expecting a second child. Everyone hoped it would be a boy. The heir to the throne showed no signs of wishing to marry, nor did the remaining brothers, and the King was ageing rapidly. Even the parents hoped as much, and when the Duchess of York gave birth to a second daughter on 21 August 1930, no girls' names had been chosen. The Duchess particularly wanted to call her Ann Margaret, but the King objected, and she was named Margaret Rose instead.

Though the Duke of York never completely lost his awe of his father, the relationship between both had eased considerably. 'Delighted to have Bertie with me,' the King had written to Queen Mary two years earlier; 'have had several talks with him & find him very sensible, very different to D[avid]'.[5]

In 1929 Princess Mary's husband succeeded his father as Earl of Harewood, and she became Countess. Two years later her aunt Louise, the reclusive Princess Royal and Duchess of Fife, died after several years of ill-health. In the New Year Honours List of January 1932 the title of Princess Royal was bestowed on Mary. Such elevation, however, made little difference to her way of life. She continued to make regular appearances in public, especially where engagements involved nursing and the Women's Services, but she and her family continued to spend as much time in Yorkshire and as little in London as they reasonably could.

The grounds of Harewood House contained a forty-acre lake. During a particularly severe winter in the early thirties, the surface froze over, and family and estate staff enjoyed three weeks' continuous sport. The highlight was an ice hockey match one Saturday afternoon, arranged by the Earl, who was a particularly skilled skater. His chief gardener Geoffrey Hall, whose team included the Countess in goal, tried hard to bring him down during the match, but to no avail. Mr Hall was quite accomplished at the sport himself, and the Countess asked him to teach her sons. Gerald, the younger, made a good pupil, recalled the gardener, but although he taught George to skate as well 'I do not think he ever forgave me.'

The Duke of Gloucester was now performing his first ambassadorial duties abroad. With the King's worsening health, there was less justification for allowing the Prince of Wales to travel too far in case he should suddenly succeed to the throne; and the Queen considered it would be prudent to keep him at a safe distnace from Beryl Markham in an effort to try and prevent the liaison from becoming too strong for their own good. In the summer of 1929 Henry was sent to attend the Coronation of Hirohito, Emperor of Japan, and to invest him with the Order of the Garter. He himself was then invested with the Grand Order of the Chrysanthemum. The following year, he represented his father at the Coronation of Haile Selassie as Emperor of Abyssinia.

Nevertheless the affair had run its course. Soon after his return from Japan, the Duke was back at the Grosvenor with Beryl, where parties were still held, with several of their friends from Kenya among those present. There was speculation that Mansfield and his elder brother Sir Charles Markham, as titular head of the family, planned to end the marriage in court, citing the Duke as co-respondent unless he formally agreed to 'take care of Beryl'. Queen Mary informed Sir Charles bluntly that 'one simply could not cite a Prince of the Blood in a divorce petition', and the matter was settled privately in December

1929, with the establishment of a trust fund and an annuity paid by London solicitors on behalf of the Duke and his estate until her death in August 1985.[6]

Nor did the Prince of Wales show any signs of settling down. Though he and the Duke of York had been very close, maintaining something of a united front against what they regarded as their father's pettiness, after the Duke married he gradually came to resemble the King more in outlook. It was therefore to George, with whom he had so much in common, that he turned increasingly as a companion. The elder Prince was much more at home in society life, relishing the company of fast, amusing frivolous people, who frequented night clubs. He was often to be seen dancing the Charleston in the small hours with frenzied energy.

Tiny Winters, a jazz musician who saw both Princes regularly at the Embassy Club in London, recalled one occasion when they stayed all night. The moment they left, an exhausted band 'shot out to catch the buses.' As they did so, they ran into the royal brothers, who had just run into the street themselves and were having a riotous time playing with each others top hats, climbing up lamp posts and putting them on the iron bars, then chasing one another as they kicked their hats all over the road.

King George's forebodings that his youngest son would 'get into bad company' after leaving the navy and taking up residence at York House were soon realized. A natural taste for the glamour of society life and showbusiness personalities was actively encouraged by the Prince of Wales, and after the restrictions and discipline of service life, the temptation of this garden of earthly delights proved more than he could handle. It was unfortunate that his period of freedom coincided with that following the Prince of Wales's return from his gruelling tours abroad and his determination to embark on an existence of nightclub hedonism. There were affairs with at least two aristocratic girls, whom it was rumoured at various times he was keen on marrying. One was 'Poppy' Baring, who said herself that she 'couldn't bear the royal family'. However, the Prince seemed to have overcome her objections, and told his parents at the end of the month that he wanted to marry. Initially the King and Queen raised no objections, but ten days later it was all off; 'unfavourable reports' about her had reached the ears of His Majesty.

Rumours of Prince George's scandalous behaviour multiplied. How much was based on fact and how much was gossip is open to conjecture, but there was talk of unsavoury liaisons with an Argentinian diplomat, an Italian aristocrat, and the playwright Noel Coward, who in later life 'seemed rather proud of it [his affair with the Prince] and at times was almost a bore on the subject.'[7]

Matters came to a head when Prince George met a vivacious American woman, Kiki Whitney Preston, who introduced him to cocaine and morphine. After trying for several months to separate them, the Prince of Wales persuaded her to leave the country, and then told his brother that she had gone to live permanently abroad. Disconsolate, heavily dependent on narcotics, and at a thoroughly low ebb, Prince George offered no resistance when the Prince of Wales took him firmly in hand, as 'doctor, gaoler and detective combined'.

The episode brought out the best side of the Prince of Wales's character. He dutifully sacrificed the chance of a holiday with Mrs Dudley Ward, in order to put his brother back on the right track, and by the end of 1929 'the cure' had worked. 'It really is a terrible and terrifying thing to happen to anyone, and far worse to one's brother,'[8] he wrote to the King in January 1930. The whole business resulted in a great, if only temporary, improvement in relations between father and eldest son, and the former was grateful; 'Looking after him all those months must have been a great strain on you, and I think it was wonderful all you did for him.'[9] Apart from one anxious moment a couple of years later when Prince George met Kiki Preston unexpectedly at Cannes and had to be removed almost by force, the crisis had passed and he had evidently learnt his lesson.

Despite the self-indulgence, there was another side to the Prince's character. A talented pianist, he was the first member of the royal family since Queen Victoria's youngest son, the

Duke of Albany, to show a pronounced interest in the arts. As a bachelor he built up an excellent collection of antique furniture, first editions, Georgian silver, porcelain, and pictures. Regarded, albeit in a kindly way, as 'somewhat of a Bohemian' by his parents, George was very different in outlook and temperament from his brothers.

After leaving the navy in 1929 he was attached to the Foreign Office, becoming the first Prince to be a civil servant. Not finding the work sufficiently demanding, and sharing concern for the plight of the unemployed, he moved two years later to the Home Office, becoming an official factory inspector.

He began this role in April 1932. On his own insistence his royal status was played down to a minimum, so that in the early days he appeared to be just an ordinary trainee factory inspector learning his job. Accompanied by a senior inspector, he began his tours of factories in the London area at 10 a.m., working through till 5 p.m. Dressed as inconspicuously as possible, he gained an extraordinary insight into working conditions, many of them leaving much to be desired in the way of safety measures. Men who had no idea of his true identity poured out their troubles and grievances and found a sympathetic and eager listener. He clambered over ladders and scaffolding, came to understand the monotony of assembly lines, made his way up and down dimly lit staircases and tramped across concrete floors until his feet ached. During the summer months he spent long days going to firms making lift equipment, paint, fine chemicals, photographic materials, wirelesses, and clothing. When he got back to York House at night he prepared detailed reports of his findings to present to his superior the following morning.

Inevitably he was soon recognized, and owners of small firms and premises thought it a great honour to be visited by the King's son. They showed him such hospitality that his carefully-timed schedules of visiting were held up. In addition, his public engagements were increasing in number, and the Home Office were dismayed that 'social and other functions' were allowed to take precedence over his inspection work.

And still the Prince of Wales showed no sign of wishing to marry. He saw Mrs Dudley Ward, who had divorced her husband in 1931, every day while they were in London. Although the King referred to her scathingly as 'a lacemaker's daughter', she was always spoken of as being 'very good for him'. The same could not be said for the young, frivolous, American-born Thelma, Lady Furness. Her second marriage was already on the rocks by the time she met the Prince of Wales. Whereas Freda Dudley Ward had curbed his self-indulgence and irresponsibility, Lady Furness actively encouraged his high-spirited behaviour. They led a pleasure-seeking life, dining and dancing at London clubs, and once went on safari to Africa. They spent cosy weekends living in apparent domestic bliss at Fort Belvedere, leading a quiet life as she watched him pottering in the garden, pruning his trees and playing the bagpipes. In one way, though, her influence was beneficial. She taught him needlepoint, in the hope that it would give him something to occupy himself during evenings at home instead of drinking, on the grounds that 'the hand that holds the needle cannot hold the brandy snifter.'

Yet the Prince was never more than superficially faithless to Freda, who was still the strongest influence in his life.

Fort Belvedere, a grace and favour house situated on land bordering Windsor Great Park near Sunningdale, provided the Prince with some respite away from the clatter of London. Here he might be seen in plus-fours and loudly-patterned sweaters, working in the garden. The house and garden had been neglected, becoming untidy and overgrown; the Prince threw himself heart and soul into modernizing it, decorating the house, adding bathrooms and a swimming pool. At weekends he would invite his brothers over to help clear the shrubbery. He enjoyed every moment at the Fort, and begrudged the time he had to spend away from it.

The Yorks, living at Royal Lodge, were near-neighbours of the Prince at Fort Belvedere. Though they did not share his social life, they remained good friends on a family basis, and never gave up hope that he would eventually find himself a suitable wife.

One evening at their London home they were entertaining a woman friend when the Prince of Wales rang to invite them round to York House. When they arrived, they found 'almost nobody else', except for Princess Marina of Greece. The Yorks' friend later recalled that he danced with her the whole evening, and she 'could see that the Duke and Duchess of York were thrilled. Then Freda Dudley Ward arrived back next day and that was the end of that.'[10]

By now he found Buckingham Palace particularly gloomy. To Lady Diana Cooper, he described how he and his brothers 'froze up' whenever they stepped inside, how bad-tempered their father was, and how the Duchess of York was 'the one bright spot there. They all love her and the King is in a good temper whenever she is there.'[11] As he aged, the King clung more and more to the ways of his youth, paticularly sartorial fashions. This caused endless friction between father and son. One morning at breakfast the Prince, was rebuked by the King for not wearing gloves at the ball the previous night, and ordered to 'see that this does not happen again'. When the Prince arrived at the Palace sporting trousers with the latest fashion in turn-ups, the King took one look at him and asked sarcastically, 'Is it raining in *here?*'

The other Princes likewise found their father's attitude petty and niggling, though they knew better than to provoke arguments over such issues. After an altercation at Balmoral between the King and the Prince of Wales on how to wear the kilt correctly, Prince George remarked wryly to a minister in attendance that he never knew what to do with all the knives and forks and other accessories demanded by the kilt.

In January 1931, Lady Furness held a weekend house party at Burrough Court, near Melton Mowbray, to which she invited the Prince of Wales. A married couple who were also on the guest list suddenly fell ill, and in their place she invited Mr and Mrs Ernest Simpson.

Like Lady Furness, Mrs Simpson was born in America, and was already once divorced. In 1928 she made a second marriage to Ernest Simpson, a native of New York who had served in the Coldstream Guards and become a naturalized British citizen. Though Mrs Simpson had lived in England for several years, she still clung fiercely to her 'American ways and opinions', and her Baltimore accent was very pronounced. Hard-faced and by no means attractive, she was always elegant and well-dressed, and the Prince of Wales found her sympathetic, understanding and witty. Though she made little impression on him at their first meeting, she and her husband invited him to dine at their London flat a year later, and soon an invitation to spend a weekend at Fort Belvedere followed. The association, as she remarked in her memoirs, 'imperceptibly but swiftly passed from an acquaintanceship to a friendship.'[12] Mutual friends and members of the household soon noticed that the Prince appeared to be infatuated by her as never before.

They were horrified with the way she behaved; she was harsh, domineering and rude to everyone. Because the Prince never complained, she treated him worst of all. Once the other guests had departed from the Fort, the servants saw or heard her nagging and taunting him until he was reduced to tears.

Other acquaintances were prepared to give them the benefit of the doubt. Alfred Duff Cooper concluded after a lengthy conversation with her that she was a pleasant and sensible woman, 'but she is as hard as nails and she doesn't love him.' Early in 1934, Lady Furness decided to join her twin sister Gloria on a visit to California. When she told the Prince that she would be away for five or six weeks, she noticed, his face took on a resigned look. When she told Mrs Simpson, the latter remarked that 'the little man is going to be so lonely'. Jokingly, Lady Furness asked her friend to 'look after him' for her while she was away.

The Prince of Wales invited the Simpsons to stay at Fort Belvedere again and to dine at the Dorchester. For the next few weeks, they were rarely out of each others company. When Lady Furness returned to England in March, she noticed an undoubted coolness towards her from the Prince; although formally cordial, he appeared personally distant. Puzzled, she asked Mrs Simpson, only to be told blandly that 'the little man' loved her very much, and was just lost without her.

At the end of the month, Lady Furness drove the Simpsons down to Fort Belvedere. On the following evening, at dinner, she saw that the Prince and Mrs Simpson seemed to be indulging in little private jokes throughout. When he picked up a piece of salad with his fingers, Wallis playfully slapped his hand. Lady Furness caught her eye and shook her head sternly. Wallis looked straight back; 'That one cold, defiant glance had told me the entire story.'[13] She left the Fort the following morning, never again to see or hear from the Prince.

One month later, it was the turn of Freda Dudley Ward. Her eldest daughter had been seriously ill after an operation for appendicitis. For several weeks she was so preoccupied with the girl's health, that it was not until she was on the way to recovery that she realized the Prince of Wales had not telephoned or visited for some time, although he was still in England. She put a call through to the switchboard at St James's Palace. The operator, who knew and liked Mrs Dudley Ward, replied in tones of great distress: 'I have something so terrible to tell you, that I don't know how to say it.' After being encouraged, she went on sorrowfully, 'I have orders not to put you through.'[14]

It was therefore some consolation to the family that Prince George was about to redeem himself and settle down. He had first met Princess Marina of Greece and Denmark, a granddaughter of Queen Alexandra's brother King George, in 1923, and though he was immediately taken with her, she returned home before anything could come of it. When he met her again ten years later, on another visit to England, it was evident that they had eyes for nobody but each other. Marina's brother-in-law, Prince Paul of Yugoslavia, acted as matchmaker by inviting Prince George to come and stay at Bohinj, his summer home in the Slovenian mountains, when Princess Marina was there in August 1934.

The family were relieved and delighted when the engagement between them was announced. Princess Victoria, the King's spinster sister, summed up the elder generation's feelings: 'Of course it is the best thing for him. Marina is a sweet child and so pretty and I do hope she will look after him and give him a happy home.'[15]

Like her great-aunt Princess Alexandra of Denmark in 1863, Princess Marina arrived in England with no fortune to her name, for her family had suffered as a result of turbulent political events since the Great War. However, she had grace, beauty and intelligence. As Prince George told Prince Paul of Yugoslavia with some glee, when the British public gathered, waiting to welcome her at Victoria station in September, they expected 'a dowdy princess – such as unfortunately my family are.' When she stepped out of the carriage, they could hardly believe their eyes, and shouted good-naturedly, 'Don't change – don't let them change you!'[16]

In October, Prince George was created Duke of Kent, a title that had been vacant since the last holder, the father of Queen Victoria, had died in January 1820. At a Buckingham Palace reception a couple of days before the wedding, among the guests were Mrs Simpson. The Prince of Wales introduced her to his parents, who both greeted her politely. As Queen Mary would later recall, this was the only occasion on which she had ever received the woman who would cause such bitterness among everyone involved. Mrs Simpson later recalled that it was only a brief encounter – a few words of perfunctory greeting, an exchange of meaningless pleasantries, before they moved away. 'But I was impressed with Their Majesties' great gift for making everyone they met, how ever casually, feel at ease in their presence.'[17]

The good manners of the King and Queen concealed their inner indignation. Already King George had learned with despair and anger of his son's attachment to a divorced, remarried woman with two husbands living. From all that he heard, he thought her unsuitable as a friend, disreputable as a mistress, and unthinkable as Queen of England. At least

Mrs Dudley Ward had been a better class of person, and had conducted her liaison with more discretion.

The rest of the family never lost their respect for Mrs Dudley Ward and the dignity with which she behaved after the Prince of Wales jettisoned her. In particular the Duke of Kent remained friends with her to the last. To Lord Mountbatten, she had always been a good influence on the future King Edward VIII, unlike the others. Mrs Simpson's influence, he remarked, 'was fatal.' Though Mountbatten liked to think of the Prince of Wales as his best friend, he was disgusted by his callous abandonment of her. While he found Mrs Simpson amusing, he was convinced she would never make a suitable Queen.

The Kents' wedding was celebrated at Westminster Abbey on 29 November. That morning, as the Duke was about to don his full-dress uniform as a Royal Naval Commander, he realized that he only had a few pounds' change on him. Calmly, he put on an ordinary suit and made his way, virtually unrecognized, through the dense crowds around St James's Palace, to cash a cheque at his bank in Pall Mall. On his return, the Prince of Wales and the Duke of York asked him in astonishment why he could not have sent somebody else. Shrugging his shoulders, he told them that it had given him something to do. Nancy Astor, Conservative member of Parliament for Sutton, Plymouth, and a close family friend, might have been forgiven for raising an eyebrow at this remark. Only a few days before he had written to thank her for the gift of a jewellery box; 'I am going nearly mad with so many things to do – I never knew getting married was so much hard work!'[18]

There were two wedding ceremonies, one at Westminster Abbey, and one according to the rites of the Greek Orthodox Church at the chapel of Buckingham Palace. Among the guests were royalty from Britain, Denmark, Greece, Yugoslavia, and from the dethroned imperial houses of Germany and Russia. Mr and Mrs Simpson were there as well. They had bought their present, a pair of vases fitted as electric lamps, in a sale at Fortnum and Mason's for £10. It was a sum they had handsomely recouped by charging an American friend £50 in order to have his name placed on the guest list for a reception at the Palace.

Afterwards, King George appeared to be in better spirits than he had been for a long time. In writing to the Archbishop to thank him for officiating, he commented that he would 'never forget the beautiful service in the Abbey, so simple and yet so dignified', or 'the enormous crowds in the streets and especially the ones outside the Palace, who showed their love and affection for us and the family.'[19]

The following year marked the occasion of King George's Silver Jubilee. Celebrations were kept to a minimum in order to spare the King's health. On the eve of his seventieth birthday he was increasingly aged, tired and bent. His personal appearance shocked his family and friends. He had taken to dining alone in his room because the effort of dressing for dinner each evening was too much. Some people wondered privately whether his failing strength was equal to the planned festivities, but it was recognized that to cancel or delay them would give rise to rumours that he was dying.

So on 6 May 1935, the twenty-fifth anniversary of their accession to the throne, the King and Queen took pride of place in a procession to St Paul's for a service of thanksgiving. He noted afterwards that he had never seen so many people in the streets before, and their enthusiasm was most touching: 'I'd no idea they felt like that about me. I am beginning to think they must really like me for myself.' Only one problem marred the proceedings, when a group of elderly prebendaries delayed the royal family's departure from St Paul's by leaving before their turn. 'Too many parsons getting in the way,' the King remarked wryly. 'I didn't know there were so many damned parsons in England.'

According to 'Chips' Channon, the star of the day's proceedings was Queen Mary, who had suddenly 'become the best-dressed woman in the world.' However he had praise for most other members of the family, as they drove to the cathedral: the Duchess of York 'charming and gracious, the baby princesses much interested in the proceedings and waving'; the Kents, 'that dazzling pair', and the Prince of Wales 'smiling his dentist's smile and waving to his friends.'[20]

Over the celebrations, however, hung the behaviour of the King's eldest son. 'He has not a single friend who is a gentleman,' he told Mensdorff bitterly. 'He does not see any decent society. And he is forty-one.' Mensdorff pleaded that the heir to the throne had many attractive qualities, including charm, but the King replied that that was a pity. 'If he were a fool, we would not mind. I hardly ever see him and don't know what he is doing.'[21]

To a lady-in-waiting, he remarked, 'I pray to God that my eldest son will never marry and have children, and that nothing will come between Bertie and Lilibet and the throne.' To his Prime Minister, Stanley Baldwin, his forebodings were just as prophetic; 'After I am dead, the boy will ruin himself within twelve months.'

Six days after the thanksgiving service, the King had a long and serious talk with the Prince of Wales about the future when he ascended to the throne, and regretting that he had never married. To this the Prince of Wales replied that he could never marry, as such a life had no appeal to him. When the King accused him of keeping Mrs Simpson as his mistress, the Prince reacted with anger and gave his word of honour that he had never had any immoral relations with her. He then begged the King to invite her to the Jubilee ball at Buckingham Palace and to Ascot, which the King did with reluctance. It was a decision which caused the rest of the royal family as much mortification as it had the King to approve.

The Duke of York was especially shocked. He had already noticed with bitterness that Mrs Simpson was accepting large sums of money from the Prince of Wales, as well as jewellery – particularly family heirlooms bequeathed to the Prince by Queen Alexandra, who had taken it for granted that he would make a suitable marriage and would need them to give to his Queen Consort. On hearing about the interview that had passed between father and son, he was aggrieved that the Prince of Wales should have lied so blatantly about his relatioship with Mrs Simpson. He was sure that the two were lovers, suspicions soon to be confirmed by the Prince's staff who testified that they had been seen in bed together.* It is doubtful whether the Prince was aware that he was not the only object of her affections at the time. A confidential Special Branch report sent to the Commissioner of the Metropolitan Police at about the time of the Jubilee revealed that Mrs Simpson was also involved with a married lover, Guy Trundle, an engineer and salesman for the Ford Motor Company living and working in London, was was said to be receiving large sums of money and expensive gifts from her in addition to personal favours.

Yet there were signs that at least the Duke of Gloucester was about to settle down. He had been abroad during the Duke of Kent's wedding, and the Queen wrote to him that she hoped he would think about marying on his return. He needed very little encouragement.

For some years he had been a regular visitor to the home of the Duke of Buccleuch at Langholm. At first, the main attraction of the place seemed to be its facilities for shooting, with the Duke's sons Walter and William as companions. But after a while, he appeared quite taken with their sister Alice. A sense of guilt after the Markham affair, and a frustrated ambition to command his regiment, the 10th Hussars in India, disappointed and depressed him. Sensing something of his loneliness, the Duke's family always paid him special attention when he came to stay. He regarded William as his best friend, and came to enjoy his visits more and more. Maybe he felt

---

* As Duke of Windsor, to the end of his days he denied that his wife had been his mistress during her second marriage. He successfully sued one author, Geoffrey Dennis, whose *Coronation Commentary*, published in 1937, referred to her having been his mistress, and some twenty years later threatened to take the official biographer of the late King George VI, John Wheeler-Bennett, to court if he did not drop the word 'mistress' from his book.

something of the spirit of family life with them that he saw the Duke of York enjoying.

Soon after the Jubilee celebrations, the Duke stayed at Windsor with Queen Mary; Alice was also there. One day in August the couple were walking the Duke's dogs in Richmond Park. Alice later wrote in her memoirs that 'there was no formal declaration on his part, I think he just muttered it as an aside.' He was thirty-four; she was only twenty-one months younger, reckoned she had 'had a very good innings,' and felt that it was time she did something more useful with her life.[22]

The King's pleasure at being about to acquire another daughter-in-law took something of a knock on Alice's first day at Balmoral. Asked what she was going to do that day, she replied, 'Stalking.' The King was stunned. End of conversation. Later, while they were out on the moors, her fiancé told her that she could not have made a worse *faux pas*. As far as the King was concerned, ladies were not even permitted to watch grouse-shooting, so the idea that one should intend to go out stalking was absolutely unheard of.

It was arranged that the wedding should take place that November. However the bride's father had been ill for some time, and died on 19 October. The ceremony went ahead on the date planned, 6 November – but quietly in the Chapel of Buckingham Palace, instead of at Westminster Abbey. Princesses Elizabeth and Margaret were bridesmaids, attired in Kate Greenaway dresses shortened at the King's request, as he wished 'to see their pretty little knees'. Not everything went smoothly at the ceremony. When signing the Register, the King made 'unfavourable comments' on the quality of the pen he was handed to use, and Queen Mary was disappointed to be told that the Archbishop's primatial cross was not an antique. When the couple failed to cut the stiff icing on the cake with the traditional officer's sword, the King was visibly irritated.

The Gloucesters spent their honeymoon quietly in England, hunting at Boughton and shooting in Northern Ireland. They had been told that the Kents' foreign honeymoon a year earlier was considered 'extravagant' at a time of economic recession, and were also discouraged from their original idea of a skiing holiday on the continent, as the Prince of Wales and Mrs Simpson were doing likewise, and if the foursome met unexpectedly it would be embarrassing for all concerned.

As far as King George V was concerned, another shadow hung over the nuptials of his third son. 'Now all the children are married except David,' he wrote grimly in his diary that evening.

The strain of the Jubilee celebrations had told on King George's declining strength, and he did not attend the Armistice service at the Cenotaph on 11 November. By the end of the month Princess Victoria, the unhappy spinster to whom the King had always been so devoted, was seriously ill. Her passing away on 3 December, the family believed in retrospect, also sounded the death knell for her sorrowing brother. He was so distressed by the news that he cancelled the State Opening of Parliament planned to take place that same afternoon, and after his sister's funeral he never appeared in public again.

Christmas was celebrated as usual at Sandringham. After delivering his festive broadcast to the nation on 25 December, a tradition which had begun three years earlier, he turned to simpler, more domestic pleasures, and particularly enjoyed watching his Kent grandson in his bath. The Duke and Duchess of Kent had become parents on 9 October with the birth of a son, whom they named Edward. In her will, Princess Victoria had left them her home, Coppins, a large, rambling house near Iver in Buckinghamshire, and part of their Christmas was spent discussing the transformation of the house. The whole family was present – the Duke and Duchess of York, watching their daughters romp around a twenty-foot Christmas tree; and the newly-wed Gloucesters, planning their move into the Royal Pavilion, Aldershot, lent to them as their first married home. All of them were too preoccupied with their immediate concerns, and with their fahter's failing strength, to notice the melancholy attitude of the Prince of Wales. Later he summed up his own feelings that Christmas: 'I was caught up in an inner conflict and would have no peace of mind until I had resolved it.'[23]

On the afternoon of 16 January 1936, as he was shooting in Windsor Great Park, the Prince of Wales was handed a note written by Queen Mary. She had advised him that the royal physician, Lord Dawson of Penn, was 'not too pleased with Papa's state at the present moment', and he should come to Sandringham, but in a casual manner so as not to alarm him.[24]

Next morning, he flew to Sandringham in his private aeroplane. Later that day he telephoned Mrs Simpson to tell her that the King was unlikely to live for more than two or three days. The Dukes of York and Kent joined them, leaving the Duke of Gloucester who was at Buckingham Palce, recovering from laryngitis. On 20 January, shortly after midday, the King received his Privy Counsellors for the last time. Propped up in an armchair, wearing his dressing-gown, he was too weak to do more than answer 'Approved' when the Lord President read out the order paper, and make two shaky marks signifying the initials G.R. on the document. Shortly before midnight, in the words of Lord Dawson, his life moved 'peacefully to its close.'

Queen Mary's first act as widow was to kiss the hand of her eldest son, the new sovereign. Immediately afterwards, the new King telephoned Mrs Simpson with the news.

6

'He has many ideas of his own'

The new King's reaction at his father's deathbed was one of grief so intense that the rest of the family were astonished. Just before his father's death, the Prince of Wales became hysterical, cried loudly, and kept on embracing his mother. Considering that he had been the least close of them all to his father, it seemed strangely out of character. Was it a reaction to the guilt he was experiencing, at having disliked his father while he was alive and at having caused him so much anxiety, maybe even shortening his life?

In retrospect, a more chilling construction was later put on his behaviour. Sir Alan Lascelles, the late King George V's assistant private secretary, was convinced that Edward and Mrs Simpson had planned to run away together in February, but the King's death had forestalled them. Through his procrastination, and a reluctance to resolve the dilemma of his private life, he had allowed a situation to develop that could have been sorted out more easily and with less fuss while he was heir to the throne than could be once he was King.

King George V was the third British sovereign to die within the first four decades of the twentieth century. Considerable unease had been voiced on the passing of each one, and doubts expressed on the adequacy of his or her successor. Despite initial misgivings, though, King Edward VII and King George V had been worthy constitutional sovereigns at a time of national and international upheaval. Despite, or perhaps because of their contrasting personalities, father and son had each been 'the right King at the right time', and their deaths were followed by widespread grief that transcended the rituals of conventional mourning.

As the news of King George V's death broke across a stunned nation, people in all walks of life wondered what the reign of his eldest son would bring. 'He [George V] was really beloved for there never was a man who did his duty better,' Lady Astor wrote to Grand Duchess Olga (25 January 1936). 'I feel the new King will do it just as well, but in a different way. It is a much easier thing being a Constitutional Monarch than any other, but it may be hard for the new King because he has many ideas of his own.'[1] His great-uncle, the octogenarian Duke of Connaught, declared that he had 'the great advantage of having visited every part of the Empire and of being known personally by all its inhabitants.'[2]

Meanwhile, *The Times* commented that no man was 'more willing to make friends, and none has a greater regard for the obligations of friendship.' It also paid tribute to his 'genuine interest, which more "democrats" profess than feel, in all sorts and conditions of people, and he is rich in a study that is admirable and endearing in any man and inestimable in a Sovereign – the study of mankind.'[3]

Tom Jones, deputy secretary to the cabinet, told the Prime Minister, Stanley Baldwin, that he was impressed with the King's quick intelligence, his freedom from humbug, social sympathies and above all his sense of duty; he would 'rise to the new responsibilities though he may discharge them in his own way.'

The Times leader who noted a parellel between King Edward VIII and his grandfather, who bore the same regnal name. 'Men, not books, are his library, as they were for the last King Edward, and he has the same power to learn from them.' In his memoirs, the King would observe of his father, 'by the gravity of his temperament it was to [Queen Victoria], rather than to the livelier example of his own father, that he looked for a model of the Sovereign's deportment.'[4] He saw himself as embodying the traditions of King Edward VII's *joie de vivre*. So, with some displeasure, did his uncle the Earl of Athlone.

According to the latter, as a boy he had taken 'an unhealthy interest' in his grandfather's private life. Athlone tried to discharge him, only to be asked by his nephew, 'Wasn't my grandfather very popular with everyone?' He was told that 'It was all right in his time, but nobody would stand it today!'

The body of King George V had lain in the church at Sandringham, and the coffin was transported by gun carriage to London. In the funeral procession the King and his brothers followed the gun carriage on foot, Queen Mary and the Princess Royal riding in a carriage. As the cortege turned into Westminster Palace Yard, the Maltese Cross surmounting the crown which had been secured to the lid of the coffin rolled off and fell to the ground. A company sergeant-major, bringing up the rear of the two files of Grenadier Guardsmen flanking the carriage, bent down swiftly to retrieve the cross. Two members of parliament overheard the King exclaim: 'Christ! What will happen next?' A fitting motto, remarked one to the other, for the coming reign.

Initially, the King and the Duke of York enjoyed a good relationship. The brothers had always been close, and at first the King went out of his way to accord the respect due to the heir of the throne. One of his first official acts was to order the inclusion of the Duke and Duchess of York after the names of the sovereign and Queen Mary in the prayer for the royal family said throughout churches each Sunday, notwithstanding the church's objection that no precedent existed for praying for the heir presumptive 'when there was no direct heir of the body.' He also arranged for the Duke of York to see certain secret telegrams and papers, and in recognition of his brother's interest in tradition and ceremonial, appointed him to the committee entrusted with arrangements for the Coronation.

The Duke of Gloucester was the brother to whom the King felt least close; as the latter remarked, they had very little in common apart from a mutual interest in horses and riding. Yet the King treated him with equal respect and consideration.

Knowing how deeply Harry was attached to the army, King Edward had encouraged him to persist with his plan for attending Staff College at Camberley and thus continuing an active military career when the rest of the family had had scant enthusiasm for the idea. Soon after King George V's funeral, the Duke reported to Camberley to begin this new phase of his career. His brother had given him a promise that he would not be expected to undertake ceremonial military duties while studying at college.

The Gloucester's official London residence was now York House, but for the time being, Aldershot was home. The Pavilion had been built during the Crimean War, partly on the suggestion of Prince Albert, and used as a royal residence ever since. Inside the building, he and the Duchess formed a collection of Chinese porcelain, sporting books and drawings.

In one way, the Duke showed himself as impatient of time-honoured royal tradition as King Edward. Queen Victoria had ordered a great mound of earth to be deposited by the employment of labourers with shovels and carts and wheelbarrows, in front of the Pavilion, to prevent people from looking through the windows. To improve the view, Prince Henry promptly had the obstruction removed by a bulldozer.

Another duty entrusted to the Duke of York by the King was the preparation of a report on economies which could be made at Sandringham. As Prince of Wales, he had disliked the Norfolk home where in his cynical phrase, his father's 'private war with the twentieth century had ended in the almost complete repulse of the latter.'[5] The family had their suspicions that King Edward wanted to sell it, and the report to be made was probably a compromise arrangement by which the King would be persuaded not to do so. The Duke of York and a mutual friend, the Earl of Radnor, spent a fortnight surveying the estate. Their report on retrenchment and economies that could be made was read by the King but thrown aside as being too moderate. He made his own cuts, dismissing members of staff and only telling the family once it was a *fait accompli.*

The King's penny-pinching at a time when he was

showering his mistress with lavish gifts lost him much sympathy from his servants and household. Shortly after his accession, a sanction was obtained that no man in royal employment should be dismissed without being offered alternative employment, but this rule was soon quietly dropped by the King. Servants resented having their wages cut when they spent much of their time loading furniture, plates and cases of champagne for despatch to Mrs Simpson's flat. The King's personal instruction that soap supplied for the guests in the royal residences, which was collected up after the guests had left and finished in the servants' quarters, should in future be brought to his own rooms, was also ill-received below stairs.

At the time of her brother-in-law's accession, the Duchess of York was in low spirits. Early in the new year she had been struck down with influenza, and was still very weak when the King died. She grieved for him, noting that unlike his own children she was never afraid of him, and in all the years she had known him, 'he never spoke one unkind or abrupt word to me.' As yet she attached little importance to the King's infatuation with Mrs Simpson, though a tasteless remark by the latter did nothing to raise her standing with the Duchess. She was told that early in February, during a conversation about court mourning, Mrs Simpson remarked that she had not worn black stockings since she gave up the Can-can.

It was noticed that the Yorks no longer visited Fort Belvedere, so much did they dislike what they heard of the King's subservient behaviour towards Mrs Simpson. The Gloucester's did, but with deep misgivings. They were unhappy about the liaison, but the Duke felt personally obliged to go. The Kents did likewise, but the Duke was saddened that his eldest brother, who had always been so close, now appeared so remote and distant. Against her better judgement, the Duchess of Kent regularly invited her brother-in-law and Mrs Simpson to tea at Coppins and at their London home in Belgrave Square.

For the time being there was nothing to be done but to maintain a dignified silence. Queen Mary confided to Lady

Airlie in February that she did not like to talk to David about 'this affair', as she did not wish to give the impression of interfering with his private life, as he was the most obstinate of her sons. If she opposed him over anything, she knew from past experience, that would make him more determined than ever. Though he was utterly infatuated, her hope was that violent infatuations 'usually wear off.'

One thing that rapidly wore off was the King's devotion to his paperwork. Entering into this aspect of duty with initial enthusiasm – not unlike a child with a new hobby – he read diligently at first through all the documents in the official red boxes despatched to him by government departments, initialling them all by hand. This proved to be his undoing, because it was only a matter of time before the royal autograph was conspicuous by its absence.

Worse was to come. Whitehall officials soon noticed that documents containing official secrets were coming back after protracted delays, with circular marks left by wine or cocktail glasses. Apart from such revealing sloppiness, there was another pressing consideration which weighed heavily on the government – that of King Edward VIII and his attitude towards Nazi Germany.

Like so many other aspects of his life and reign, this needs to be put into perspective. In November 1933 Count Mensdorff, former Austrian Ambassador in London, had noticed with surprise how sympathetic the Prince of Wales appeared to Hitler's regime, saying that it was 'the only thing to do,' and that 'we will have to come to it, as we are in great danger from the Communists too.'[6] Like many others of his generation, he admired the achievements of National Socialism in reducing unemployment and providing better housing for the working classes, and regarded stories of Nazi brutality as communist-inspired scaremongering. In European terms, he saw the immediate balance of continental power as lying between a degenerate and enfeebled France and a resurgent, more decisive Germany. Russia and international communism, he was convinced, posed a far greater threat to the west than fascism. In a speech to the British Legion in June 1935 he had proposed that a group of its members ought to visit Germany, as there was no more suitable body of men to stretch forth the hand of friendship to the Germans than 'we ex-servicemen'. His audience cheered him loudly, but the government were dismayed that the heir to the throne should express such views so publicly and risk displeasing Britain's French allies.

Mrs Simpson was foolish enough to voice her approval of Germany, and Joachim von Ribbenstrop, German Ambassador in London, appeared to go out of his way to cultivate her approval and friendship, knowing how much she influenced the King. Although rumours that she was a paid German agent were disbelieved by all but the most credulous, her Germanophile leanings were viewed with unease at the Foreign Office. She was known to share the King's views on French decadence and the superiority of German National Socialism.

As a result, foreign office papers were carefully screened, and Baldwin restricted documents sent to those which merely required the royal signature. This was in contravention of the constitution, by which the monarch was entitled to see all papers, but the King was so preoccupied with his personal and private life that he never noticed.

Courtiers and servants found him similarly slapdash, impractical and inconsiderate in his dealings with them. During the day it was difficult for them to contact him as he was still living at Fort Belvedere, although he kept an office at Buckingham Palace. He did not like being disturbed with official business while he was at the Fort. Officials could only go there when invited, and once they had arrived, they were generally kept hanging about for hours, without being offered anyting to eat. As the King never ate lunch himself, he did not see why other people should. He was impatient with other people's routines, and typical of his lack of consideration was his habit of deciding it was time for him (and them) to do some work, and start telephoning just as they were sitting down to dinner. Alec Hardinge, private secretary to the King, and formerly assistant private secretary to King George, was irritated at regularly being phoned five times during an evening. Once he was at Buckingham Palace, noticed Hardinge, he 'shut himself up' giggling with Mrs Simpson for hours on end, while the royal footmen informed the waiting secretaries gravely that 'the lady is still there.'

The King and Hardinge were exact contemporaries, the latter being the elder by one month. Although from the same generation, they had nothing in common regarding character and personality. Hardinge was an ultra-conservative, a man of tradition and habit who had admired and respected everything King George V stood for. He and his wife were close friends of the Duke and Duchess of York, and Lady Hardinge had been a bridesmaid at their wedding.

It was the perceptive Lady Hardinge who was disturbed by a conviction, as early as March 1936, that nobody seemed to share. She was convinced that King Edward VIII was not satisfied with having Mrs Simpson as a mere mistress and companion, but was determined to marry her regardless of the consequences. Later, he told Walter Monckton that he had made up his mind to marry her as far back as 1934. Secretive by nature, however, he kept his counsel to himself. To divulge his intentions would have resulted, as he knew well, in plans by family and courtiers to leave no stone unturned to prevent him from doing so.

The Yorks and their household noticed with alarm how the King was changing, and how his infatuation with and dependence on Mrs Simpson was increasing. One afternoon in April, the King and Mrs Simpson drove over to Royal Lodge, Windsor, where the Yorks were living, as he wanted to show them an American station wagon he had just bought. The brothers went for a drive in the vehicle, leaving the Duchess and her future sister-in-law together. Exercising the utmost self-control, the Duchess restricted conversation to subjects of a strictly impersonal nature.

The princesses' governess, Marion Crawford, was shrewd in her observations of the King and Mrs Simpson. She noticed her 'distinctly proprietary way' of speaking to the King, suggesting to him how the view from the window at Royal Lodge would be improved if certain trees and part of a hill were removed. To do such a thing in the presence of the Duke of York, who as a labour of love had transformed the garden from a virtual wilderness, was extremely tactless. As for the King himself, how he had changed. Formerly so youthful and relaxed, now he appeared haggard and distraught, fumbling incessantly with his tie, appearing not to listen when people were talking to him. He made plans with his nieces, and then forgot all about them. That evening, after the King and Wallis had departed, the governess observed that the Duke and Duchess made no allusion to the visit, as if it was an unwelcome interlude which they were determined to forget.

That summer, the King – under the alias of Duke of Lancaster – chartered a yacht, *Nahlin*, for a holiday cruise around the Adriatic. With Wallis, he left England on 8 August, flying to Paris and boading a private coach attached to the 'Orient Express.' When the train paused at Salzburg, they strolled together along the platform, only to be ambushed by photographers. Hours later, the pictures were being wired around the world. In British newspapers, they were published with the image of Mrs Simpson discreetly painted out. The press in other countries felt no such obligation, and copies of cuttings landed on the desks of offices in Whitehall, as well as that of Queen Mary. On board *Nahlin*, the King was quite unconcerned by the publicity. Every time the yacht put in to port, he and Mrs Simpson strolled casually through the streets, hand in hand.

During the course of this cruise, the King paid the first visit to Turkey ever made by a British sovereign, and President Kemal Ataturk was particularly impressed by the friendliness of a ruler representing a state which he had previously regarded as an enemy power. He also visited Tsar Boris in Sofia, and the Bulgarian press paid tribute to 'the democratic spirit he displayed'. These visits were of a relatively informal nature, free of the protocol and trappings of official state visits, and suggested that after the insularity of King George V, a new democratic spirit had indeed succeeded to the British throne.

However, the holiday was destined to be remembered less for the effect it had on these two Eastern European countries than for the King's apparent disregard for customary standards of royal dignity and discretion. During a visit to Vienna, he visited a public bath house and wandered around the steam room naked, astonishing some of the more conservaitve Austrians. His habit of wandering around on the yacht deck clad only in shorts and binoculars, or around the streets of Adriatic towns with a bottle of lemonade in his hand, likewise hardly accorded with what was expected of him.

On the yacht, personal feelings did not take long to surface. Apart from the King and Mrs Simpson, the luxurious state rooms accommodated an assortment of friends, including two of the King's secretaries, Godfrey Thomas and Tommy Lascelles, plus Alfred and Diana Cooper, the Duke of Kent's equerry, Humphrey Butler and his wife, and Wallis's friends Herman and Katherine Rogers. One evening after they had returned from visiting King George II of Greece and his English mistress, Wallis asked why he did not marry her. With what must, with hindsight, seem an amazing lack of tact, one of the company replied innocently that it was impossible for the King to marry a woman who was a commoner and already married. Such plain speaking could not have failed to touch a raw nerve, and suddenly it seemed as if the King had fallen into one of the moods of depression which his entourage had noticed with concern ever since his Empire tours shortly after the Great War.

Further evidence appeared of Mrs Simpson's tendency to taunt her submissive companion in front of others. When the King went down on his hands and knees to pull a corner of her dress out from underneath the chair, she stared at him coldly, remarking, 'Well, that's the *maust* extraordinary performance I've ever seen.' She then proceeded to criticize his manner and meanness, and his attitude to King George of Greece. Diana Cooper was so angry that she left the room in protest. She realized that Wallis was bored stiff, and when bored the King's dog-like devotion irritated her. Her 'commonness and Becky Sharpness' were getting on everyone's nerves, and the sooner the cruise ended, the better for all of them. It was impossible to enjoy antiquities with people who showed no interest in visiting them, and who referred to Delphi as Delhi.

When the King flew back to London a month later, leaving Wallis to visit Paris for some shopping, he dined with Queen Mary. Still she could or would not bring herself to say a word with him about carrying on such a liaison with a married woman in full view of the world's press. The only personal question she put to him was an enquiry as to whether he did not find it terribly hot in the Adriatic. Later that month, Queen Mary knew, her son was planning to take up the threads of tradition again, and stay at Balmoral. Little did anyone know that he was about to make an appalling gaffe which forfeited him considerable sympathy from not only the family, but also from his hitherto admiring subjects.

'GREAT ENTHUSIASM MARKS ARRIVAL OF THE KING' proclaimed a banner headline on the Aberdeen *Evening Express*, 23 September, the day the King arrived at the castle. Within four days, this enthusiasm had quickly evaporated.

Some months earlier, the King had been asked by the Lord Provost of Aberdeen to open the new Royal Infirmary. He had declined on the grounds of court mourning for his father. However, full mourning officially ended on 20 July, six months after King George V's death. King Edward delegated the duty to the Duke of York, a move which puzzled the people of Aberdeen, as observance of mourning (if indeed that was the genuine reason) surely applied equally to both brothers. The Yorks themselves were equally surprised at first, but the Duke performed the opening ceremony and was warmly welcomed. Meanwhile the King, who had said he would not be in Aberdeen that day, took the wheel of his private car and drove sixty miles from Balmoral to the city's railway station to meet Mrs Simpson off the train. Although he was wearing motoring goggles, which he had naively supposed would be sufficient disguise, almost everyone at the station recognized him – apart from a policeman, who told him to move his car as it was in a no-waiting area. He complied good-humouredly.

The *Evening Express* accordingly noted on its front page, alongside a photograph of the Duke and Duchess of York opening the infirmary, that His Majesty had made a 'surprise visit in car to meet guests'. Though it discreetly refrained from mentioning the guests (Mrs Simpson, and her American friends Herman and Katherine Rogers), and merely referred to their travelling from London by train, those who knew the King did not need to be told. Aberdeen, they remarked sadly, would never forgive the King.

Nobody was more angry than the Duchess of York. She felt that her husband and herself had been made to look thoroughly foolish, deputizing for the King who had enough free time to drive such a distance in order to meet friends, while saying blandly that he could not do a job of work.[7]

Not content with letting his brother and sister-in-law suffer such an insult in public, the King compounded it with the Court Circular in *The Times* and the *Daily Telegraph* on 24 September. It gave precedence to the arrival of Mrs Simpson and the Rogers at Balmoral Castle, and only in the following paragraph did it mention the Duke and Duchess of York's opening ceremony at Aberdeen. In fact, during their sojourn at Balmoral the King and 'Queen Wallis', as the American press had enthusiastically dubbed her, seemed to be going out of their way to offend the rest of the family and courtiers. In front of others, she would send the King out of the room to order champagne for them while she was playing bridge, making suggestions as to the repositioning of furniture, and declaring loudly that 'this tartan's got to go.' With characteristic understatement, the Duke of Gloucester, staying at nearby Abergeldie, wrote to Queen Mary that it was 'lovely being here but somehow everything seems different.'

On the evening of Saturday, 26 September, the King gave a dinner and reception at Balmoral. The Duke and Duchess of York had been invited, but Elizabeth was so angered by his behaviour that she did not want to go. However the Duke felt obliged to attend for the sake of family unity, especially as the Kents would be there as well and the Duchess of Kent was six months pregnant with her second child. He did not want to cause any unpleasantness himself, and persuaded her to accompany him.

It should have been the official host or hostess who welcomed the guests that evening, in this instance the King. Either Wallis was ignorant of such court etiquette, or more probably she intended to make what one observer present called 'a deliberate and calculated display of power.' As the Duchess of York preceded her husband into the drawing room, Mrs Simpson walked forward to greet her. With a 'freezing expression', the Duchess ignored her, walked straight past, and announced as if to nobody in particular, 'I came to dine with the King.'[8] The Duke of York seemed embarrassed, and the startled King immediately broke off his conversation with other guests to come and greet his brother and sister-in-law. Though Mrs Simpson sat at the head of the table, the Duchess led the women from their seats at the end of dinner. She and the Duke left as soon as they conveniently could.

The following morning, crowds gathered in the pouring rain outside Crathie Church to watch the royal family's arrival. The King, whose casual churchgoing had already been noted with regret by the court, arrived by car with the Duke of Kent. The Duke of York also attended with his daughters. But the Duchess, who so rarely missed divine service on a Sunday, was conspicuous by her absence.

On Monday, the Court Circular laconically reported Saturday's proceedings: 'The Duke and Duchess of York dined with The King this evening.'

Not everybody was immediately infected with the sour atmosphere. On the contrary, the Duke of Kent wrote on 2 October, shortly after leaving Balmoral, that he could never believe how any place could change so much and have such a different atmosphere: 'It was all so comfortable and everyone seemed so happy – it really was fun.'[9] He had evidently found the Highland home much more free-and-easy this time than it had been under the forbidding eye of his mother and father.

Two months later, however, the Duke of Kent was starting to see his eldest brother as no mere playful maverick who was good company despite his little lapses. By then, he was telling others bitterly that Mrs Simpson was using him as a weapon to provoke the King into displays of jealousy. At Balmoral, she did this to such marked effect that by the end of dinner one night, the King was 'beaten into a frenzy of jealousy and desire.'[10]

To Queen Mary, the Duchess of York wrote from Balmoral on 11 October of the 'great sadness and sense of loss for us and all the people. It will never be quite the same for us . . . It is very sad, and I feel that the whole difficulty is a certain person.'[11]

7

'It isn't possible!'

September had been a bad month for the royal family; October was to bring more portents of the impending crisis. Hardinge was informed by the Press Association that Mrs Simpson's divorce petition was to be heard at Ipswich Assizes on the 27th of the month. Aghast, he discussed the news with Baldwin, who went to see the King on 20 October to warn him what a scandal his 'friendship' with the lady was causing, and to ask him to try and prevent the divorce from going through. The King firmly declined. As yet, Baldwin took a less serious view of matters than Hardinge, who called upon the Duke and Duchess of York to warn them that the King's abdication was a definite possibility.

The Duke was appalled, and seemed reluctant to believe that matters could come to a head like this. Respecting the importance of family unity and the sanctity of the crown, he was shocked at the thought that the royal family's name should be dragged through the mud, and at the prospect of taking over from his brother in what he saw as the worst possible circumstances. Knowing how Mrs Simpson's hold over the King was gaining momentum, he hoped fervently that the King could be convinced that marriage with a twice-divorced woman was unacceptable to the vast majority of his subjects and that it was his duty as sovereign to reject the idea unconditionally. Legally or constitutionally, though, there was no bar to the King marrying Wallis once her divorce was made absolute. The King's marriage was outside the scope of the Royal Marriages Act of 1772, which required members of the royal family to obtain the monarch's consent before marrying.

It would, however, be unconstitutional for the King to marry against the advice of his ministers.

Hardinge told the Duke of York he intended to get Baldwin to make it clear to the King that marriage to Mrs Simpson was unacceptable, and if he planned to go ahead, he would be rejecting the Prime Minister's advice, therefore acting against the British constitution. At the same time, Hardinge planned to gather up such a weight of evidence to demonstrate to the King that this marriage would be unacceptable to his subjects at home and throughout the Empire.

Such plans were doomed to failure. A younger, more ruthless Prime Minister than Baldwin might have influenced King Edward VIII better, but nearly seventy years of age and close to retirement, he lacked the necessary firm touch with his royal master. Moreover, everyone involved underestimated the strength of the King's devotion to Mrs Simpson and his determination to put their personal interests, and what he considered his duty, namely his duty to her, before any other consideration.

Though the British press still adhered to a gentleman's agreement that the name of Mrs Simpson should not appear in their columns, it was becoming an increasingly open secret that the King intended to marry her. Mrs Simpson's decree nisi was granted on the grounds of Ernest's adultery, but suspicion was rife that everything had been arranged for the convenience of her and the King. On 10 November, her name was publicly mentioned for the first time in the House of Commons. During question time, the Coronation was referred to, and John McGovern, Labour member for Shettleston, Glasgow, declared angrily that they need not bother to talk about it in view of the odds at Lloyd's that there would be no Coronation. To cries of 'Shame!' he retorted, 'Yes – Mrs Simpson!'

Abdication rapidly progressed from a grim but remote possibility, to inevitability. London was alive with rumours at all levels of society. Even friends of the King acknowledged, albeit with reluctance, that if the King married Wallis, he would have to abdicate immediately, otherwise there would be renewed Socialist (and perhaps Republican) agitation, the formation of a King's party, a Yorkist party, and a general election in which the King's marriage and its acceptability or otherwise would be a major issue; an unfortunate distraction at a time of recession and severe unemployment at home, and sabre-rattling from the dictators abroad.

The Duke of York was the person who had most right to be kept informed, but he found his brother infuriatingly impossible to contact. The King would issue invitations for his brother to see him at a certain time, and then suddenly postpone the appointment for no apparent reason.

On 16 November the King invited Baldwin to Buckingham Palace, and told him that he intended to marry Wallis Simpson at the earliest possible opportunity, whether his ministers approved or not. If they did not, he was prepared to abdicate. Later that evening he went to see Queen Mary at Marlborough, and told her and the Princess Royal.

Since King George V's death, mother and daughter had drawn very close to each other. Whenever she and her husband were at their London residence, the Princess Royal spent as much time as reasonably possible with the Queen, and during the crisis she was her mother's greatest support. They were 'astounded and shocked' at his threat – or intention – to relinquish the throne. The Queen told him firmly that he must give up Wallis or the throne; and it was his duty to give up the former. To this, he countered that he felt unable to function as King without marrying her, and therefore his ultimate duty was to leave the throne. When he asked them to receive Wallis as his wife, they refused, and on being asked why, the Queen replied coldly, 'Because she is an adventuress!' He regarded this as an insult which he might one day forgive but never forget.

Over the next few days, the King informed his brothers of his decision. 'Because we had always been a somewhat complicated quartet,' he later recalled, 'I preferred to see them separately, knowing that each would act in his own fashion.'[1] Although Hardinge had prepared him for it, the Duke of York was so dumbfounded by the implications for him, his wife and children, that he was literally speechless. The Duke of Gloucester seemed philosopical enough and appeared little moved, his chief concern being as to how any additional royal duties would affect his army career, especially as he was the next brother in line, and would be Regent for his niece Elizabeth if anything should happen to the King. The Duke of Kent, who had always been closer to King Edward than any other member of the family, appeared genuinely upset, but 'reconciled to my decision,' the King thought. In fact, the Duke was furious. Although too angry to say much at the time, he told others afterwards that his brother was 'besotted on the woman, one can't get a word of sense out of him!'[2]

As the Duke of York was unable to express what he felt, the Duchess interceded on his behalf. On 23 November she wrote to the King, begging him to be kind to Bertie – 'I wish that you could realize how loyal and true he is to you, and you have no idea how hard it has been for him lately.' The letter, which she implored him to keep a secret from Bertie, was penned more in sorrow than in anger, 'We both uphold you always. We want you to be happy more than anything else, but it's awfully difficult for Bertie!'[3]

On 18 November, King Edward began a long journey through the depressed areas of South Wales, inspecting the unemployment blackspots of the Rhondda and Monmouth valleys. The King's sympathy for men out of work for so long and their families seemed sincere enough as he spoke to several of them directly. It was a long and demanding schedule, and he ended it almost an hour late as he made a detour, not in his original programme, to visit the Bessemer Steel Works – a vast derelict area which had employed a workforce of nine thousand only a few years earlier. Hundreds of men awaited him, sitting on piles of twisted, rusting metal where the works had been demolished. When he arrived, they rose to their feet and sang an old Welsh hymn; plainly moved, the King stood bareheaded. When they had finished, he turned to one of the officials accompanying him, and said, 'These works brought all these people here. Something must be done to find them work.'[4]

At dinner that night, he was told of plans to reopen derelict pits and steelworks in South Wales and Monmouthshire. On the next day, he made another long tour. At Pontypool he told a crowd who had come to see him that 'You may be sure that all I can do for you I will. We certainly want better times brought to your valley.' At Blaenavon he told the Chairman of the Unemployed Men's Committee that 'Something will be done about unemployment.'

It was an apparently genuine display of concern for his subjects, and he was obviously moved by the misery and despair he saw all around him. What the men and women he addressed did not realize, of course, was that he had told his Prime Minister and family a couple of days before that he was about to abdicate. While honest enough in telling them that something would be done about unemployment (as he had it on the authority of his officials), his assurance that he personally intended to do all he could for them had in retrospect a rather hollow ring.

In some sections of the press, the King's visit was given enthusiastic coverage. In particular the *Daily Mail* published a long leader comparing his decisive statements and sense of urgency with the prevaricating attitude of his government towards defence and rearmament in the face of the dictators' movements abroad, notably Germany and Italy. It might be too much to suggest that the King had deliberately chosen to appeal to his subjects, by demonstrating the depth of his social concerns, as a prelude to what looked like being a struggle with his ministers over the issue of his private life. Yet his sense of timing indicated something of the sort. The vast majority of the public still knew little if anything about Mrs Simpson; to them, he was their King who had shown such promise as Prince of Wales, and who was determined to be a more modern monarch than his father had been. His tour of Wales could only have increased his popularity with them.

The *Daily Mail* leader was inspired by its owner and

editor Lord Rothermere, whose son Esmond Harmsworth was responsible, jointly with Lord Beaverbrook, for arranging the gentleman's agreement to mention Mrs Simpson and the divorce case as discreetly as possible. Harmsworth saw a possible way out of the impasse, by proposing that Mrs Simpson and the King should marry morganatically. She would therefore not take her husband's rank, and any children of the marriage would be barred from the succession, while their claim on their father's estate would be limited to his personal property. There were several precedents for morganatic marriage, among them that of Duke Alexander of Württemberg, Queen Mary's grandfather, whose marriage to a commoner gave rise to the house of Teck; that of Prince Alexander of Hesse and the Rhine to Julie Hauke, whose marriage in 1851 founded the Battenberg dynasty, anglicized to Mountbatten in 1917; and most notable of all, that of the Austrian heir Archduke Francis Ferdinand to Countess Sophie Chotek in 1900, a controversial but happy union shattered on its fourteenth anniversary at Sarajevo by the bullets of Gavrilo Princip.

Asked whether she would be prepared to marry King Edward under these conditions, Mrs Simpson said she could not comment with propriety. The King was interested, but his friend Walter Monckton – who had become a confidant of the King and an unofficial mediator between him and Baldwin, replacing the distrusted Hardinge – warned that the cabinet was unlikely to approve a morganatic marriage; special legislation would be required, but even then it was unlikely to pass Parliament. Neville Chamberlain was certain that if the morganatic marriage should be arranged, it would be a mere prelude to making Mrs Simpson Queen with full rights.

None the less, telegrams were sent to the Dominion governments asking them to choose between three options: the King should marry Mrs Simpson and she would be recognized as Queen; the morganatic marriage proposal; or the King should abdicate in favour of the Duke of York. The Dominions were almost unanimous in their refusal to accept the first or second. Joseph Lyons, the Catholic Prime Minister of Australia, was the most hostile of all, declaring that the King should abdicate whether he chose to marry her or not. Baldwin showed the King Lyons' telegram, which was dismissed coldly with the retort that 'there were not many people in Australia.'

The Duke of York was all too aware of the third proposal; he felt like the proverbial 'sheep being led to the slaughter.' If the worst happened and he had to take over, he wrote to the King's assistant private secretary, Sir Godfrey Thomas on 25 November, he would do his best 'to clear up the inevitable mess, if the whole fabric does not crumble under the shock and strain of it all.'[5]

The name of Mrs Simpson was gradually becoming known to a dumbfounded public; she was receiving anonymous threatening letters, and threats were made to blow up her house. By the end of November, 'Chips' Channon observed, there was 'no hope for the King.' The Lord President of the Council and former Prime Minister Ramsay MacDonald, whose humble upbringing and socialist sympathies had not prevented a deep respect for and devotion to King George V, remarked angrily that his successor had 'done more to harm his country than any man in history.'[6] The diplomatist Harold Nicolson, recently elected to Parliament as National Labour member for Leicester West, commented that King Edward still imagined his country to be with him. What he did not know was that the upper classes minded her being an American more than they objected to her being divorced. The lower classes did not mind her nationality so much as the fact that she had had two husbands already.

With the impending storm, it was obvious that the press could not be expected to hold back much longer. The catalyst for the flood gates of Fleet Street to burst came from an unexpected quarter.

On 1 December Dr Walter Blunt, Bishop of Bradford, addressing the Lambeth Conference, commending the King to God's grace, 'which he will so abundantly need – for the King is a man like any other – if he is to do his duty properly. We hope that he is aware of this need. Some of us wish that he gave more positive signs of such awareness.' Though he was concerned not with his sovereign's private life, but rather with his lack of regular churchgoing, informed opinion was preoccupied so much with the former that his remarks were misinterpreted.

The Bishop's address, soon to be known as 'the blunt instrument', dealt a mortal blow to the newspaper proprietors' agreement. On 2 December his words were reported in the *Yorkshire Post*, and the remaining provincial papers followed suit. Convinced that public opinion was on his side, the King, in isolation at the Fort with an increasingly distressed Wallis, was shocked when he saw the *Birmingham Post*. 'They don't want me,' he remarked sadly as he showed it to Baldwin.

On 3 December the national dailies broke ranks. The Duke and Duchess of York had been in Edinburgh, where the former was installed as Grand Master Mason of Scotland. As they stepped off the train at Euston early that morning, they were aghast at being confronted by a throng of photographers and a wall of newspaper placards, announcing boldly THE KING'S MARRIAGE. The Duke hastened to see Queen Mary, and then to talk to his brother, in the presence of Monckton. The King, he reported, was 'in a great state of excitement', saying he would temporarily leave the country as King after broadcasting to his subjects, and then leave it to them to decide what should be done.

This, probably inspired by Mrs Simpson, was a petulant attempt to appeal to the people over the heads of their elected representatives, and it never had more than a remote chance of success. The publicity that had broken about them convinced the King that it was essential to send Wallis out of the country, and she decided to join Herman and Katherine Rogers at their villa near Cannes. An old friend, Lord Brownlow, was asked to escort her. When he arrived at Fort Belvedere on the evening of 3 December, he found the King tired and overwrought, dreading her departure 'almost like a small boy being left behind at school for the first time.' Watching her depart without saying goodbye to any of the staff, a footman remarked triumphantly to the butler, 'Well, that's the end of that.' 'Don't be too sure,' replied the butler. 'We'll keep our fingers crossed.'[7]

That evening, the King went to see Queen Mary at Marlborough House. With her he found the Duke and Duchess of York and the Princess Royal. He explained to his mother that he had refrained from seeing her during the preceding few days as he he was anxious to avoid causing her pain. But he had decided that he could not live alone as King, and must mary Mrs Simpson.

Before leaving, he told the Duke of York to come and see him at the Fort next day. The Duke rang to confirm the arrangement next morning, and was told to wait until Saturday 6 December. The Duke rang again that day, and was told 'Come & see me on Sunday.' Sunday evening he rang again, to be informed that 'The King has a conference & will speak to you later.' The King did not speak to him later. On Monday afternoon the Duke rang again and the King said he might be able to see him later. At last, the King returned the call on Monday evening to say he would see him after dinner. 'No, I will come and see you at once,' was the Duke's firm reply, and ten minutes later the brothers were face to face. The Duke of York's 'awful & ghastly suspense of waiting was over'. He found his brother pacing up and down the room, and 'he told me his decision that he would go.'[8]

Although not supported by documentary evidence, it was rumoured that serious consideration was given to offering the crown to the Duke of Kent, and that King Edward VIII's prevarication was part of a plot to alter the line of succession. The Duke of York, it was believed by some, would never be able to undertake all the arduous duties demanded of a King; he would never be able to speak in public; he would be a recluse or at best a 'rubber stamp', and the government required a few days to decide whether he – and eventually his daughter – would really provide personalities dynamic enough to win back the lustre of the monarchy after abdication.[9] There were also doubts about the Duchess of York, who was thought to lack the sufficiently commanding presence expected of a

Queen, to be too retiring and too dedicated to a quiet domestic life. The Duke of Gloucester was next in line after the Duke of York; he did not inspire confidence, and his marked taste for alcohol made him a problem. On the other hand the Duke of Kent was good-looking, debonair, married to a strikingly attractive European princess, and already had a son to succeed him. If chosen to do so, they would avoid 'laying so heavy a future burden upon the shoulders of any woman.'[10]

That Queen Victoria had shouldered such a burden for over sixty years rather distracted from the force of the last argument; and the Duke of Kent's youthful liaisons and dalliance with drink and drugs, albeit firmly in the past, cast doubts on his suitability as King. Moreover, nobody thought to explain why in a more egalitarian age a striking-looking European princess should make a better Queen Consort than a woman of Scottish aristocratic birth. In any case, the crisis was traumatic enough, and this was not the time for tampering with the succession or the dynastic rights of each prince.

These arguments, though, persisted among – and perhaps even originated with – the 'smart set' who had befriended and idolized the King, both as heir and sovereign. Yet for all his lack of charisma, apparently fragile appearance, and above all, as Baldwin stated, the fact that he 'had no chance to capture the popular imagination as his brother did', the Duke of York had many of his father's virtues – a sense of decency and duty, capacity for hard work, commonsense, and sound judgement. Above all, he had courage; the determination that had won him his wife, and had helped him to control his speech impediment, had led his never-easily-pleased father to tell Lady Airlie that 'Bertie has more guts than the rest of his brothers put together.'[11] Baldwin reassured the Duke of York that King George V had appeared 'uninspired and dull' in comparison with his father, but by perseverance, reliability and example to his people, he had soon gained for himself the much-loved position he held at his death.

Prince Albert certainly needed 'guts'; for the uncertainty of it all was placing an almost intolerable strain on him. The

Duchess was ill with influenza and had taken to her bed, and in her absence it was on the Duke of Kent that he leaned most for support. The brothers were at the Fort on the afternoon of 8 December, talking to Baldwin and reassuring him that he had done all he possibly could. They were surprised and shocked by the King's indifference to the gravity of the situation, and the Prime Minister told them that he refused to discuss anything, but merely paced up and down the room, saying, 'This is the most wonderful woman in the world.'

Meanwhile, on 7 December, the day after arriving at Cannes, Mrs Simpson had issued a statement declaring her readiness 'to withdraw forthwith from a situation that has been rendered both unhappy and untenable.' Before doing so, she had read it over the phone to the King, who readily agreed as he saw that it would silence those who thought she was being callous towards everyone else involved. Yet it never occurred to him for a moment – though others, especially members of the government, believed as much – that she had any intention of 'actually asking to be released from the claims of my love.'[12]

Her solicitor, Theodore Goddard, was asked by Baldwin to go to Cannes and find out what her intentions were. During the course of a long conversation with her, she told him that she was prepared to give the King up, but felt that wherever she went he would follow her. She was in such a state of nerves that she offered to withdraw her divorce petition against Ernest Simpson, and he took a signed statement from her to this effect. Goddard believed that she was being perfectly sincere in all that she said. He knew, however, that it would be worthless if the King remained obdurate.

At dinner on 8 December, the King was the life and soul of the party. It was no wonder that the Duke of York appeared dull by contrast, according to Major Dugdale, Baldwin's private secretary. 'And this is the man we are going to lose,' the Duke whispered to Monckton beside him.

Next day, after discussions on family business, the Duke of

York returned to Marlborough House to report to his mother, broke down and 'sobbed like a child.'

On the morning of 10 December, all four brothers were present at the signing of the Instrument of Abdication. With a degree of calmness which astonished the others, King Edward signed several copies of the Instrument and then five copies of his message to Parliament, one for each Dominion Parliament.

There were still difficulties to be resolved in what was an unprecedented situation. Never before had a British monarch voluntarily abdicated the British throne. The last King to be deposed, James II (in 1688, coincidentally also on 11 December), had never formally renounced the throne and still called himself King during his remaining twelve years of exile abroad. Edward was suddenly worried about how badly off he would be, and requested that the terms of his father's will should be strictly observed as regards his life interest in Balmoral and Sandringham; they should be treated as absolutely his, for him to dispose of as he thought fit. There was uncertainty as to whether he would be provided for by government, and whether the life or freehold interest in Balmoral passed to the crown under Scottish law.* A few minor alterations were agreed and signed. Neither his brother nor Lord Wigram realized that he had made huge savings in his personal fortune for such an eventuality. When they did, it added to the anger and resentment they already felt at his rejecting his responsibilities as King and head of the family, while being unwilling to accept the financial consequences of doing so.

Another issue to be settled was the outgoing sovereign's future title. As he was born the son of a Duke, he would be

---

* Within two days of his accession, he had been disturbed at finding out that King George V had left him a life interest in Sandringham and Balmoral and their contents, but no personal bequest of money, as had been left to his brothers and sister. King Edward VII had drawn up his will along similar terms, not leaving his son and heir any money on the perfectly reasonable assumption that as Duke of Cornwall he had built up an adequate surplus from Duchy revenues.

119

Lord (instead of plain Mr) Edward Windsor, and under such a name he could stand for election to the House of Commons. The chance that Mrs Simpson might persuade him to do so did not escape their notice. Only by confirming him as HRH Duke of Windsor could he be barred from doing so, and the Duke of York maintained that he could not speak or vote in the House of Lords;* but he would not be deprived of his position in the army, navy or Royal Air Force.

At 1.52 p.m. on Friday, 11 December, 'that dreadful day', in the phrase of the new King, Britain witnessed her third sovereign in eleven months. Prince Albert, Duke of York, was now King George VI. He had chosen his regnal name a few days earlier, preferring to take the same one as his father in order to demonstrate a sense of continuity with the latter's reign, and in preference to the name of Albert, which he recognized had too Germanic a ring.

That evening the family held a farewell dinner at Royal Lodge, with guests strictly limited to family – Queen Mary, the Princess Royal, the four brothers, the Queen's brother the Earl of Athlone, and his wife Princess Alice, who had been staying at Marlborough House with the Queen ever since the beginning of the crisis. This dinner, recalled the Earl of Athlone, was relatively cheerful, although 'it might have been quite a gloomy occasion.' Now that the uncertainty of it all was over and everyone knew the worst, the sense of relief that they felt was partly responsible; alternatively, most of the diners were probably becalmed as if unable to realize the gravity of it all.

The Duchess of York was confined to bed with influenza and a high temperature, but wrote sympathetically to her brother-in-law to say how she regretted not being there to see

---

* This was technically incorrect. Royal dukes can speak in the House of Lords. The sons of King George III, and King Edward VII as Prince of Wales, had previously done so; as would Prince Charles and Richard, Duke of Gloucester many years later. The former King Edward VIII's title was created by Letters Patent on 8 March 1937.

him before he left. Wishing him happiness in his new life, and promising to mention him in her prayers, she said how she often thought of 'the old days and how you helped Bertie and me in the first years of our marriage.'[13]

After dinner, Edward left for Windsor Castle to make a farewell broadcast to his subjects. Queen Mary had tried to disuade him on the grounds that it would be hardly necessary for him to do so; he ought to spare himself the extra strain and emotion, and in any case the Prime Minister had said everything there was to be said. Though she refrained from saying so, she had her doubts lest he might say anything controversial.

Sir John Reith, director of the BBC, announced over a microphone in an improvised studio at the Augusta Tower: 'This is Windsor Castle. His Royal Highness, Prince Edward.' Even this dignified moment was not without a touch of farce. As the Prince moved across to face the microphone, he accidentally kicked the table leg. Several million tense listeners sitting beside their wireless sets firmly believed that Reith had angrily banged the door on their former sovereign as he went out of the room.

'At long last I am able to say a few words of my own,' he began, at first a little nervously, as he told how he found it impossible to carry the heavy burden of responsibility and to discharge his duties as King without the help and support of the woman he loved. He thanked his family for their comfort and Baldwin in particular for the full consideration with which he had been treated, and commended to everyone the new King, who had 'one matchless blessing' – a happy home with his wife and children.

Returning to Royal Lodge afterwards, he found the atmosphere less tense than before. To Queen Mary, it was 'the dreadful goodbye' before his departure abroad – 'the whole thing was too pathetic for words.' The Queen gave no outward show of her emotions, but the Princess Royal was in tears. So was the Duke of Kent. As the Duke of Windsor bowed to the new King, he cried out, 'It isn't possible! It isn't happening!'[14]

Shortly after midnight, in the small hours of 12 December, Monckton drove his friend to Portsmouth, where they arrived soon after 1.30 a.m. for him to board the destroyer *Fury*. Monckton had told Reith that 'there would be a ghastly reaction in a week or two' when the King realized what he was doing. In retrospect, though, the Duke of Windsor would observe of this momentous journey away from his throne that he was entering 'life in the real world – the world which by my own free will I had chosen.'[15]

The Prince and Princess of Wales with their family on the steps of Marlborough House, *c.* 1889. *From left*: Prince Albert Victor; Princess Maud; the Prince and Princess of Wales; Princess Louise; Prince George and Princess Victoria.

The Duke of Clarence and Princess May of Teck at the time of their engagement, photographed by Downey, December 1891.

The Duke and Duchess of York on their wedding day, 6 July 1893.

The Duchess of York, *c.* 1898.

King Edward VII and Queen Alexandra.

York Cottage, Sandringham, with the Prince of Wales (inset).

Prince Edward and Prince Albert of York, 1897.

Prince Edward, 1905.

The Prince of Wales' children, from a postcard, *c.* 1907.

Prince John and Prince George, *c.* 1911.

The Russian imperial family's visit to Osborne, August 1909. *Seated, from left*: the Princess of Wales; Tsar Nicholas II; the Tsarevich, Alexis (*on ground*); King Edward VII; Grand Duchess Anastasia (*on ground*); Empress Alexandra; Prince of Wales; Grand Duchess Marie. *Standing, from left*: Prince Edward; Queen Alexandra; Princess Victoria; Grand Duchess Olga and Tatiana.

The funeral procession of King Edward VII, High Street, Windsor, 20 May 1910. Princes Edward and Albert, in naval uniform, follow behind William, German Emperor, King George V, and the Duke of Connaught.

The children of King George V, photographed by Downey, 1910. *Front row, left to right*: Prince John; Prince Henry; Prince George. *Back row, left to right*: Prince Albert; Princess Mary; the Prince of Wales.

Prince John on his cycle, *c.* 1911.

King George V and Queen Mary
in Coronation robes.

The Prince of Wales in military
uniform, c. 1918

Prince Albert in RAF uniform,
c. 1918.

Family group on Buckingham Palace balcony after the homecoming of the Prince of Wales, flanked by his parents, Queen Alexandra (*far left*) and Viscountess Lascelles (*far right*), 21 June 1922.

Family group for the christening of George Lascelles, 1923. *From left*: King George V; Lady Harewood (*seated*); Princess Mary, Viscountess Lascelles; Queen Mary (*seated, holding the infant*); Viscount Lascelles.

Family group on the Duke of York's wedding day, 26 April 1923. *From left*: Prince of Wales; Princess Mary (*seated*); Prince Henry; King George V; Prince Albert, Duke of York; Queen Mary; Prince George.

The Duke and Duchess of York after their wedding, 26 April 1923, with Queen Alexandra (*far left*), King George V, and Queen Mary

The Duchess of York with
Princess Elizabeth, 1926.

Princess Mary, Viscountess
Lascelles, 1927.

Prince George.

The Duke of York.

H.R.H. Princess Nicholas of Greece   H.R.H. Prince George   H.R.H. Prince Nicholas of Greece

H.M. The King   H.R.H. Princess Marina   H.M. The Queen

Family group on Prince George's engagement, August 1934. *From left:* Prince Nicholas of Greece; King George V; Princess Marina; Prince George; Queen Mary; Prince Nicholas of Greece.

The family on Buckingham Palace balcony during the Silver Jubilee celebrations, June 1935. *From left*: the Duke of York; Mary, Princess Royal and Countess of Harewood; King George V; Princess Margaret; the Hon. Gerald Lascelles; the Earl of Harewood; Princess Elizabeth; the Hon. George Lascelles; Queen Mary; the Duke of Gloucester; the Duchess of Kent; the Duke of Kent; the Duchess of York.

The Duke and Duchess of York.

The Coronation ceremony, 12 May 1937.

King George VI and Queen Elizabeth with Princesses Elizabeth and Margaret after the Coronation.

King George VI and Queen Elizabeth inspecting bomb damage at
Buckingham Palace, September 1940.

The Duke of Kent visiting the Church Army hostel at Livingstone House,
Stonebridge Park, 9 May 1939.

Group at the christening of Prince Michael of Kent, Windsor Castle, 4 August 1942, exactly three weeks before the Duke of Kent's death. *Seated, from left*: Princess Elizabeth; Lady Patricia Ramsay; Queen Elizabeth; Prince Edward of Kent; Queen Mary; Princess Alexandra; the Duchess of Kent, holding Prince Michael; the Dowager Marchioness of Milford Haven; Crown Princess Martha of Norway; Princess Margaret; Princess Helena Victoria. *Standing, from left*: Princess Marie Louise; Prince Bernhard of the Netherlands; King George VI; the Duke of Kent; King Haakon VII of Norway; King George II of the Hellenes; Crown Prince Olav of Norway.

King George VI, Queen Elizabeth and Princess Elizabeth at Sandringham Park, August 1943.

Funeral procession of King George VI, 15 February 1952, including (*left to right*) the Dukes of Edinburgh, Gloucester, Windsor and Kent, and Earl Mountbatten of Burma (*in naval uniform*).

Queen Elizabeth II and the Duke of Gloucester, at the Queen's Birthday Parade, 5 June 1952.

8

'I never wanted this to happen'

King George VI succeeded to the throne with reluctance and grave misgivings. One of the first people to see this, apart from his wife, was his cousin Lord Louis Mountbatten. As they were at Fort Belvedere on the first night of his reign, the new King turned to his cousin in great distress, saying, 'I never wanted this to happen; I'm quite unprepared for it. David has been trained for this all his life. I've never even seen a State Paper, I'm only a Naval Officer, it's the only thing I know about.' Mountbatten was immediately struck by history repeating itself. He told the King how, just after the Duke of Clarence died, his father Prince Louis of Battenberg had told the then Prince George, in response to a similar confession how wrong he was. 'There is no more fitting preparation for a King than to have been trained in the Navy.'[1]

The comparison was not appropriate in all respects. Prince George of Wales had had eighteen years to prepare for the inheritance of the crown. Prince Albert, Duke of York, had had barely a month's warning that it was inevitable he would succeed his brother.

All the same, by experience and temperament he was uniquely well-fitted for the throne. His father's hope that nothing would stand between him, 'Lilibet' (Princess Elizabeth) and the throne had been fulfilled. Apart from his courage, the fact that he had lived and worked as a member of a ship's company gave him a deep understanding of humanity and human nature, as had his experiences of physical suffering and feelings of inferiority, and knowledge of the working and living conditions of the working class in industry.

Moreover, as had been pointed out in his brother's farewell broadcast, he had a happy family life. The future Queen Elizabeth had had her misgivings about marrying into the royal family, but she rose to the challenge magnificently. As the second youngest of a large family, she had never suffered from shyness. Being married to a man who was shy and vulnerable, she had learnt to protect as well as support him; now she needed to more than ever. The last two Queens Consort had been overshadowed by their husbands, in addition to other handicaps. Queen Alexandra's premature deafness had prevented her from doing much more than play a ceremonial role in visiting hospitals and the like. Queen Mary had a keen grasp of social questions, and as had been remarked, would have made a good factory inspector; but the rigid face she showed to the public, and her fear of upstaging the irascible King, held her in check. It was evident to those who knew her that Queen Elizabeth promised to be a very different Consort from her predecessors.

At his Accession Council on the morning of 12 December, in the uniform of Admiral of the Fleet, the King looked pale and haggard. Though he addressed his Privy Council in a low, clear voice, the hesitations in his speech were evident. Reading from a prepared statement, he declared his adherence to the strict principles of constitutional government, and his resolve to work before all else for the welfare of the British Commonwealth of Nations. With his wife and helpmeet by his side, he took up 'the heavy task' before him, and looked for the support of all his people. His first act on succeeding his brother, he confirmed, would be to confer on him a Dukedom, and he would henceforth be known as His Royal Highness the Duke of Windsor.

Family life offered him some light relief from the almost overwhelming responsibilities of his new position. As he returned to 145 Piccadilly from the Accession Council, his daughters curtsied to him in the hall. Deeply touched, he stood still for a moment – as if this had brought home to him the change in his position as much as anything else – before stooping down to kiss them warmly. At lunch, he said teasingly: 'Now, if someone comes through on the telephone, who should I say I am?'

For the girls, there were subtle differences at home that day. 'That's Mummy now, isn't it?' Princess Elizabeth remarked to Lady Cynthia Asquith as she saw a letter on the hall table at their London home addressed to Her Majesty The Queen. Princess Margaret, learning to write, grumbled that she had only just learned how to spell York, and now she was not allowed to use it as part of her name any more as she had been told to sign herself 'Margaret all alone'.

The Duke of Windsor's immediate destination on leaving England was Schloss Enzesfeld, the home near Vienna of Baron and Baroness Eugene de Rothschild. The six months following his abdication, while he was not permitted to meet Wallis in order that the decree would be made absolute, were the most miserable of his life. With no artistic or cultural interests to occupy his mind, cut off from the life of royal duty in which he had been brought up, and separated from the woman for whom he had surrendered so much, to say that he was bored and lonely would be an understatement. He slept in a room almost entirely bare except for several large photographs of Wallis. His chief diversions, according to his equerry 'Joey' Legh, were playing the jazz drums 'very loud and long to a gramophone record', drinking brandy, and doing an impersonation of Churchill trying to persuade him not to renounce the throne – 'Sir, we must fight . . .'

Major Edward Metcalfe, a friend of several years' standing, broke off a skiing holiday nearby to come and join him. He soon noticed how hard the Duke found it to reconcile himself to his status as a former King. On the evening of his arrival, at dinner the Duke was told that King George VI wanted to speak to him on the phone. Not wanting to interrupt his meal, he said he could not take the call just now but asked for it to be put through at 10 p.m. To this, the answer was that the King would talk at 6.45 p.m. the next day as he was too busy to talk any other time. 'It was pathetic to see HRH's face,'

Metcalfe told his wife. 'He couldn't believe it! He's been so used to having everything done as he wishes. I'm afraid he's going to have many more shocks like this.'[2]

This did not put the Duke off persistently phoning his brother. Some of the calls were concerned with money, connected with the Duke's sale of his life tenancy of Sandringham and Balmoral, and his income from the Privy Purse; others were with unsolicited advice about politics and foreign affairs, for he assumed that the inexperienced King could not do without the benefit of his superior advice. Needless to say, this advice frequently ran counter to that which he was getting from government ministers.

Queen Elizabeth was particularly concerned at the effect her brother-in-law's telephone calls were having on her husband. She noticed that outbursts of temper often followed a phone conversation with his brother, especially if any of them touched on the matter of receiving Wallis into the royal family. She was insistent that the phone calls should cease, a proposal strongly supported by the King's secretariat. At last, the King told his brother that he could no longer go on phoning him like this. The Duke was astonished, but had no choice but to concede.

For the King and Queen and the rest of the family, it was a traumatic Christmas at Sandringham. Queen Mary, who had seemed such a tower of strength during the whole crisis, retired to her room on Christmas Eve and did not come out again until New Year's Day. Queen Elizabeth believed that the abdication had very nearly killed her; 'there is indeed such a thing as a broken heart and hers very nearly collapsed.'[3]

On Christmas Day the Duchess of Kent gave birth to a daughter, named Alexandra. This was a happy culmination for the Kents, of an otherwise unsettling year. The diplomat Sir Robert Bruce Lockhart, one of the Duke of Windsor's friends, and not the most reliable of witnesses, described the Duke of Kent as 'a nervous wreck' who was capable of doing anything and wanted to kill Mrs Simpson. The Duke of Kent was undoubtedly shattered by the events of the last few weeks, having been so devoted to his eldest brother, but rumours concerning his demeanour at this time were undoubtedly exaggerated.

To make matters worse, the new year had barely opened before the press discovered that the Duke and a certain 'Mrs Allen' had visited the London Phrenological Institution at Ludgate Circus, where they had had their heads 'read' by a Miss Bool, who claimed to be able to reveal a person's abilities and characteristics by examing the contours of his or her head. Within a few days it was suggested that Mrs William Allen, wife of a wealthy business man and former Member of Parliament for West Belfast, was having an affair with the Duke, and that the cuckolded husband had instituted divorce proceedings. Only an angry disclaimer from William Allen himself, published in *The Times*, put a stop to this ill-informed speculation.

Although the abdication had also left its mark on Queen Elizabeth, she managed not to let it show. 'I can hardly now believe that we have been called to this tremendous task . . . and the curious thing is that we are not afraid,' she wrote to the Archbishop, Cosmo Gordon Lang 'I feel that God has enabled us to face the situation calmly.'[4]

Three months later, Harold Nicolson was particularly struck by her manner at a dinner party at Buckingham Palace. Her smile, he thought was indicative of how she would have enjoyed the party if only she had not been Queen of England. 'Nothing could exceed the charm or dignity which she displays, and I cannot help feeling what a mess poor Mrs Simpson would have made of such an occasion. It demonstrated to us more than anything else how wholly impossible that marriage would have been.'[5]

To Lady Diana Cooper, the atmosphere at Windsor under King George VI and Queen Elizabeth was very different to that of King Edward VIII's entertainments at Fort Belvedere; the latter had been an operetta, while the former was an institution.

It was largely through the Queen's efforts that Buckingham Palace took on a more homely air. To transform a building with six hundred rooms, largely neglected during King Edward VIII's reign, was no easy task, but fresh flowers, new carpets and curtains in the rooms used by the King and Queen, helped to create a better atmosphere. Disliking protocol for its own sake, she scrapped the traditional custom by which children of the monarch curtsied or bowed to their parents at each meeting, so that their daughters could still rush to greet them as they always had. However, they were still required to curtsey to Queen Mary, as a mark of respect for their grandmother schooled in a different age with different standards.

The Duke of Gloucester was now third in succession to the throne. The heiress presumptive and her sister were aged ten and six respectively, and if the King should die before Princess Elizabeth's eighteenth birthday in April 1944, the Duke would be Regent; and whenever the King was abroad, he would be required at home as a Counsellor of State. Such arduous commitments, the King realized, would be inconsistent with the routine of a regimental army officer. The Duke had looked forward to the day when he would command his own regiment, the 10th Royal Hussars, and the King regretted that it should be necessary for his brother to give up his career in the army, to which he was so attached.

By way of compensation, the King promoted him to Major-General with effect from 1 January 1937. It was appropriate for the Regent Designate, though he was disappointed not to be able to go on to command his regiment, or to achieve promotion on merit alone.

The Duke of Windsor's loneliness was eased by regular phone calls to Wallis – 'of course he's on the line for hours & hours every day to Cannes', Metcalfe told his wife. They were a mixed blessing, for Wallis seemed 'to be always picking on him and complaining about something that she thinks he hasn't done or ought to do',[6] and also tormented by the fear of losing him. In particular, the fact that Baroness Kitty de Rothschild stayed there for several weeks after the Duke's arrival, without her husband, sent a shudder through Mrs Simpson. 'God, that woman's a bitch,' remarked the exasperated Metcalfe, referring to Wallis, 'she'll play hell with him before long.'[7] The rest of the royal family must have considered that she had played hell with the former sovereign quite enough already.

It was nearly two months before anybody from the family came to call. On 2 February the Princess Royal and the Earl of Harewood visited him, and he was on the verge of tears when they met on the railway station platform in Vienna. Equerry John Aird was unenthusiastic about their arrival, while conceding reluctantly that they were better than nothing; 'although they both try their best they do not add to life.' Their visit was overshadowed by Wallis phoning up after being told of a malicious story in the press about financial negotiations in the royal family. Harewood told King George VI on his return that he had tried to calm the Duke, 'but I expect she gave him Hell down the phone.'[8]

Three weeks later the Duke of Kent paid him a visit, but without the Duchess. After his initial anger, he had forgiven his brother, and had wanted to come in January. The King had however asked him to wait, as newspaper interest in the abdication had only just died down and any early visits would revive front-page news too quickly.

Watching events from Norway, Queen Maud, last surviving sister-in-law of Queen Mary, wrote on 20 February to express her sympathy for the Duke; 'it makes me *quite* low to think of *him* banished out there and that he has given up everything of his own free will all on account of one *bad* woman who has hypnotized him.' Yet she still hoped that the divorce would not be finalized – '*Do* pray still that something may happen to "her" to prevent her from marrying him!'[9]

Queen Mary's attitude was still far less indulgent. When Lord Salisbury expressed his sympathy for the ex-King, she retorted that the one who needed most sympathy was her second son: 'he is the one who is making the sacrifice.'

In mid-March Lord Mountbatten arrived for three days. As Prince of Wales, the Duke had been best man at Mountbatten's wedding, and rather rashly Lord Mountbatten was promising not only to repay the compliment, but also suggested the date for the wedding, 3 June (a date hardly calculated to find favour with the rest of the family, being the late King George V's birthday), and assuring him that he could persuade the King, the Duke of Gloucester and the Duke of Kent to attend the ceremony as well. The Duke of Windsor gently declined Mountbatten's offer to be best man, feeling sure that his brothers, would be there to act as royal supporters.

Though his motives were undoubtedly prompted by a desire for family unity, Mountbatten must have sorely underestimated the resentment against Mrs Simpson. Thinking the better of it, it was not until 5 May that he wrote to the Duke of Windsor, regretfully declining an invitation to the wedding and explaining that while his brothers had been willing to come, 'other people had stepped in to create a situation which made all the Duke's friends most unhappy.'[10]

Further ill feeling was engendered by subsequent alterations to the financial settlement made after the abdication. The Duke of Windsor was required to bear part of the cost of pensions paid to retired retainers on the Sandringham and Balmoral estates, thereby reducing his allowance from £25,000 to £21,000. The government, though contributing nothing directly to the Duke's annuity, persuaded the King to make this payment conditional on the Duke's not returning to England without express permission. The Duke was aggrieved, insisting that his brother had broken a verbal agreement made at the time of the abdication, and the exchange of letters became more acrimonious until he threatened to have the King and his family evicted from Sandringham and Balmoral.

Although the government may have been unnecessarily vindictive, the Duke was insensitive in not realizing the shock and contempt which his renunciation of the throne had provoked. Eventually he accepted the terms of the settlement, but his resentment lingered.

While the Duke was preparing for his wedding, concentration in the kingdom was focused on the Coronation of his brother, to be held on 12 May. It had been planned that a Durbar in India would follow later in the year, to mark his accession to the Indian Empire, as King George V had done, but both the King and Baldwin himself were apprehensive of the strain of an Indian visit on top of a summer burdened with Coronation festivities.

The King was deeply anxious about the Coronation ceremony, particularly the effect that his speech impediment would have on making his responses. Fortunately he could make light of the cruelly-exaggerated rumours about him. *Time* quoted him as saying that he was 'supposed to be unable to speak without stammering, to have fits, and to die in two years. All in all, I seem to be a crock!'[11]

On 12 May, the King and Queen were woken up at about 3 a.m., by the sound of loudspeakers being tested in Constitution Hill; 'one of them might have been in our room.' If nerves did not prevent them from going back to sleep, bands and marching troops from 5 a.m. onwards certainly did. The King could eat no breakfast and 'had a sinking feeling inside', at what he regarded as the most important ceremony in his life. The hours of waiting before they left for Westminster Abbey were the most nerve-racking, and it was a relief when the time came for them to drive in the State Coach to the Abbey.

Though the ceremony had been rehearsed down to the most minute detail, there were unexpected setbacks. On their arrival, the King and Queen were met by their pages and train bearers who would accompany them to their retiring rooms. The Queen's processions began first but a halt was soon called, as one of the Presbyterian chaplains had fainted. The King was kept waiting, 'it seemed for hours due to this accident, but at last all was ready.' Everything went smoothly until he knelt at the altar to take the Coronation oath. Two bishops, Durham, and Bath & Wells, were on either side to support him and to hold the form of service for him to follow. When the moment came, neither bishop could find the words, so the Archbishop held his down for the King to read, but with his thumb covering the words of the oath.

The Lord Great Chamberlain was supposed to dress the King, but his hands fumbled and shook so much that the King had to fix the belt of the sword himself. At last all the various vestments were put on, and the Archbishop handed him the two sceptres. The supreme moment came when St Edward's Crown, weighing seven pounds, was placed on his head. Then he rose to his feet and walked to the throne in the centre of the amphitheatre. As he turned after leaving the Coronation Chair he was brought to a standstill, as one of the bishops was treading on his robe; 'I had to tell him to get off it pretty sharply as I nearly fell down.'[12] At least the homage of the bishops and peers, with the Dukes of Gloucester and Kent doing theirs immediately after the Archbishop of Canterbury, went off successfully.

On the following day, the King and Queen drove through the streets of London in an open carriage and were received tumultuously. Other festivities included the Naval Review at Spithead on 20 May, and a service of public thanksgiving at St Paul's on Empire Day, 24 May.

For several weeks, the Duke of Windsor had been haunted by the possibility that Wallis's divorce might not be made absolute. A solicitor's clerk, Francis Stephenson, had served an affidavit on the King's Proctor alleging that the divorce was founded on collusion, and this could have been sufficient to prevent proceedings from going through. His theory, however, was based on rumours that Ernest Simpson had been paid up to £150,000 to divorce his wife. The King's Proctor suggested that this could hardly be called collusion, whereupon Stephenson abandoned his attempt, but the Proctor launched his own investigation into the King's alleged adultery, particularly during the *Nahlin* cruise. Not until March 1937 did the Attorney-General give a final ruling that there were no grounds for refusing the decree.

A week before the Coronation, the Duke of Windsor and Mrs Simpson were reunited. On 3 May, she was informed that the decree had been made absolute, and she called the Duke in Austria. He caught the 'Orient Express' from Salzburg that afternoon and met her at the Chateau de Cande, central France, at lunchtime the following day.

Cande, which belonged to a very rich French-born naturalized American named Charles Bedaux, had been chosen for the Windsors' marriage. After Montbatten's letter, the Duke had sadly resigned himself to the fact that none of his family would be attending, and Metcalfe accepted an invitation to be best man.

What rankled far more deeply, however, was King George VI's refusal to raise Wallis to royal rank upon their marriage. Shortly before the abdication, the then Duke of York had apparently promised to do so, at a time of considerable nervous strain and emotion, and without consulting any other members of the family or their advisers. When they learned of this, they were aghast. Queen Mary, who had promised King George V that she would never receive Mrs Simpson after his death, was particularly appalled. Queen Elizabeth and their advisers were just as vehement; it would create a disastrous impression to confer royal rank upon a woman with two previous husbands living, and who had been instrumental in the King abandoning his throne. Moreover, the rank of Her Royal Highness, once conferred, would be for life. Few people in high places believed the marriage would last. Even the Duke's ally, Churchill, had said that he fell constantly in and out of love, and 'his present attachment will follow the course of all the others.'[13] The mere possibility of Her Royal Highness Duchess of Windsor, as she would become, divorcing or being divorced by him and collecting more husbands in future, was enough to set them firmly against the idea. The title of Royal Highness was therefore reconferred on the Duke, and 'not for his wife or descendants if any' by Letters Patent on 27 May.

The Duke of Windsor was bitterly angry, and never forgave his family. In high dudgeon, he told the King that he would fight the ruling. To Herman Rogers and his staff, he said he hoped they would all recognize his wife as Her Royal Highness, and that the ladies would curtsey to her as such. 'This is a fine wedding present!' he remarked angrily to Monckton, who had handed him the King's letter announcing the decision. At first he wanted to renounce his own right to style himself

HRH, but Monckton persuaded him that he would not help himself by over-reacting. The Duke knew that 'Bertie couldn't have written this letter on his own,' and blamed the Queen and Queen Mary. It was a wound that never ceased to pain him. Writing in 1966, he still described it as a 'cold-blooded act' and 'a kind of Berlin wall' which had cut him off from country and family.

The wedding took place as arranged on 3 June. A civil marriage by the Mayor of Monts was followed by a religious ceremony at which the Reverend R. Anderson Jardine officiated. Jardine, Vicar of St Paul's Church, Darlington, was warned by the Bishop of Durham that he had 'no episcopal licence or consent' to conduct the ceremony, but went ahead anyway. He had what Monckton called 'a marked weakness for self-advertisement.' Later he had visiting cards printed with the words, 'The Duke's Vicar' beneath his name, offered himself for lecture tours in America, and secured the services of an agent in Hollywood. Sixteen people attended the wedding, and in London the following day's Court Circular made no reference to it.

Though the Metcalfes were to prove faithful friends to the Windsors, Lady Alexandra had her doubts. She shook hands with them after the ceremony, realizing that she should have kissed the Duchess but 'just couldn't . . . If she occasionally showed a glimmer of softness, took his arm, looked at him as though she loved him one would warm towards her, but her attitude is so correct. The effect is of a woman unmoved by the infatuated love of a younger man.'[14]

She had not been alone in seeing how the love appeared to be largely on one side. Ever since the abdication crisis, Queen Mary had prayed devoutly that Mrs Simpson 'would make him happy,' remarking astutely that it was 'no ordinary love' he had for her. Implicit were her doubts as to how much she really felt for him.

After the wedding, the Windsors left to stay at Count Munster's house, Wasserleonburg. The Duke brooded on how the family had ignored his wedding, though they all telegraphed their good wishes. In particular he was bitterly hurt and disappointed that his mother did not send a wedding present. There was ample evidence, he wrote to her, that the consistent humiliation was 'not only the policy of the present government, but is also Bertie's personal attitude towards myself, and further, I regret to say, your attitude and that of the whole of my family.' It could only have one result – 'my complete estrangement from all of you.'[15]

In August, the Duke and Duchess of Kent arrived to stay with her sister and brother-in-law, Prince and Princess Paul of Yugoslavia, at Paul's hunting lodge. Also there was 'the ladies' formidable mother', Princess Nicholas of Greece.

The Duke was keen to visit his brother, but as he admitted to Paul, this put him in a difficult situation. Queen Mary had given him 'strong instructions' that Marina, being a foreigner by birth should not be the first female member of the royal family to call on the Duchess of Windsor, as the feeling against her was particularly strong in England at that time. Acting as go-between, Paul phoned the Duke of Windsor, then handed him over to the Duke of Kent, who said, 'I've just arrived and may I come and see you with Paul?' The Duke of Windsor told him to wait a moment, presumably while he went to consult Wallis. After a few minutes he returned, to ask, 'Are you coming with *your wives?*' The Duke of Kent diplomatically said that they had just arrived and as their mother-in-law was in the house, it was not convenient at that moment. 'In that case, it's No,' said the Duke of Windsor curtly, and put the phone down.[16] Dismayed, the Duke of Kent referred his difficulties to King George VI, who reluctantly took Monckton's advice and directed the Duke and Duchess of Kent to call on the Windsors together. Backed up by not only Queen Mary, but also the feelings of Queen Elizabeth and her own mother Princess Nicholas, the Duchess of Kent was adamant that she would not. When the Duke of Kent and Prince Paul called at Wasserleonburg without their wives, the Duchess of Windsor retaliated by refusing to see them, and the Duke of Windsor gave his brother 'a lecture he wouldn't soon forget.'

It all added to the sense of grievance the Duke of Windsor

felt against his family. He wrote to his mother in October saying that he knew from George (the Duke of Kent) that she and Queen Elizabeth 'instigated the somewhat sordid and much publicized episode of the failure of the Kents to visit us' and now he could not see 'how any form of correspondence can give pleasure to either of us under these circumstances.'[17]

As a result, a marked coolness developed between the Duke of Windsor and the brother who once had been closest to him. When the Duke of Kent sent him a gold box as a Christmas present, it was returned with a note saying, 'The only box I have come to expect from my brothers is a box on the ear.'[18]

Minor points of etiquette were one thing, errors of judgement were another, and they played their part in widening the estrangement between the former King and his family. That summer he gave further proof of his apparent readiness to consort with the Nazi regime by his plan with Charles Bedaux to visit Germany, ostensibly to study the living and working conditions of the labouring classes in several large cities. Boredom was partly responsible; after twenty years of complaining about 'princing' and the pressures of public life, time hung heavily on his hands. Isolation from his life of duty was becoming irksome; he needed the limelight, and now he had a wife to share it with him. That it gave the infamous Bedaux an opportunity to enhance his business relations with his Nazi associates was regrettably lost on him. Moreover, he felt that he should improve his knowledge of and acquaintance with the German leaders. If war threatened, maybe he could use his influence as an honest broker and help to avert such a catastrophe.

The Duke's belief that Britain could live with German aspirations, and that war was not inevitable in 1937, was one widely shared by members of the government and the man in the street. Moreover, like King George VI, he viewed Soviet Russia as a greater menace to Western Europe than Nazi Germany.

The Duke's detractors have never ceased to hold their German visit as proof of his and his wife's readiness to give their seal of approval to the Nazi regime. To those in Britain who had viewed with misgivings his open support of

Germany as Prince of Wales, it was a vindication of his lack of soundness where foreign affairs were concerned. Although the King and Queen supported the appeasement policy of Chamberlain – who had succeeded Baldwin as Prime Minister in May, two weeks after the Coronation – they were aghast at the idea of the Duke of Windsor's consorting with the Nazis to such an extent. The Queen was particularly angry, seeing it as a deliberate attempt to recapture the spotlight from her husband, and they were dismayed at having been given no previous notice of the tour.

On 11 October the Windsors arrived in Berlin. Although the Foreign Office had directed the British Embassy staff to give them no official reception on their visit, they met all the principal Nazi leaders, including Josef Goebbels, director of propaganda, Heinrich Himmler, head of the Gestapo, and Hitler's deputy Rudolf Hess. For two weeks they toured German cities and factories, greeted everywhere with the Nazi salute and cries of '*Heil Windsor!*', to which he responded with '*Heil Hitler!*' On two or three occasions, he was seen to give a full Nazi salute.*

The climax of their German tour was a visit to Berchtesgaden to take afternoon tea with the Fuhrer. Although no detailed accounts of their conversation survive, Hitler's interpreter remarked afterwards that they talked chiefly about social and industrial welfare conditions, and that the Duke said nothing to indicate his apparent sympathies with the ideology and practices of the Third Reich.

Hitler was satisfied with the meeting. Afterwards, he spoke of the abdication as a severe loss for Germany, and thought that permanent friendly relations with England could have been achieved if he had stayed on the throne. As for Wallis, 'she would have made a good Queen.'

---

* Though bitterly censured for so doing, he was not alone. On a visit to Berlin in May 1938, the England soccer team were photographed in Berlin, likewise raising their arms high in a full Nazi salute at the insistence of the British Ambassador, Sir Nevile Henderson.

Press reaction in Britain and in the United States was mixed. It was seen that the Duke had given the Nazis unwitting proof that he was an ardent advocate of their cause, and that they had used him as a propaganda weapon. Yet Winston Churchill (briefed by his son Randolph, who had been present on the tour), who was no friend of Nazi Germany, wrote to congratulate him afterwards as 'it all passed off with so much distinction and success.'[19] Meanwhile Bedaux was drawing up plans for a similar tour of America, but there was such an outcry that the idea was abandoned.

Behind King George VI's anger at his brother's behaviour lay a deep sense of unease. After visiting the King and Queen at Balmoral in October, their conversations with Sir Ronald Lindsay, British Ambassador to Washington, the impression that the King did not yet feel safe on the throne, and he was like a medieval monarch with a hated rival claimant living in exile. To some extent this was the case. One year ago, King George VI had been Duke of York, and was confident of being so for many years to come. Elevated swiftly to the throne in unexpected and dramatic circumstances, he still did not feel really established as a monarch. To have the brother to whom he had always looked up and respected, now courting the limelight, only compounded his insecurity.

None the less, the taxing year ended successfully. On 26 October the King opened Parliament in State, an ordeal which had worried him almost as much as the Coronation. But he practised in the study at Buckingham Palace, first with the crown on his head, reading first his father's speech and then the draft of his own, watched by Logue. Although there were still minor hesitations in his speech, he was proud of himself at carrying off the ordeal well.

That Christmas, he broadcast to the nation again. Although he did not intend at this stage to continue his father's tradition of an annual broadcast at Christmas, he took the opportunity to say a few heartfelt words of thanks 'for the love and loyalty you gave us from every quarter of the Empire during this unforgettable year now drawing to its end. We have promised to try and be worthy of your trust, and this is a pledge that we shall always keep.'[20]

The Duke and Duchess of Gloucester had reason, albeit briefly, to celebrate. During a relaxing summer at Birkhall, near Balmoral, the Duke enjoyed an excellent shooting season and in September he wrote to Queen Mary to report that the Duchess was expecting a child. The Queen was thrilled, knowing how much they hoped for a family of their own. Unfortunately the Duchess suffered a miscarriage some weeks later.

Immersing themselves in work to keep themselves occupied after this setback, they were soon kept busy with the acquisition of their own country home, Barnwell Manor, Northamptonshire. The Duke's military activities prevented him at times from devoting proper attention to his landowning responsibilities, particularly as events in Europe looked ever more threatening. A rather weary letter to Queen Mary remarked on 'having this tiresome house on top of everything else. We were unlucky to acquire it when we did.'[21] To the Duchess, therefore, fell the tasks of supervising fencing, hedging, roads, livestock, payment of accounts and the arrangement of furniture, carpets and curtains. They were jobs she tackled with vigour, and with its shooting and farming facilities Barnwell Manor indeed was to become a home to them and their family in every sense.

Meanwhile, the Duke and Duchess of Windsor celebrated Christmas with Herman and Katherine Rogers at Cannes. Their first Christmas card as a married couple showed a drawing of them by the French artist Etienne Drian. Edward was portrayed as a small, wistful figure seated in a chair. Perched on the arm, towering above him, was the strong-faced, determined figure of his wife. It suggested an unhappy boy in the custody of a large, autocratic nanny, and was referred to derisively among members of the royal family as 'David and the Giantess'.[22]

With the worsening European situation, it was necessary for Britain to cultivate her allies. In the summer of 1938, King George VI and Queen Elizabeth paid their first official state visit abroad, to France. It was due to begin on 28 June, but five days earlier the Queen's mother, the Countess of Strathmore, died at the age of seventy-five, and it was postponed for three weeks. As she did not wish to wear bright colours so soon after her mother's death, but could hardly be dressed in black on such an important occasion – and in fashionable Paris, of all places – her clothes were made in white. 'A radiant Winterhalter,' as Lady Diana Cooper described her, she enchanted the French, while Paris headlines proclaimed that 'today France is a monarchy again.' At Villers-Bretonneux, where the King unveiled a memorial to the eleven thousand Australians who fell in France during the Great War, the Queen walked forward spontaneously and scattered on the ground an armful of red poppies picked in the neighbouring fields and given to her that morning by a French schoolboy. Watching the incident on a newsreel film in Berlin, Hitler remarked that the Queen was 'the most dangerous woman in Europe.'

By this time, divisions in the British government for or against appeasement were becoming marked. Neville Chamberlain's policy of appeasement was supported by the King, not out of any intention to surrender to the dictators, so much as to avoid precipitating another world war. The conflict of 1914–18 and its attendant horrors were by no means a distant memory, and the idea of plunging country, Commonwealth and Empire into a further conflict appalled him. No reasonable effort, therefore, should be spared in attempting to avoid this. The anti-appeasement faction, led by Churchill and Anthony Eden, who had resigned from the Cabinet earlier that year in protest, strongly deprecated Hitler's bullying tactics towards the smaller European nations.

In March, Nazi Germany had annexed Austria; later, Hitler threatened to bring the German-speaking areas of Czechoslovakia, the Sudetenland, under German rule. King George offered to send a letter to Hitler as one ex-serviceman to another, begging him to help spare Europe from the disaster of war, but Chamberlain dissuaded him on the grounds that an insulting reply might be his only reward. In September, the Prime Minister flew to confer with Hitler at Berchtesgaden, and thus began meetings which culminated in the signing of the Munich agreement on 30 September, sacrificing the integrity of Czechoslovakia for the fragile prospect of lasting peace in the continent. The King was dissuaded from going to meet Chamberlain at Heston airport on his return to England, but sent a letter to be handed to him as he stepped off the plane, inviting him to come at once to Buckingham Palace so he could express his heartfelt congratulations without delay. Chamberlain and his wife duly appeared on the palace balcony with the King and Queen, and received a grateful reception from the crowds below.

This royal endorsement of Chamberlain's action was to prove somewhat contentious, in view of the official parliamentary opposition's denunciation of the Munich agreement. 'In the circumstances,' commented historian John Grigg, half a century later,* 'this has to be regarded as the most unconstitutional act by any British sovereign in the present century.'[23]

The men and women of London, like the King and Queen, warmly endorsed Chamberlain's actions, and believed him when he declared that he had brought home 'Peace with honour'. In Parliament, though, he was criticized by the Churchill-Eden faction and opposition parties. When Alfred Duff Cooper resigned from the Cabinet on 2 October, the King remarked as he accepted the seals of office that although he disagreed with Cooper's decision, he 'respected those who had the courage of their convictions.'

If King, Queen and Prime Minister were united on the threatening European situation, they were not in total agreement on the vexed question of what to do about the Duke of Windsor. Chamberlain thought that, once the dust had settled on the abdication crisis, he should be treated as a younger brother of the King who could take some of the work off the latter's hands. The King was not anxious for the Duke to return so soon, but according to Monckton, he was 'not fundamentally against the Prime Minister's view.'

* In a review of *George VI*, by Sarah Bradford.

But the Queen was vehemently opposed to the idea, feeling that the Duke still posed a threat as a potential rallying point for any who might be critical of King George, who was 'less superficially endowed with the arts and graces that please.'

As an interim measure, Chamberlain decided he would test public opinion on a meeting between the Windsors and other members of the royal family. The Duke and Duchess of Gloucester had gone on holiday to Kenya and Uganda, playing polo, shooting and taking photographs, and he arranged for them to call on the Windsors in Paris on their way back to England.

At the meeting in November, the two exchanged friendly handshakes, the Duchess of Gloucester kissed her sister-in-law, and they enjoyed a leisurely lunch in the Windsors' hotel suite. In the evening they went out to dine at a fashionable restaurant. While the Windsors revelled in this sign of reconciliation and both Dukes made tentative plans for them to visit England again – perhaps in time for Christmas festivities at Sandringham, according to an optimistic forecast by the *Daily Mail* Paris correspondent – the Duchess of Gloucester was uncomfortable. She did not feel 'in the least chic' with the red dust of Kenya hardly out of her hair, wearing a simple blue dress as she had not brought any smart clothes from England with her, while the Duchess of Windsor positively sparkled in a fetching purple creation, diamond clips in her hair.

If the Duke of Windsor expected his former subjects to clamour immediately for his and his wife's return, he was to be disappointed. When the Gloucesters returned home, the Court Circular recorded discreetly that they had 'arrived from abroad', while making no mention of their reunion in Paris. Some other English papers did, with the result that 'a lot of old ladies duly wrote furiously disapproving letters',[24] which the Duchess found quite upsetting.

Queen Elizabeth showed no sign of softening her attitude. When it was mentioned to her that the Duchess of Windsor had done much for the Duke, and stopped or at least curtailed his drinking – 'no more pouches under his eyes,' she retorted, 'who has the lines under his eyes now?'

In December 1938 the Duke and Duchess of Windsor were pressing to be allowed to come and visit England, ostensibly for the purpose of the latter being introduced to members of the royal family. The King made it plain in a letter to Neville Chamberlain that neither the Queen or Queen Mary had any desire to meet her, suggesting at the same time that perhaps the Duke would take such a decision in a more kindly manner from the Prime Minister than from his brother and sovereign. The Duke was furious, complaining at 'their attitude towards my wife and myself', insisting that he would 'never allow this attitude on their part to be used as a reason for keeping me out of my country.' The government supported the King, and were prepared to impose financial sanctions if necessary. Ever since April 1937, ministers had suggested that the £21,000 annual allowance paid to the Windsors should cease if the Duke attempted to return to England without permission. An annuity of £50,000 had originally been suggested but withdrawn on the recommendation of Sir Horace Wilson, personal adviser to Stanley Baldwin. He warned that Mrs Simpson was quite capable of returning to England, aided by what she expected to be a generous provision from public funds, and that it 'must not be assumed that she has abandoned hope of becoming Queen of England. It is known that she has limitless ambition, including a desire to interfere in politics.'[25]

Yet public opinion was by no means against the former monarch. In January 1939 a Gallup poll taken to find out what the general public reaction would be to the Windsors returning to live in the country, 61 per cent replied Yes, only 16 per cent No, and 23 per cent 'did not know'.

In the summer of 1938, Lord Gowrie, Governor-General of Australia, wrote to Sir Godfrey Thomas, now private secretary to the Duke of Gloucester, that he hoped the Duke would at some future date come to Australia to fill the position which was currently his. Loyal Australians were mildly aggrieved as the Dominions of Canada and South Africa had already had royal Governors-General, while they had had none. The idea appealed to the Duke, but such an appointment would have to wait at least until Princess Elizabeth came of age in 1944. As Regent designate, the Duke of Gloucester's presence near his brother was required at home. Should anything happen to the King, the Duke would have to hurry back several thousand miles, and moreover at a time when he might be somewhat out of touch with affairs in Britain. Under such circumstances, the Duke of Windsor might be regarded as a more practical choice of regent than a brother almost at the opposite end of the world.

In October, however, the King announced that the Duke of Kent would be the next Governor-General of Australia, a post which he would take up in November 1939, making his official residence Government House in Canberra. The idea appealed greatly to the Duke, who looked forward to making his mark there as an individual. He would be the King's personal representative, and it would give him a chance to introduce a new and more relaxed style into what had always been a very formal office.

Now the omission was to be remedied. The *Sydney Sun* called it 'the greatest compliment the Throne can pay to the Australian people.'

The Duchess of Kent did not share everyone else's enthusiasm. Family considerations made her dread the undertaking, for she would be twelve thousand miles away from her mother and sisters. Barely a month went by without at least one of her relatives coming to stay at Coppins. Still, she accepted the imminent duty with good grace. The Duke immediately started finding out as much as he could about Australia, and she shared his homework, as they read every book on the Dominion they could lay their hands on, studying old maps and documents from the Public Record office, including the original Letters Patent constituting the office of Governor-General, and the log of HMS *Sirius* which accompanied the first settlers who had gone to the then newly-discovered continent.

The Duke chose the colour scheme for the Governor-General's house, and planned exactly where the new furniture would be placed. Oatmeal-coloured silk tweed curtains, pale blue satin-covered sofas and chairs, and white Grecian rugs were sent over from England. Arrangements were made to ship the children's toys and Prince Edward's Shetland pony, and after the Duke was given three racehorses (by the Aga Khan, Prince Aly Khan, and Lord Derby), he decided to take up racing and registered his colours in Australia. The first part of the long journey would be made by air, and they would stop off in India to visit some of the Indian princes. After they had gone, Coppins would be put up for sale.

With the shadows of war looming larger over Europe, the Duke of Windsor accepted an invitation from the National Broadcasting Company in the United States of America to broadcast an appeal for peace worldwide. The timing was unfortunate, for the King and Queen were about to embark on a crucial state visit to America and Canada, the first by a reigning British sovereign and his consort. When the Duke's intentions became known, even Lord Beaverbrook was dismayed, and published an editorial in the *Daily Express* on 8 May urging him to wait until after the state visit. Yet the Duke went ahead, much to the King's anguish, but the BBC refused to relay it in Britain.

However, nothing could diminish the King and Queen's triumph in the United States. They sailed on the liner *Empress of Australia*, after refusing to leave on HMS *Repulse* on the grounds that a warship could not be spared by the Royal Navy. On 17 May they landed at Quebec, where large crowds greeted them with great affection. The Governor-General of Canada, the novelist John Buchan, wrote to a friend that although he had always been deeply attached to the King, 'I realize now more than ever what a wonderful mixture he is of shrewdness, kindliness and humour,' while the Queen had 'a perfect genius for the right kind of publicity.'

On their three-day visit to the United States, the reception was equally warm as they drove to Hyde Park, Washington, the presidential residence. On their arrival Franklin D. Roosevelt had a tray of cocktails waiting for them. 'My mother thinks you should have a cup of tea,' he said. 'She doesn't approve of cocktails.' 'Neither does my mother,' said the King, smiling, as he reached out his hand to take one. During their twenty-four hours together, much mutual goodwill was established between King and President, and their wives, and the King spent some time talking with him to find out what help could be expected from America in the event of a war between Britain and the fascist powers. Roosevelt assured him that if London was bombed, 'the USA would come in.'

When they arrived back in Britain on 22 June, there was a new confidence about the King and Queen. No longer did they feel overshadowed by the former King Edward VIII. At last they had achieved international popularity in their own right, and on their own merit. Watching them as they drove through London, Harold Nicolson observed the sovereign's 'happy schoolboy grin', while his consort was 'one of the most amazing Queens since Cleopatra. We returned to the House with lumps in our throats.'[26]

This new mood of self-assurance was timely, for within a few weeks it was to be submitted to the most gruelling test imaginable. Chamberlain's faith in his 'Peace with honour' had been all but shattered by March when Hitler annexed the rest of Czechoslovakia, and on 22 August, the announcement of the Nazi-Soviet pact made war in Europe inevitable. One week later the Duke of Windsor sent a telegram to Hitler, urging him to desist, which was answered by a reply blaming British belligerence, and to King Victor Emmanuel III, who replied that Italy would remain neutral in the event of conflict.

That same month, the Duke and Duchess of Kent went to Yugoslavia for a last family holiday with Princess Nicholas. Most of their luggage, and the racehorses, were already on their way to Canberra. Disturbed by the gathering storms of war, the Duke cut his visit short and flew back to England, telling his wife that it would be best if he went home to make sure of the facts. A few days later, she received a telegram asking her to return home at once.

The governments of Britain and France stood by their guarantees to Poland, and mobilized their forces on 1

September as Poland was invaded by German forces. An ultimatum was issued demanding the withdrawal of German troops within forty-eight hours. No reply was received, and at 11.00 a.m. on Sunday 3 September, Chamberlain broadcast to the nation that war was declared.

In his diary, the King confided that at the outbreak of war in 1914 he was a midshipman, keeping the middle watch on the bridge of HMS *Collingwood* in the North Sea. Now, they were at war again, and he was no longer a midshipman in the Royal Navy, but Admiral of the Fleet. Now that the 'crises' following the Munich agreement were over, and 'the result of the breakdown of negotiations is War, the country is calm, firm & united behind its leaders, resolved to fight until Liberty & Justice are once again safe in the World.'[27]

In Europe, the Duke of Windsor was deeply pessimistic, and did not hesitate to say so. He and the Duchess were bathing at their house at Antibes when he was told that the British Ambassador was on the telephone from Paris. Ten minutes later he came back, and told her that Britain had just declared war on Germany. 'I'm afraid in the end this may open the way for world Communism.'[28]

King George VI's gloomy fears in 1936 that 'the whole fabric' of monarchy 'might crumble under the shock and strain' of the abdication crisis had been totally unfounded. The crown, he had proved beyond doubt, was in the best possible hands. Now the future of Britain and the Empire faced a far greater and even more daunting struggle.

9

'Thank God for a good King'

From the outbreak of war, King George VI never appeared in public except in uniform, by way of showing that he was on active service. During the first few months of conflict, he made several visits to his forces in the field, and in the first week of October went to see the fleet at Scapa Flow. It was a diffcult time for the monarch who was at once the Supreme Commander of his country's armed forces, yet as a constitutional sovereign prevented from playing any active part in the waging of the war. 'I wish I had a definite job like you.' he wrote to Lord Mountbatten on 23 October. 'Mine seems such an awful mixture, trying to keep people cheered up in all ways, and having to find fault as well as praising them.'[1]

Meanwhile the Windsors travelled across France and on 12 September reached Cherbourg, where they were met by Lord Mountbatten who escorted them back to England on board HMS *Kelly*. During the cross-channel journey, the Duke and Mountbatten chatted happily about old times, but as they approached Portsmouth, the Duke was apprehensive. To the Duchess, he confided that he did not know whether it would all result in reconciliation. 'War should bring families together, even a Royal Family. But I don't know.'[2]

They docked at Portsmouth at 10 p.m., and went to stay at the Metcalfes' house near Coleman's Hatch, Sussex. Still acting as an intermediary, Monckton was asked to tell the Duke that the King would receive him, but not the Duchess, at Buckingham Palace on 14 September.

The brothers met after the King and Queen had returned home from a tour of the London docks, and the Queen was not present. The King noted in his diary afterwards that they talked for an hour, and 'there were no recriminations on either side.' To Chamberlain, he wrote that his brother was apparently not at all worried 'as to the effects he left on people's minds as to his behaviour in 1936. He has forgotten all about it.'[3]

The Duke was offered a choice of two posts, that of Deputy Regional Commissioner in Wales, or as a member of the Military Mission in France. Though he expressed a preference for the former, on reflection the King and Queen realized that it would be inconvenient to have him and his wife in Britain during what might be a long war, so he was persuaded to take the latter. As the King remarked to his Minister for War, Leslie Hore-Belisha, all his predecessors had succeeded to the throne after their own predecessors had died; 'Mine is not only alive, but very much so,' and it would be expedient for the Duke to leave for Paris at once. The Duke did so, but not before asking – in vain – if it could be mentioned in the press that he was not being paid for his war service. He had enquired whether the Duke of Gloucester was being paid for his, and was told that no member of the royal family ever accepted payment for service in the army.

The Windsors remained in England for a further fortnight, while details of staff, uniforms and military instructions were seen to. No member of the royal family communicated with them during this time. Making a sentimental journey back to Fort Belvedere one day, they found the lawn overgrown, their garden a mass of weeds, and the shuttered house damp and slowly decaying. The Duchess told Lady Metcalfe gloomily that they realized her husband had no place in his own country, and she saw no reason for them ever to return. While some of their defenders might have regarded the family's treatment of them as needlessly petty during a time of war, even the sympathetic Lady Metcalfe found it impossible not to be critical; 'their selfishness and self-concentration is terrifying.'

The Duke was required to give up his rank of Field-Marshal for the duration of the war, in order to become an acting Major-General. He was to work with No. 1 Military Mission, an appointment with somewhat vague terms of reference, but its real task was apparently to spy on the notoriously secretive and suspicious French, who refused to tell their allies much about their defences and fortifications. They had not yet allowed any Englishman to inspect the Maginot Line, the basis of their defensive system.

At last, noted the Mission's Chief of Staff, they were to have a heaven-sent chance of visiting the French front. The French Commander-in-Chief, General Gamelin, raised an objection to the Duke's going anywhere in the French war zone. He made three important tours of French army zones during the autumn, and compiled penetrating reports on French lack of preparations for attack and the poor state of morale, and the in-fighting between the French commanders whom he thought were more hostile to each other than to the Germans.

Unfortunately, the Duke's presence was overshadowed by a trifling incident in October when he met the Duke of Gloucester, who was Chief Liaison Officer between the British and French armies. Gloucester tried to avoid his brother, and only met him rather reluctantly when Edward asked pointedly to see him. A few days later, the brothers set out with Lord Gort, the British Commander-in-Chief, to tour the British Expeditionary Force. When the headquarters guard of the Coldstreams turned out and presented arms, the Duke of Windsor walked ahead of his brother (who was senior in rank) and took the salute. Gloucester and Gort were horrified, seeing further evidence of his refusal to ignore the changes in rank brought about by his abdication. When the Duke of Windsor made a brief visit to London early in January to report to the Chief of the Imperial General Staff, Sir Edmund Ironside, none of the family made any attempt to get in touch with him.

In December the King made his first visit to the BEF in France, and inspected the British troops in their positions. Widely reported in the French press, it helped to draw attention to the Anglo-French alliance by increasing awareness in France that British forces were fighting in their country.

It was agreed by the King and his advisers that the first Christmas of war should be marked by a personal message from the sovereign. King George had declined to continue his father's tradition, partly because of his antipathy to the microphone, and partly as King George V's four Christmas broadcasts had become so legendary that he was doubtful of his ability to reach the same standard.

He need not have worried, for the message he gave his people on 25 December 1939 soon passed into immortality. A few days before the broadcast, he was sent a collection of verse, *The Desert*, printed privately in 1908. The author, Marie Louise Haskins, was a tutor and lecturer in Social Sciences at the London School of Economics. In the book's introduction, he found precisely the words he was looking for: 'I said to the man who stood at the gate of the year: "Give me a light that I may tread safely into the unknown." And he replied: "Go out into the darkness and put your hand into the hand of God. That shall be to you better than light and safer than a known way."'

Shortly after the outbreak of war, the Duke of Kent's Australian appointment was postponed, and the Australian Prime Minister, Robert Menzies, told him that he looked forward to His Royal Highness assuming the duties of Governor-General 'when the present troubles were overcome.'

Determined to do something worthwhile at home, the Duke accepted a post at the Admiralty. Initially he had a desk job, which he found so irksome that he transferred to the RAF and dropped his honorary rank of Air Vice Marshal so that he would not be superior to officers under whom he had to work. In time he was promoted to Air Commodore, and became Chief Welfare officer of the RAF. In addition, he undertook a certain amount of work on behalf of the Ministry of Labour, inspecting factories engaged in war production and civil defence services.

Being fascinated by machinery and everything mechanical, he would ask searching questions as to how something functioned. If shown the intricate mechanism of a bomb, he would want to find out exactly how it was made. One of his private interests was antique clocks, which he collected, having over a hundred at Coppins. A duty visit from which it was difficult to drag him away was at a watch factory in High Wycombe, where he was fascinated to see precision pocket watches being made for RAF pilots. That was the only time which he broke his golden self-imposed rule of being back at Coppins by 4.30 in the afternoon, after the daily visits, to have tea with his children.

Collecting fine pictures and *objects d'art* was still one of the Duke's major relaxations. With some of the inheritance left him by his father, he continued to purchase paintings, porcelain and silver. In 1940 he was thrilled to acquire a group of three paintings by Claude Lorrain, which were added to a private collection already containing works by Van Dyck, Guardi, Lely, Reynolds, and Richard Wilson.

On the outbreak of war, the Kents gave up their London house at Belgrave Square and made Coppins their only home. The Duke indulged himself freely in gardening, a hobby which the Duchess was more than happy to leave him as she had never enjoyed doing so herself.

In March 1940, the King spent several hours inspecting the Dover Patrol and for a while, he acted as ticket-collector for BEF troops. A sergeant hurried to the barrier to catch his train, and thrust his papers hastily into the hands of a man in naval uniform standing by the ticket collectors. Suddenly he gave a gasp of surprise, stood to attention, and saluted, as he recognized his sovereign.

By this time, the war was about to enter a more threatening phase. On 9 April, Germany attacked Denmark and Norway. Within a month Norway was in Nazi hands, apart from a small pocket of allied resistance at Narvik. Parliamentary confidence in the leadership of Chamberlain collapsed, and after a crucial vote in the House of Commons, his normal majority of over two hundred reduced to eighty-one, he tendered his resignation. Like him, the King – and indeed the opposition parties – would have preferred Lord Halifax as his successor, but the latter was unenthusiastic.

There was only one obvious choice – Winston Churchill. Less than a year previously, the King had told Roosevelt that only in very exceptional circumstances would he consent to Churchill becoming Prime Minister. He had not only been one of the most vocal parliamentary champions of King Edward VIII, but had also argued persistently against Chamberlain's policy of appeasement with which the King had identified himself. Early in his parliamentary career he had briefly resigned the Conservative whip, and while his refusal to behave as lobby fodder demonstrated a commendable streak of independence, many of the party which he had long since rejoined were dismayed at his persistent rebellion against official Conservative policy.

However these were exceptional times, and the King accepted him, albeit with reluctance. Premier and sovereign were very different in character, one was shy and modest, while the other was theatrical and full of confidence in his own abilities. Luckily, Churchill possessed charm and tact, and knew well that he had not been the King's first choice. Moreover, it was a time for national unity, and both were determined to stand together. Within a few weeks, formal audiences were replaced by regular Tuesday luncheons, at which they served themselves from a side-table, discussing state business at Buckingham Palace undisturbed save by the occasional air raid.

Churchill's partisanship of the former sovereign was now history. 'He is a very loyal servant of King George and is no longer – it must be said – interested in the Duke (of Windsor),' his physician, Lord Moran, noted three years later. 'When they tell him that the Duke has asked for an appointement, the P.M. sighs and arranges the day and hour.'[4]

By mid-May, the Germans had virtually overrun France. One afternoon the Duke of Windsor burst into their house in Boulevard Suchet, Paris, gave the Duchess two hours to pack, and rushed her down to a hotel in Biarritz. He returned to

Paris to hear that the Duke of Gloucester had been winched out of Boulogne and flown back to the security of Buckingham Palace, as the British army was in retreat. Metcalfe had remained with the Duke of Windsor as an unofficial (and unpaid) aide-de-camp, and on 27 May bade him goodnight as usual. When he telephoned the Duke's home next morning for daily instructions, he was astonished and hurt to be told by a servant that His Royal Highness had left for Biarritz two hours earlier. After twenty years of devoted friendship he had been abandoned at the drop of a hat, to find his way back across a panic-stricken France to England on his own.

The Duke had gone to join his wife in Biarritz, and they left for the Château de la Croë. On their way, they heard that King Leopold III of the Belgians had surrendered to the Germans. To the Duke, it was confirmation that Europe was lost.

Their whereabouts provided a grave problem not just for themselves, but also for King George VI. After the Germans entered Paris, they set out for the Spanish frontier, and on arriving at a hotel in Barcelona, the Duke cabled to the Foreign Office for the attention of Churchill, to say that as he had received no instructions he had arrived in neutral Spain to avoid capture and was proceeding to Madrid. The Foreign Office knew that the return of the Duke and Duchess would raise complications. But if he was to remain in the Iberian peninsula, he ran the risk of being captured by the Germans. Deciding that the former was the lesser of two evils, Churchill then telegraphed to the Duke that they would like him and his wife to return home as soon as possible. A flying boat would be sent to Portugal to collect them, and they were to go to Lisbon.*

With German forces advancing towards the Pyrenees, there was a grave risk that Spain, convinced of British defeat, would

---

* The Foreign Office inadvertently ordered 'Their Royal Highnesses to proceed to Lisbon', an accidental elevation of the Duchess to the rank which she still coveted. This earned a swift written rebuke from Sir Alexander Hardinge, the King's principal private secretary, who ordered that such an official error must never occur again.

have to enter the war on the side of Germany if she was to survive. Nazi propagandists in Madrid were trying to persuade the Spanish goverment that Britain was disunited and close to defeat. To have the former British sovereign and his wife, both cold-shouldered by Britain's government, royal family and court alike, was indeed providential. Ribbentrop, German Foreign Minister, discussed with his country's ambassador in Madrid the chances of detaining the Duke and Duchess of Windsor and establishing contact with them.

Astonishing reports of the Duke's indiscretions were circulated. According to Marcus Cheke, a junior secretary in the British Embassy, Madrid, he predicted the fall of Churchill's government and its replacement by a Labour one which would negotiate peace with Germany. The King would abdicate, revolution would follow, and he himself would be recalled to his throne. Britain would then lead a coalition of France, Spain and Portugal, leaving Germany free to march on Russia. Such extraordinary schemes, Cheke suggested in mitigation, were put into his head by Frenchmen and Spaniards who were 'playing Germany's game.'[5]

How indiscreet the Duke really was in his conversation, and how much his remarks were distorted by others in the retelling, is open to debate. What was beyond doubt, however, was his refusal to accept an invitation to come home to England unconditionally, instead asking Churchill first if he would be given a job, and secondly whether the royal family would recognize and receive the Duchess. It would be better, answered Churchill, for the Duke to come to England as arranged, when everything could be considered. The Duke would not accept without definite assurances.

At this critical juncture of the war, the exasperated Prime Minister settled matters by reminding the Duke that he had taken active military rank, and 'refusal to obey direct orders of competent military authority would create a serious situation.' A thinly veiled hint of possible court-martial proceedings was raised. The Duke felt bitterly at being threatened 'with what amounted to arrest, thus descending to gangster methods in your treatment of your old friend and former King.'[6] By the time his letter of complaint reached Churchill, the word 'dictator' had replaced 'gangster' on the advice of the Duchess.

A way was found out of the impasse when the Duke was offered the post of Governor and Commander-in-Chief of the Bahamas. Lord Halifax said it was 'quite a good plan that they should go to the Bahamas, but I am sorry for the Bahamas.' Grudgingly the Duke accepted, telegraphing to Churchill that he was sure 'you have done your best for me in a difficult situation.'[7] To the government's relief, the Windsors sailed from Lisbon for their new destination on 1 August.

By this time, the French government under Marshal Petain had sued for an armistice. Britain and the Empire now faced the fascist powers alone, and in July Hitler gave final orders for the Luftwaffe to prepare the way for an invasion of Britain.

During the battle of Britain, while the RAF and Luftwaffe fought for control of the skies, and as German bombers mercilessly attacked British cities, the King refused to leave his capital, but travelled to Windsor each evening to sleep. When it was suggested that Princesses Elizabeth and Margaret ought to be evacuated to America, the Queen replied: 'The Princesses could not go without me; I could not leave the King; and the King will never leave.'

By insisting on staying in London, the King and Queen established themselves and the monarchy ever more firmly in the public affection. On 9 September, a bomb fell on the north side of Buckingham Palace and exploded early next morning. There were no casualties, but all windows were shattered by the explosion.

Three days later, they had the narrowest of escapes. While the King and Queen were upstairs talking with Hardinge, they heard the roar of an aircraft above them, saw two bombs falling past the opposite side of the palace, and then heard two resounding crashes as they fell in the quadrangle, thirty yards away. They all looked at each other, and then ran into the passage. 'The whole thing happened in a matter of seconds,' the King wrote in his diary. 'We all wondered why we weren't dead.'[8] Although it was soon common knowledge that the Palace had been bombed, the full truth was not revealed until after the war. Not even Churchill knew for some time. The King was particularly shaken, and suffered a shock reaction for several days, being unable to read and concentrate for long at a time, and perpetually glancing out of the window.

However, the Palace bombing had inestimable propaganda value. As Mountbatten wrote to the King, if Goering could have realized the depth of feeling which his bombing had aroused throughout the Empire and America, 'he would have been well advised to instruct his assassins to keep off.' The King now noted that he and the Queen had found a new bond with the bombed citizens of London – 'nobody is immune from it.' As for the Queen, 'it makes me feel I can look the East End in the face.'

They regularly paid informal visits to the most heavily-bombed areas of London, inspecting the rubble and the ruins. On one occasion, a man called out, 'Thank God for a good King,' to which the King answered, 'Thank God for a good people.'

Harold Nicolson was astonished to learn at a lunch party in July 1940 that the Queen was practising every day in the grounds of Buckingham Palace with a rifle and a revolver. If Hitler invaded, she told him, she would go down fighting with a gun in her hand. 'They did me all the good in the world,' Nicolson wrote to his wife afterwards. 'We shall win. I know that. No doubts at all.'[9]

The King and Queen were proud to do their bit in economizing for the war effort. Food rationing was strictly enforced at the Palace, but as the King had always eaten sparingly, frugal meals were no great hardship. Offering a sandwich to a visitor, he apologized and admitted, 'I don't know what's in these – sawdust, I expect.' He usually preferred draught beer to drink, though at one luncheon meeting he produced a rare bottle of French wine, keeping the source of his supply a secret, much to Churchill's chagrin. The Big House at Sandringham was closed for the duration of the war, and when the family came to Norfolk they used Appleton, the small house on the estate in which Queen Maud of Norway (who had died in 1938) had stayed on her visits to England.

In every room at Buckingham Palace and Windsor Castle, a notice was displayed drawing attention to the need for fuel economy. A line was painted in red or black five inches from the bottom of each bath. No central heating was in use at either dwelling, and fires were only lit in bedrooms on doctor's orders. Only one light bulb was permitted in each bedroom, no mean sacrifice in view of the size of the rooms.

The King's daughters contributed from their pocket money to the Red Cross, the Girl Guides and the Ambulance fund. They collected tinfoil, helped to roll bandages, and knitted socks for the forces. Family life provided the King with a respite from the cares of state and wartime pressure. Parents and daughters were a very closely-knit group, despite the girl's contrasts in character. Princess Elizabeth was more serious minded and better organized, in many ways the opposite of her extrovert sister. 'What a good job Margaret is the younger one!' the elder generation would exclaim with an indulgent smile.

The King's tastes were as middle class as those of his precedessors. He did not enjoy opera or serious theatre, preferring the music-hall and musical plays. One of his favourite forms of relaxation in the evening was sitting at home with the family, listening to radio programmes such as Tommy Handley's *ITMA*, or Richard Murdoch's *Band Waggon*.

Like his father and grandfather, he could be a martinet where dress was concerned. When King Peter of Yugoslavia called upon him wearing uniform of the Royal Yugoslav Air Force, the King noticed a thin gold watch chain threaded through the upper pockets of the tunic, and he asked if that was part of the uniform. When told it was not, he ordered King Peter to take it off – 'it looks damned silly and damned sloppy.' And when his daughters joined the Girl Guides, he forbade them to wear the regulation black stockings as they were 'so unbecoming', suggesting that they wear knee-length beige ones instead.

In one way, though, he differed markedly from his predecessors. One day following a severe attack of colitis, Lord

Woolton, Minister of Food, had a private audience with the King. The latter took him to his room, remarking how unwell he looked, and pulled up an easy chair for him to sit in. It had been rare for non-royal visitors seeking an audience with King Edward VII or King George V to be invited to sit down in the monarch's presence, let alone have a chair personally fetched for them.

By 1941 the threat of German invasion had receded, and Hitler's attack on the Soviet Union brought Communist Russia – a nation for which Churchill had had nothing but the deepest contempt – into the war on the side of the democracies. Though the United States was still sympathetic to the allies, not until a Japanese bombing raid on Pearl Harbour, Honolulu, did America declare war. Simultaneously a Japanese attack on Malaya and Hong Kong sank two vessels of the British fleet, the battleship *Prince of Wales*, and the cruiser *Repulse*. To the King it was 'a national disaster'. 'And to think they made me travel 10,000 miles to give the Garter to that damned Mikado,'[10] the Duke of Gloucester remarked drying, recalling the investiture he had been sent to make some eleven years earlier.

In his Christmas broadcast at the end of the year, the King said, 'The range of the tremendous conflict is ever widening. It now extends to the Pacific Ocean. Truly it is a stern and solemn time. But as the war widens, so surely our conviction deepens of the greatness of our cause.'[11]

There had been one happy event to cheer the family. On 18 December 1941 the Duchess of Gloucester gave birth to a son at Lady Caernarvon's Nursing home, Barnet. Named William, he was christened at Windsor in February 1942. Meanwhile the royal doyen of the British Army, the Duke of Connaught, Queen Victoria's last surviving son, had died in his ninety-second year on 16 January. Symbolically and militarily the Duke of Gloucester, his great-nephew, inherited the position left by his death.

Although Britain and the United States were now 'married' after many months of 'walking out', as Churchill told the King in January, and though they were confident of ultimate victory, the first few months of the year brought more diasasters for the allied cause. In particular the surrender of Singapore to Japan dealt British prestige a severe blow in the Far East.

The King was irritated at the constant criticism of Churchill's leadership. Acknowledging that they were 'going through a bad patch at the moment,' he wished 'people would get on with the job and not criticize all the time, but in a free country this has to be put up with.'[12] Later that month he was encouraged by Churchill's changes in the Cabinet. 'The House of Commons wants Winston to lead them; but they don't like the way he treats them. He likes getting his own way with no interference from anybody and nobody will stand for that sort of treatment in this country.'[13]

With further bad news from the East Indies and Africa, and a renewed bombing attack by the Luftwaffe on British cities, morale was falling. On 1 July 1942 a motion of censure on the government, particularly on Churchill, was moved by a backbench Conservative member, Sir John Wardlaw-Milne. In the midst of his analysis of faults in the direction of the war, Wardlaw-Milne suddenly suggested that the Duke of Gloucester should be appointed Commander-in-Chief of the British army. At this, the House 'rocked with disrespectful laughter', and Churchill smiled genially as he saw that any serious challenge to his leadership had instantly collapsed.

The hapless Wardlaw-Milne had no chance to explain that all he wanted was an end to inter-service rivalry and a reduction of politically-motivated military interventions. To the House, it looked like a demand for a return to the Napoleonic era, when an earlier royal Duke – King George III's second son Frederick, Duke of York – had 'marched his men up to the top of the hill and marched them down again.' The Duke of Gloucester, in India at the time, was not impressed. 'What impertinence on the part of Wardlaw-Milne without asking anybody & me in particular,'[14] he wrote to the Duchess on 4 July.

The Duke of Gloucester was representing the King in the Middle East, after an awkward time as second in command of the Twentieth Armoured Brigade, having been demoted from Major-General to Colonel so as not to embarrass the commanding officer, a Brigadier. Such distinctions of military rank made it hard for him as the King's brother to be what he would have preferred to be, an ordinary cavalry officer. Though genial and well liked by his junior officers, he was not suited to the higher levels of the army. He had hated his time in France as liaison officer under Gort, where other senior officers had looked down on him, making rude remarks behind his back about his stupidity, his drinking and his braying laugh. If they thought he was too much of a fool to be unaware of their unkind comments, they were wrong. The Duke was very bitter about their treatment, found them impossible to get on with, and was relieved to be posted elsewhere to more congenial company.

As the war progressed, the Duke of Kent found himself away on duty much of the time, often engaged in routine tasks such as inspecting RAF bases. Inspecting factories, shipyards and bomb damage did not satisfy a heartfelt desire to serve to his utmost in the war effort; 'It's not very exciting to spend an awful lot of time looking at ablutions.' A welcome break from routine came when he was sent on a mission across the Atlantic to report on the results of the Commonwealth Training Plan, a scheme for training air crews overseas, and he completed it with visiting aircraft factories in America and staying a few days with President Roosevelt.

The Duke and his wife knew what it was like to experience the pangs of divided family loyalties, for the Duchess's brother-in-law Prince Paul was Regent of Yugoslavia until his nephew King Peter came of age. In March 1941 Paul was pressed into signing a tripartite pact with the Axis powers guaranteeing Yugoslavia freedom from attack if the country would permit German troops and ammunition to pass through its territory to Greece. Exhausted and war-weary, surrounded by conflicting demands on all sides, he signed the pact and then abdicated, while a new government took power with King Peter nominally in charge. Yugoslavia's enthusiasm on entering the war was soon crushed when Luftwaffe raids on Belgrade killed seventeen thousand people in three days. King Peter escaped first to Greece and then to Britain, flying in an RAF Sunderland flying boat to Poole Harbour, where he was met by the Duke of Kent.

When the Duke was in England, he and the Duchess spent their time playing happily with the children, going to Badminton to visit Queen Mary (who had left London for the duration) and taking her shopping in Bath. Prince Edward and Princess Alexandra were lively, even sometimes unruly children, but Queen Mary treated them with grandmotherly indulgence and 'amused forbearance.'

The Duke of Kent also played his part in visiting bombed cities and hospitals. 'These raids are appalling but I was in the East End yesterday & their spirit is wonderful,' he wrote to Lady Astor, 'but there is terrible damage to the poor people's houses.' He had nothing but contempt for Joseph Kennedy, the American Ambassador in London, who had made no secret at an Embassy dinner of his conviction that Germany would invade and Britain was doomed; 'He seems to live in a world of his own & not to know what is going on.'[15]

He was touched to receive a letter from a veteran of the South African and Great Wars, a Mr F.W. Paget and his wife, of Liverpool. In thanking him for visiting their son in Devonport Military Hospital shortly before he passed away, the writer begged him: 'Do please write back to my poor invalid wife and cheer her up. She is so pleased to hear you paid her son a personal visit before he died.' It was a request to which the sympathetic Duke was glad to accede.

Because of his friendship with Nancy Astor, the Duke of Kent took a particular interest in Plymouth, one of the worst-hit cities outside London. 'I like Plymouth,' he wrote to her in February 1942, '& the people are so friendly & it is so easy to walk about talking to them.' He was incensed when shown a letter from the Controller of Salvage, in response to a query about the clearance of blitzed material in Plymouth, blandly assuming that, 'taking the country as a whole, about 90% has been left in the streets not cleared away! Anyway I've now written to Works & Buildings . . . perhaps something will be done!'[16]

Late in 1941 the Duchess was expecting again. On 4 July 1942, she gave birth to a second son at Coppins. He was christened on 4 August at Windsor with the names Michael George Charles Franklin, the last after his proxy godfather Roosevelt, who was proud to be honoured thus as his godson had been born on Independence Day. Guests at the ceremony included several royalties temporarily driven from their countries by the Nazi invaders, including the widowed King Haakon of Norway and his son Crown Prince Olav, and Prince Bernhard of the Netherlands.

On 23 August the Duke of Kent left Coppins to set off on another RAF welfare tour, this time to Iceland. Next evening, he and his party arrived at Invergordon, a flying-boat base on the Cromarty Firth which had been chosen as it was easily accessible by rail from London. The 900-mile flight to Iceland was expected to take about seven hours. Fifteen people would be on board the Sunderland flying boat and depth charges were carried, in case enemy submarines were spotted.

Despite heavy rain on the morning of 25 August, visibility over the Cromarty Firth was reported to be good, and the forecast was for further improvement. At 1.10 p.m. the aircraft took off.

A farmer and his son were rounding up their sheep that afternoon. They heard the sound of an aircraft overhead, but could not see it because of the mist; then there were two explosions. After a thirty-minute flight, the flying boat had crashed into a hill. Of the fifteen men on board, only one had survived. The Duke of Kent's body, clad in his flying suit, had been flung clear of the wreckage.

That evening at Coppins, the Duchess was about to retire to bed for an early night when the telephone rang. Her old Nanny Kate Fox, 'Foxy', who had come out of retirement to help her look after Prince Michael as a baby, took the call. Numb with shock, she slowly climbed the stairs. Somehow

Marina sensed the worst, and the moment her nurse opened the bedroom door, she cried out, 'It's George, isn't it?'

At Balmoral the King and Queen were dining with the Duke and Duchess of Gloucester, when the steward entered the dining room and whispered to the King that Sir Archibald Sinclair, Secretary of State for Air, was on the telephone and needed to speak to him urgently. A few minutes later the King returned, grim-faced and silent. The Duchess of Gloucester, sitting next to him, thought that something had happened to Queen Mary. Then he cancelled the next course, and called the Queen, Duke and Duchess into another room to tell them the news. They all left for London later that evening.

Though the family knew that George faced exceptional risks as an airman and was an easy target for enemy planes, they were stunned by his death. As ever, Queen Mary's self-control came to her rescue. Grief-stricken at the loss of her favourite son, her first thoughts, however, were of what her daughter-in-law was going through, and planned to visit her the next day.

On her arrival at Coppins early in the morning, she found the Duchess in a state of shock, weeping uncontrollably one moment, staring into space the next. At his funeral on 29 August in St George's Chapel, Windsor, she was heavily veiled and inconsolable. The King had attended many funerals there already, but none had moved him quite like this; 'Everybody there I knew well but I did not dare look at any of them for fear of breaking down.'[17]

In his office at Government House, Nassau, the Duke of Windsor heard of his brother's death from a news broadcast on the BBC Empire Service. At first his reaction was one of shocked incredulity. Attending a memorial service for him in the cathedral at Nassau on the day of the funeral, he broke down at the beginning and wept like a child all the way through. It was the only time his equerry had ever seen him lose his self-control. For several days he wanted to be left alone, and not even Wallis could console him.

The tragedy brought about a temporary thaw in the relationship with his mother, who wrote that her thoughts went out to him, knowing how devoted he was to George, 'and how kind you were to him in a difficult moment in his all too short life.'[18] To the Duke, his brother's death brought home to him as nothing else could 'the utter useless cruelty of this ghastly war.' He wrote a letter of condolence to the Duchess of Kent, and told Queen Mary he was doing so, but it never arrived; and he was accused of acting out of spite, as if he had still not forgiven her for refusing to call on his wife in France in 1937.

King George VI and Queen Mary knew that Marina had not merely been devoted to but utterly dependent on her husband, and with three small children, one a baby of seven weeks, she had to have somebody to give her mutual support. Foxy was too old and too distressed to be relied on. The most obvious choice was her sister Olga, Princess Paul of Yugoslavia. This however presented a problem. They were in Kenya, where Paul was a political prisoner under British jurisdiction. Though sympathetic to the allied cause, he had been persuaded against his better judgement to sign a tripartite pact on behalf of Yugoslavia with the Axis powers, in his capacity as Regent for his nephew King Peter, still a minor. In Britain, he was regarded as a traitor. All the same, King George sent a destroyer out to fetch the Princess, and after a long journey through Africa, Portugal and Ireland, she arrived at Poole Harbour. On 17 September she reached Coppins, for an emotional reunion with her sister.

On 4 November, the Duchess put on her Commandant's uniform to fulfil the first public engagement of her widowhood, a visit to a Wrens training centre in London. Later it was announced that she was to assume many of his patronages including those of the Royal School for the Blind at Leatherhead, and the Shaftesbury Homes. She was also appointed Colonel-in-Chief of the Royal West Kent Regiment, a battalion from which had taken part in the ceremonial guard-of-honour at St George's Chapel on the day of the funeral.

It has been asserted that there was always a gulf between the Duchess of Kent and her in-laws. Despite her background of poverty, she was always conscious of her royal and imperial descent, being a great-granddaughter of Tsar Alexander II. Her reserved disposition was taken for an air of superiority, and it was said that she never felt properly absorbed into the British royal family, apparently regarding the Queen and the Duchess of Gloucester as 'those common little Scottish girls'.[19] This may or may not have been malicious gossip. Yet although her in-laws perhaps regarded her as cold and distant, they were fully supportive of her in her grief. They knew that she had been an ideal wife for the mercurial Duke of Kent, and that few other women would have been able to treat his moods as sensibly as she did – by ignoring them until they passed.

She was anything but superior in her dealings with people at Iver, where she became a familiar figure with a ready smile and greeting for everyone as she walked to and from church on Sunday morning, or pottered around the village on weekdays. As a mother she was devoted to her children, although she was careful to impress on them that nothing would ever be theirs for the asking. Her financial position was far from secure, for her husband's annuity from the Civil List died with him, and no provision was then made for royal widows. In November 1943 she had to sell at auction some furniture left to him by his great-aunt Louise, Duchess of Argyll, in order to help maintain her standard of living.

10

'Much hard work ahead to deal with'

In the autumn of 1942, the tide began to turn for the allies. Fortuitously, good news arrived one October night. Mrs Roosevelt was staying with the King and Queen at Buckingham Palace, where she was taken aback by the chilliness, and by the simple meals which though still served on gold and silver plates, according to Lord Woolton, 'might have been served in any home in England and which would have shocked the King's grandfather.'[1] During dinner Churchill, a fellow guest, seemed to be showing signs of anxiety. At length he made his apologies and went to telephone his office at Downing Street for news of the battle developing at El Alamein, North Africa. He returned with a spring in his step, singing *Roll out the barrel.*

A few days later, the King received confirmation that the Eighty Army, under General Montgomery, had defeated the German and Italian forces at El Alamein. 'A victory at last,' he commented, 'how good for the nerves.'[2]

In June 1943 the King visited the allied forces in North Africa. The journey could only be made by flying, and the day before his departure he summoned a solicitor to help place his affairs in order – 'I think it better on this occasion to leave nothing to chance.' He also appointed five Councillors of State – the Queen, the Duke of Gloucester, the Princess Royal, Princess Arthur of Connaught,* and the Countess of Southesk.

---

* Daughters of the King's late aunt Louise, Princess Royal and Duchess of Fife.

167

Remembering the fate that had befallen his brother, it was as well to be prepared for the worst.

The plane was scheduled to stop at Gibraltar for refuelling, but dense fog surrounded the Rock and they had to fly straight on to Algiers, landing there on 12 June. Though the King had made his journey under the alias of 'General Lyon', his arrival was soon common knowledge.

For two weeks he undertook a gruelling programme. He was touched to receive a moving and dramatic welcome from three thousand British troops on the beach, where he was recognized and the men burst spontaneously into the National Anthem. On 20 June he visited Malta, sixty miles from the Italian forces in Sicily. The island was battle-scarred and exhausted after the raids of 1941–2, and he had awarded her people the George Cross. Now he wanted to pay a personal tribute and show his appreciation of the sacrifices the islanders had made. When he arrived on the cruiser *Aurora*, entering the Grand Harbour of Valletta, a slim figure in white naval uniform, the dense throngs of loyal Maltese went wild with enthusiasm. All the church bells started ringing as he landed. Hearing the cheers of the people 'brought a lump into my throat, knowing what they have suffered from 6 months constant bombing.'[3]

Apart from her duties as Councillor of State, the Princess Royal had had many other demands on her time as a result of the war effort. At the outbreak of hostilities she had been Contoller of the Auxiliary Territorial Service, and in the following year she was promoted to Chief Controller, a duty which entailed inspections all over the country, visiting troops and service canteens. In August 1941 she was promoted to Controller-Commandant of the ATS , and on the death of the Duke of Kent she was appointed President of Papworth Hospital.

Queen Mary had moved out from Marlborough House with great reluctance after the King told her gently but firmly that her continued presence in London would cause great anxiety to them all. While she stayed at Badminton, Gloucestershire, with her niece the Duchess of Beaufort, the Princess Royal visited her regularly and spent long periods there whenever possible. Like other guests, ladies-in-waiting, soldiers and evryone else, she was always drafted into the Queen's 'wooding squad', helping to clear ground, thin plantations, and strip ivy – Queen Mary's particular aversion – from trees, walls and buildings. The Duke of Kent had made time to visit her as his duties allowed, and the Duke of Gloucester did likewise. Harry's appearance, however, was a mixed blessing. His increasing fondness for a glass of whisky moved her to write to the Duchess, suggesting firmly that the Duke bring his own supply next time, 'as we have *not* got much left and it is so expensive.'[4]

Without any experience of colonial administration, the Duke of Windsor acquitted himself well as Governor-General of the Bahamas. Initially he had been bitter to find himself sent to a group of small islands where the heat was intolerable except during the winter holiday season, and where the society was very provincial. Although it seemed an insignificant post, it was still a job of work, and he knew that if he discharged it well, it would increase his personal standing in Britain, particularly in the eyes of those who looked on him with little favour.

Government House, Nassau, was badly planned and unbearably hot in summer. Accommodation was inadequate, the shabby house itself was riddled with termites, and the garden had been neglected. Under pressure the islands' Legislature reluctantly made some financial provision for structural repairs, but it was left to the Duke and Duchess to pay for most of the sorely needed redecoration.

At first their presence gave a boost to the holiday trade on which the island economy was largely dependent, until the United States' entry into the war put a virtual end to tourism. When the colony was threatened with starvation, he encouraged efforts to boost agricultural production, and he founded an infant welfare clinic which had been badly needed for some time.

Many charges were made against the way in which they conducted themselves while in the Bahamas. Apparently the Duke gave offence by refusing to patronise and support concerts, art exhibitions and other cultural events, as previous governors had done. He stayed away from such functions, which he admitted bored him.

The Duchess's rumoured extravagance, spending vast amounts on her wardrobe at a time of interntional privations, made her unpopular. It was said that she hated every moment of the job, calling Nassau 'this moron paradise', and crossing out the heading Government House on official stationery, substituting the world 'Elba'.

Much has been made, too, of the Duke's racist outlook. To Lord Mountbatten, he later admitted that during his tenure of office, black men were not permitted to enter Government House by the front door. When a liaison officer was needed by American contractors building airfields in the Bahamas, the Duke vetoed the obvious candidate purely because he was black. A white man, Karl Claridge, was appointed instead, and shortly afterwrds Nassau experienced its first riot. A mob of several thousand broke windows, looted shops, and martial law was declared. Order was retsored, but only after two people were killed and twenty-five injured.

However, his racial attitude reflected prevailing prejudices held by many white Britons and Americans. He was considerably more enlightened than most in the Bahamian House of Assembly, in his insistence that if black islanders were backward, then they deserved to be educated, fed and housed properly. The whites saw this as a threat to their entrenched financial superiority. Even less did they support his determination to foster local enterprise, and improve the black population's working conditions and education.

It was also unfortunate that his governorship should have been overshadowed by his mishandling of the Sir Harry Oakes murder case. A self-made millionaire and baronet, famed as much for his irascible temperament as for his fortune, Oakes had lived in the Bahamas for several years for tax reasons. On the morning of 8 July 1943 he was found murdered in his bed. The Governor reacted by imposing strict censorship on all news leaving the islands, but he was too late. Etienne Dupuch, proprietor and editor of one of the main Bahamas papers, *The*

Tribune, had already heard the news and cabled it to press agencies all around the world. The censorship thus created a rather foolish situation whereby the Bahamas papers could reproduce articles from the American press, pointing out that readers would be interested to learn from U.S. sources some of the facts they could not learn at home, as well as some of the incorrect reports that could have been avoided by more prudent handling of the situation.

The Governor compounded his error of judgement by appointing two Miami detectives, assigned to look after him on his visits there, to investigate the case. Normally he would have been expected to call in the local police force, the CID, or the FBI. One detective, Captain E.W. Melchen, was competent enough, but his partner, Captain James Barker, proved otherwise. Oakes's son-in-law, Alfred de Marigny, who was known to have quarrelled with him, was charged with the murder. The Duke disliked Marigny, who had been less than respectful towards the royal governor. The latter had virtually made up his mind that Marigny was the guilty man. He was arrested and tried, but acquitted. The prosecution's case was largely circumstantial and rested chiefly on a fingerprint put in evidence by Barker, and under cross-examination he was virtually forced to admit that the print was a forgery. No further attempt to apprehend the murderer was made, though after Marigny's acquittal by a 9–3 verdict, the jury added a rider that he be deported on the grounds of being an undesirable. Though this recommendation was beyond their jurisdiction, the move was carried out. The killing of Oakes, news of which was greeted by the Duchess with a characteristically tasteless comment of 'Never a dull moment in the Bahamas', and its aftermath, cast a heavy shadow over the Duke of Windsor's governorship.

In all fairness, however, it must be asked whether any of his brothers could have responded much better to a no-win situation than he did. With virtually no experience of dealing with such matters, or even prior knowledge of the provincial, petty-minded island society, it would have been almost impossible for any member of his family to take on such a post and emerge with total success.

Even before the Oakes case, the Duke had been looking ahead to his future. He did not intend to remain in the Bahamas for the duration of the war, and was keen for another post, if possible in the United States or Canada. By 1944, the court was similarly preoccupied as to where he should go when war ended, particularly after he had rejected Churchill's offer of the governorship of Bermuda – as he saw it, the exchange of one backwater for another.

Alan Lascelles, who had succeeded Hardinge as the King's private secretary the previous year, was insistent that no public employment should be offered to him. Additionally, there would be difficulties if he was invited to come back to reside in England as a 'younger' brother of the King. It would be preferable for him to have some representational role, if not technically a governorship, or similar administrative post, abroad. Churchill looked with interest on both ideas, particularly as he expressed himself unaware of any legitimate reason to prevent him from coming back to live in his own country.

If Lascelles and his own family were unenthusiastic at the prospect of his return, the Duke was even less so. He replied that there was no question of his doing so unless there was a significant change in the palace's attitude towards him, and more importantly, towards his wife.

In January 1945 the Duke formally announced his resignation as Governor of the Bahamas, with effect from April. What Churchill called 'suitable openings' were never found; several other governorships and ambassadorial posts were discussed but never came to anything. They left Nassau in May, and flew to the United States for a holiday. The Duke told the press, when asked his plans, merely that he and his wife expected to 'travel a lot'.

Another family problem was the question of suitable employment for the Duke of Gloucester, made more pressing by the Duke of Kent's death. King George was very fond of his only surviving younger brother and felt responsible for him.

Both would have liked him to be given a position as the War Office, but General Sir Alan Brooke felt the Duke was not the right man for such a post. Although he was sympathetic towards the Duke, he recognized his faults. The Duke lacked the charm of his brothers and the royal memory for names and faces; he even found it difficult to remember 'the chaps in his own regiment when he saw them,' a fellow officer recalled. Being Regent Designate until Princess Elizabeth attained her eighteenth birthday was hardly adequate employment for the Duke, and for a while he had to content himself with the tedious task of inspecting hospitals, factories and civil defence units on the King's behalf until a more satisfactory solution could be found.

Knowing his brother had been interested in the Governor-Generalship of Australia, the King spoke to Churchill in October 1943. Both men agreed that it would be a good idea to appoint him to the post planned for the Duke of Kent. In November 1943, he was appointed Governor-General of Australia, and it was arranged that he would take up his duties the following year. 'Now I feel I have something definite to do makes all the difference,'[5] the Duke wrote to Queen Mary. She was pleased that at last Harry had 'a chance of showing what he is made of.'

Princess Elizabeth, heir to the throne, celebrated her eighteenth birthday in April 1944. Though the princess had spent most of the war at Windsor and in Scotland, the King realized that soon Princess Elizabeth would have to enter public life. In November 1943, a Regency Bill was passed providing for her eligibility as a Counsellor of State at the age of eighteen, instead of twenty-one as would formerly have been the case. There was also the question of a potential change in her style and title, and it was suggested that the King might be asked to create her Princess of Wales. He had no intention of doing so. As he pointed out in a letter to Queen Mary, how could he do so when it was the recognized title of the wife of the Prince of Wales; and if he did so, by what name would she be known when she married.

The Duke of Gloucester, now spared the possibility of having to take up the reins as Regent, had a new responsibility on the horizon apart from the impending Australian appointment. In February, it was confirmed that the Duchess was expecting another child that summer. Their happiness, however, was rudely interrupted by a personal tragedy when Mr Hamilton, the Duke's farm manager-worker 'and everything else' on the Barnwell estate, entered Moorfield Eye Hospital for treatment of a persistent complaint caused by shrapnel during the Great War. Soon after he was admitted, a VI flying bomb hit the hospital, killing him and six others in one of the wards. The Duke was deeply upset, and reproached himself for not having dissuaded him from going to London.

The Duchess gave birth to a second son at St Matthew's Nursing Home, Northampton, on 26 August. Queen Mary expressed a wish that 'Boy number 2' should be called Richard, 'which sounds so well with Gloucester.' The Duke was not immediately attracted by this suggestion as, the Duchess explained, he could never pronounce the letter 'R', but all the same agreed that it was a very good name. He briefly thought of naming his son Albert, as he shared the Prince Consort's birthday, but changed his mind. Appropriately the young prince, who would succeed to his father's title almost thirty years later, became passionately interested in his fifteenth-century namesake Richard, Duke of Gloucester, and patron of the Richard III Society, sharing the widespread belief that the much-maligned King was innocent of most if not all the charges levelled against him by historians.

The VI bombing raids of 1944 had posed a new threat to the royal family in London, though less intense than the blitz four years earlier. 'It is sad to lose everything,' Queen Elizabeth wrote to Lady Astor in July, 'but the amount of times I have heard people say "ah well, mustn't grumble must we" in a philosophical way after escaping with just their lives! It's a great spirit, & they deserve many years of real Peace.'[6]

Later in 1944 plans were made for allied landings on the north coast of France, Operation Overlord. Churchill informed the King that he intended to watch the D-Day landings in person, and the King decided he would too. After the protests of Lascelles, that neither sovereign nor Prime Minister should expose themselves to such risks, the King withdrew his intention, and Churchill was persuaded to do likewise.

In June, the King visited Normandy to meet General Montgomery, decorated some of the troops personally, and in the following month visited the allied armies in Italy. By the end of the year, German forces were in retreat on the western and easter fronts. The Allies held a series of summit meetings to plan for peace as well as for victory, culminating in the Yalta Conference presided over by Churchill, Roosevelt and Stalin in February 1945. The King was concerned at concessions made to Stalin, with what he viewed as an inordinate sphere of influence in Eastern Europe to Russia. He had always viewed Russia as a long-term threat to the West. The conference turned out to be Roosevelt's farewell, for he was already ailing and he died in office on 12 April.

Though the British and American advance eastwards was delayed by German resistance in the Low Countries and on the Rhine, the Third Reich was close to destruction. On 25 April, American and Russian armies met on the River Elbe, and five days later Hitler committed suicide in his bunker. On 2 May, the German forces in Italy surrendered unconditionally, and Berlin capitulated to the Russians. Hitler's successor, Admiral Doenitz, opened negotiations for the surrender of Germany, which was signed on the morning of 7 May. War was effectively over in Europe the following day.

That same day, Churchill was lunching with the King and his family at Buckingham Palace. King and Prime Minister 'congratulated each other on the end of the European war.' There was no more fear of being bombed at home, and no more living in air raid shelters, but Japan was still to be defeated and the task of peacetime reconstruction in Britain would 'give us many headaches & hard work in the coming years.'[7]

At 3.00 in the afternoon, Churchill broadcast to the nation that victory had been achieved over 'the evil-doers who are now prostrate before us', and the King's speech was broadcast at

9.00 in the evening. He spoke of the work that awaited them in the restoration of their country after the ravages of war 'and in helping to restore peace and sanity to a shattered world.'

The people of London, albeit war-weary and aware of the sacrifices that lay ahead, still demonstrated in jubilant affection their loyalty and devotion to the crown. Crowds gathered around Buckingham Palace, and gave them a tremendous ovation when they appeared on the balcony. They were called out eight times during the afternoon and evening.

In order to allow Princesses Elizabeth and Margaret some of the excitement, the King allowed them out in the care of a party of young officers with whom they joined the revelling crowds in the Mall and Whitehall; 'poor darlings, they have never had any fun yet.'[8]

On 9 and 10 May, the King and Queen made a series of state drives through East and South London, constantly halted by cheering crowds. They were impressed that the horses drawing the royal carriage behaved so well and seemed undeterred by cheering, jostling crowds. On mentioning this with surprise to his equerry, Sir Dermot Kavanagh, the King was told that he had prepared for such an eventuality for some weeks, and had conditioned the animals to strange noises by installing a wireless in the royal stables and making them listen to the BBC Forces programme.

On 13 May, they attended a National Service of Thanksgiving at St Paul's, and three days later a similar ceremony at St Giles's, Edinburgh. On 17 May, the King received addresses from both Houses of Parliament in the Great Hall of Westminster. His delivery on replying to them was almost perfect, and a spontaneous touch gave his speech a dramatic and moving quality, when he alluded to the Duke of Kent's death. His voice suddenly faltered and broke.

Exhausted by the celebrations, but deeply touched by the nation's loyalty, the King and Queen returned to rest at Windsor. 'I have found it difficult to rejoice or relax as there is still so much hard work ahead to deal with.'[9]

11

'I really want a rest'

The declaration of victory in Europe had brought a widespread feeling of relief, but the rejoicing was muted. War was not yet over in the Far East, and the country suffered from an overwhelming war-weariness. At the Thanksgiving Service at St Paul's, the King's face looked lined and drawn. He remembered all too clearly the cold grey aftermath of the Great War, when Europe was decimated by a raging epidemic of influenza, and his father had been concerned with the possibility of social revolution.

In order to avoid prolonging a tired caretaker government, Churchill called a general election in July. The King thought the outcome would be uncertain, perhaps leaving no party with a clear working majority, but those who had predicted a spectacular swing to the left were proved correct. When the results were published on 26 July, three weeks after polling, Labour came to power with an overall majority of 180 seats. Churchill was saddened and surprised at his defeat, and when he went to tender his resignation, the King told him he thought 'the people were very ungrateful after the way they had been led in the War.' They did not appreciate at once that it had been less a rejection of Churchill himself and his war record, more an indictment of some aspects of his campaign (notably his unwise comparison between British socialists and the Gestapo) and of his party's pre-war policies. Writing to him later, the King told Winston, 'I shall miss your counsel to me more than I can say. But please remember that as a friend I hope we shall be able to meet at intervals.'[1]

King George found it difficult to establish a close working

relationship with his new ministers. The crisp, businesslike, matter-of-fact manner of the incoming Prime Minister, Clement Attlee, had little in common with the charm of Churchill or his expansive, often emotional turn of phrase, and unlike the latter he did not confide in his sovereign so freely. The King liked and respected Ernest Bevin, a bluff, no-nonsense Foreign Minister who shared his distrust of Russia, and the radical Aneurin Bevan, Minister of Health, who had also been handicapped in childhood by a stammer. Yet the one new minister whom he never took to was Hugh Dalton, appointed Chancellor of the Exchequer after the King raised doubts about his suitability as Foreign Secretary. Dalton, son of the Reverend John Dalton who had been tutor to the future King George V, was an able but uncouth, unpopular member of the government who seemed to go out of his way to pour scorn on his privileged upbringing, notwithstanding the advantages it had brought him.

Christmas was spent at Sandringham for the first time since 1940. After a few days of reflection, the King realized how exhausted he was. 'I have been suffering from an awful reaction from the strain of the war I suppose & have felt very tired especially down here but I hope I shall soon start to feel well again,' he wrote to the Duke of Gloucester in January 1946. 'I really want a rest, away from people & papers but that of course is impossible.'[2]

King George VI was exhausted by overwork, but time hung heavily on his elder brother's hands. The war had changed him and his wife too. 'The two poor little old things were almost pathetic,' Lady Diana Cooper noted sadly after meeting them in Paris in September 1945, the first time she had seen them for four years. 'She is much commoner and more confident, he much duller and sillier.'[3] He had decided that he and the Duchess would settle in France, and in October 1945 he came alone to stay with his mother at Marlborough House. Queen Mary had looked forward to the reunion, assuring him what a joy it would be to meet again as she had genuinely missed him over the years. None the less there was no question of her welcoming her daughter-in-law. To the Countess of Athlone, she had expressed the hope that he would not 'bother me too much about receiving her', as nothing had altered her views about 'that unfortunate marriage.' It proved a happy reunion and there was a measure of reconciliation, but largely as the Duke was careful not to raise any contentious issues.

Once he was back in France, his friends and acquaintances were struck by his apparent inability to find any interests, beyond his gardening or the occasional game of golf. When the name Graham Greene was mentioned to him, he thought it referred to a golf course. Art and music, apart from jazz, had never really interested him. 'I never saw a man so bored,' the American authoress Susan Mary Alsop wrote. She quoted his personal description of the day's activities to her. 'I got up late, and then I went with the Duchess and watched her buy a hat, and then on the way home I had the car drop me off in the Bois to watch some of your soldiers playing football, and then I had planned to take a walk, but it was so cold that I could hardly bear it . . . When I got home the Duchess was having her French lesson, so I had no one to talk to, so I got a lot of tin boxes which mother had sent me last week and looked through them. They were essays and so on I had written when I was in France studying French before the Great War . . . You know, I'm not much of a reading man.'[4]

That a former King of England should have been reduced to such a hollow existence was sad; but that he had allowed himself to become such a martyr to self-pity was sadder still. The Duchess seemed unable or unwilling to resign herself to the fact that he had become a far less important person simply by marrying her. In a France slowly recovering from the ravages of war, she spent much of her time and money on clothes and preparing for evenings of entertaining jet-setters and self-made millionaires. After dinner she would drag the Duke off to a nightclub till the small hours.

The Duchess's domination of him was still liable to reveal itself in embarrassing outbursts. At a dinner party one evening, the Duke asked the butler to give the chauffeur a message, whereupon the Duchess raised her hands high and brought them crashing down angrily on the table, setting the plates and glasses rattling. Their guests watched in horrified silence. 'Never, never again will you give orders in my house!' she hissed at him. Realizing the effect she had had on those present, she explained to her neighbour with a smile that the Duke was in charge of everything that happened outside the house, she was responsible for the inside. Instead of standing up for himself, the Duke cringed, muttering incoherent apologies for the next ten minutes.[5]

It was not an isolated explosion. Another time, a guest overheard her scolding him for leaving papers on the dining room table; 'I've got twenty people dining here in two hours. Why don't you leave this mess somewhere else?' His reaction was to ask her if she was going to send him to bed in tears again that night. Any intentional irony in his words was lost on her.

As Governor-General of Australia the Duke of Gloucester and his family moved into their official residence at Canberra, capital of the Commonwealth of Australia, a few months before the end of the wr. One of the Duke's first duties was to preside over the celebrations of VE-Day. At the time of the German surrender, he and the Duchess were in Adelaide, the capital of South Australia. They were due in Melbourne the next day for an investiture in recognition of soldiers who had rendered distinguished war service, but convention dictated that the Governor-General's place on such a momentous day was in Canberra. They therefore had to fly six thousand miles from Adelaide before breakfast, and after putting in an appearance at the jubilations in the city streets, needed to make another flight of three thousand miles to Melbourne later the same day.

Such long-distance dashes were by no means unusual. The Duke was required to make regular appearances at the other capitals of the Australian continent, resulting in some 76,500 miles of none-too-comfortable travel during the two years he and the Duchess spent there. Routine desk work at Government House, weekly meetings of the Executive Council over which he had to preside, and expeditions to visit Australian troops in New Guinea and the Pacific Islands, were all part of the job. It was with some justification that he complained in private of being driven too hard, and with relief that he and his family returned to England so that he could resume his place as the first of the King's Counsellors of State while his elder brother was absent abroad.

The reason for his recall was King George VI's acceptance of an invitation from General Jan Smuts to visit South Africa. It happened at a difficult time, for Britain was in the grip of a severe fuel crisis during its harshest winter for many years. Coal pits were blocked by snow, ports were frozen up, and by the end of the first week in February 1947, the country was faced with electricity cuts of five hours every day in order to conserve fuel.

The King, Queen and their two daughters left from Portsmouth on the battleship HMS *Vanguard* on 1 February. He was reluctant to go, feeling that he should be at home with his people at such a time of deprivation. Offering to cut the tour short, Attlee suggested that to do so would only magnify the crisis in international eyes. All the same, the King was worried and upset that his imperturbable Prime Minister showed no concern. Was he not worried by the domestic situation, he repeatedly asked Attlee; 'he won't tell me he is, when I feel he is,' he told Queen Mary. 'I know I am worried.' The Queen wrote to Queen Mary that their tour was 'very strenuous as I feared it would be & doubly hard for Bertie who feels he should be at home.' The King was very edgy much of the time, and particularly upset by an unhappy incident in which a man who came running after their car was beaten off by the Queen with her parasol and then knocked senseless by policemen. They had all assumed that he was trying to assassinate them, when in fact he was loyally clutching a ten-shilling note in his hand which he wanted to give personally to Princess Elizabeth for her birthday.

By the end of April the exhausted King had lost seventeen

pounds in weight. Since the beginning of the year he had been suffering from cramp in both legs, an early symptom of arteriosclerosis.

During the tour, Princess Elizabeth celebrated her twenty-first birthday. On 21 April she broadcast to the peoples of the Empire, saying that, 'I declare before you all that my whole life, whether it be long or short, shall be devoted to your service, and the service of our great Imperial Commonwealth, to which we all belong.'

This tour was the last time that the family were together as a unit of four. King George was devoted to his daughters. He had never known the pleasures of a warm and close childhood himself, and the happiness he had found in his marriage made him dread the day when the family unit would be broken up.

For it was already evident to several who Princess Elizabeth's husband was to be.

Prince Philip, born on the island of Corfu on 10 June 1921, was the youngest child of Prince Andrew of the Hellenes, son of King George I, and Princess Alice of Battenberg, great-granddaughter of Queen Victoria and eldest sister of Lord Louis Mountbatten. With the turbulent fate of the Greek royal family, Prince Philip had found himself virtually a stateless exile from early infancy. He was moved from France, England, Scotland and Germany. By royal standards his parents had little money, and during his childhood they gradually drifted apart, though the marriage did not end in divorce. He was one of the many guests at the Duke and Duchess of Kent's wedding in 1934, and again at the Coronation two and a half years later. Therefore he may have met his future wife on one if not both occasions, but their first well-documented meeting was at Dartmouth Royal Naval College in July 1939. By then Philip was a tall, fair-haired, confident youth of eighteen, while his cousin Elizabeth was a shy, sheltered thirteen-year-old. By contrast eight-year-old Princess Margaret, plump and more outgoing, seemed more at ease with him.

Lord Mountbatten had become virtually a father to Philip,

with the absence of the penniless Prince Andrew and the early death from cancer of Louis's elder brother George, Marquis of Milford Haven. It was largely his influence that helped secure a college place for Philip at Dartmouth, and his influence that would discreetly press his claim as a suitor for the hand of the heir to the throne. After a conversation with Princess Nicholas of Greece, mother of the Duchess of Kent, 'Chips' Channon noted at a cocktail party in Athens in January 1941 that Philip was there; 'he is to be our Prince Consort, and that is why he is serving in our Navy.'

Philip and Elizabeth began to correspond regularly, and at Christmas 1943 he was invited to stay at Windsor Castle. By spring of the following year, King George VI was sufficiently concerned to tell Queen Mary that much as he liked Philip, who was intelligent, had 'a good sense of humour & thinks about things in the right way,' his daughter was too young to think of betrothal. She had never met any young men of her own age, so Philip 'had better not think any more about it for the present.'

After peace was declared, the King made half-hearted efforts to introduce her to other young men. Guards officers were invited to parties at Windsor and elsewhere, with the King himself leading congas round the ballroom. Queen Mary disapproved, referring to these officers scathingly as 'the Body Guard.' Like Lord Mountbatten, she thoroughly approved of Philip, and she could appreciate the virtues of what would be basically an arranged marriage. Hers had been successful enough. At length the King was persuaded, and during his visit to Balmoral in the summer of 1946, Philip proposed to Elizabeth. She accepted him, and a discreet engagement party was held. Rumours that autumn were quickly denied by an official statement from Buckingham Palace.

Early in 1947 Philip, already thoroughly Anglicized by his predominantly British upbringing, was officialy naturalized, becoming Lieutenant Philip Mountbatten, RN. Although he had been baptized into the Greek Orthodox Church, he indictaed that he would be willing to become a member of the

Church of England. In July 1947, three months after the royal family's return from South Africa, the engagement was at last made public; they were to be married on 20 November.

On the eve of the wedding, Philip was given the Order of the Garter, created a Royal Highness, and the titles of Baron Greenwich, Earl of Merioneth, and Duke of Edinburgh were conferred on him. 'It is a great deal to give a man all at once,' wrote the King, 'but I know Philip understands his new responsibilities on his marriage to Lilibet.'[6]

The ceremony at Westminster Abbey was a day of mixed feelings, particularly for the bride's father. After her departure, he wrote to her how proud he was of her and 'thrilled at having you close to me on our long walk in Westminster Abbey, but when I handed your hand to the Archbishop I felt that I had lost something very precious.'[7]

Among other royalties invited were King Frederick IX and Queen Ingrid of Denmark, King Haakon of Norway, King Michael of Roumania (shortly to be forced to abdicate), and Queen Ena of Spain. Conspicuous in his absence was the Duke of Windsor, who was not invited. Perhaps even more noticeable was the absence of the Princess Royal. Although not often seen in public, it was only to be expected that she would be there. She pleaded ill-health as the reason, though she was noticed attending a public function two days later. It was alleged that she stayed away in protest at the lack of an invitation to her eldest brother. Of all the family, Mary had always appeared the most accommodating towards him, and whenever he returned to London – with or without the Duchess – she invariably made an effort to come and meet him so they could dine together.

She met the Duchess of Windsor for the first time shortly after the war was over, and remarked tactfully that her American sister-in-law 'was really quite nice'. Her elder son summed up her reaction a little more mischieviously; 'no cloven hooves or horns'.[8]

The Earl of Harewood had died in May 1947, and their eldest son had succeeded him as Earl. Yet widowhood made no difference to Mary's life of public service, apart from a discreet interval of mourning. She maintained her charitable presidencies and patronage, and in 1948 she was installed as Chancellor of Leeds University – the first woman to hold such an office in Britain.

In his darker moods, the King was gravely worried at the outlook for the British monarchy. In February 1948, after investing Vicoria Sackville-West as a Companion of Honour, he asked after the family house at Knole, Kent. When she told him that it had been given to the National Trust, he threw up his hands with an expression of despair. 'Everything is going nowadays,' he said sadly. 'Before long, I shall also have to go.' A few weeks later her son, Ben Nicolson, Keeper of the King's Pictures at Windsor, reported after a conversation that the King had taken the fate of the recently deposed King Michael of Roumania much to heart, and was gloomily convinced that the spectre of a British republic still hung over him and his family.

If so, a public celebration that same spring must have gone some way towards reassuring him. On 26 April 1948, London was again *en fete*, as the King and Queen drove in an open landau through vast, cheering crowds to a service of thanksgiving at St Paul's to mark their silver wedding anniversary. The weather was excellent, and that afternoon they drove in an open car through twenty miles of London streets, to be received once again with spontaneous affection.

To casual observers, the King looked happy and in good health as well as good spirits, but the appearance was misleading. Since January he had been suffering from cramp in both legs. The condition became progressively worse, and by August he was in discomfort much of the time. A summer holiday at Balmoral, with moderate exercise and several days' shooting, did him good, but by October he was worse. His left foot was numb all day, and pain kept him awake at night. He insisted on maintaining his schedule of engagements as far as possible, including entertaining the King and Queen of Denmark on a visit to London, and opening Parliament in full state on 26 October for the first time since the war.

But an initial medical examination at the end of the month raised grave doubts about his condition, and the doctors recommended that a planned visit to Australia and New Zealand the following year should be cancelled. No word of the gravity of his condition should be given to the Duchess of Edinburgh, who was expecting her first child.

Becoming a grandfather on 14 November, with the birth of Prince Charles, was a great source of joy to him, and he was glad to be able to attend the christening a month later. Yet on 23 November a bulletin had been issued stating that the King was suffering from an obstruction to the circulation through the arteries of the legs, which had recently become acute. According to the doctors, there was no doubt that the strain of the last few years had 'appreciably affected his resistance to fatigue.'

There was a danger that gangrene might develop, and that the right leg might have to be amputated. Fortunately, this last measure was avoided. Unlike his father, the King was a cooperative, stoical patient, and accepted his enforced stay in bed without complaint. He enjoyed Christmas at Sandringham as usual, and by the time the royal family returned to London at the end of February 1949 he believed himself well on the way to recovery.

A consultation with the doctors on 3 March proved bitterly disappointing. They proposed that he should undergo an operation to relieve the obstruction to the blood supply in his right leg, or else he would have to continue to lead the life of an invalid – an almost unthinkable suggestion. 'So all our treatment has been a waste of time!' he remarked bitterly. The operation took place on 12 March and he made an apparently good recovery. Yet he seemed to accept that he would perhaps never be completely restored to health. Perhaps the greatest danger was that of thrombosis which could be increased by his anxious temperament if he overstressed himself again.

In the summer of 1950, the Duke and Duchess of Windsor gave their British relations two further reasons to worry. The first was a rumour that the Duke was writing his memoirs; the second was a threat to their marriage.

The Duke had begun work on his autobiography three years earlier, with the aid – and no little pleasure – of an American ghostwriter. Colonel Charles Murphy, an editor with the *Time-Life* organization. King George VI was distressed that his brother should abandon the convention that British royalty did not then give interviews or write about themselves for instant publication, but there was nothing he could do. The Duke of Windsor was bored, and needed some purpose in life; he felt he could achieve it by putting the record straight; and his obsession with money would be appeased by the amount his literary activities would earn him. An initial series of three articles based on his forthcoming book was published in *Life* in December 1947, appearing in Britain five days later.

Only persistent pressure from Murphy brought the project any further, for the Duke was easily distracted and his enthusiasm for the work was difficult to sustain. A second series of articles in *Life* began in May 1950. While the Duke and ghostwriter turned their attention to the long-delayed book, the Duchess found her own distraction. His name was James Paul Donahue Jr, a thirty-five-year-old society figure who had inherited a fortune of millions from his grandfather, the magnate Frank W. Woolworth. That 'Jimmy' Donahue was almost young enough to be her son, and a notorious homosexual, did not bother the Duchess. Both were seen regularly at restaurants and nightclubs in Paris, evidently enjoying themselves and totally preoccupied with each other. In November, when the Windsors usually left France for two months' holiday in New York, the Duchess sailed alone, leaving her husband behind to continue working on the book.

To the New York press, the fact that the Duchess was seen almost constantly in the company of Donahue made just as good copy as the liaison between the then Mrs Simpson and Edward, Prince of Wales had done fifteen years before. One columnist announced bluntly that 'The Duke and Duchess of Windsor are phfft!'

When the British Embassy drew the liaison to the attention of King George's private secretary, Sir Alan Lascelles, alarm bells began to ring. In spite of all that had happened, the King still had a soft spot for his brother, and he could not help feeling sorry for him. Much as the news vindicated his resolve not to make the Duchess Her Royal Highness, he sympathized with the brother who might suddenly find himself the third husband to be divorced by the woman born as Wallis Warfield. At the King's personal request, Walter Monckton telephoned Charles Murphy in Paris to ask if the Duke of Windsor was aware of what the American press was saying.

The Duke had been sent a large pile of press cuttings on the liaison which made him only too painfully aware. Though he would lightly dismiss rumours of an affair between them with a jovial, 'She's as safe as houses with *him*!', he was deeply embarrassed, not to say worried. Early one morning he rang Murphy to say that he was throwing up work on the book and sailing directly for New York, ostensibly because of a risk that Russia might enter the Korean War and that world conflict would result, in which case he needed to be with the Duchess. Murphy realized that this was only an excuse, and decided that he would have to accompany the Duke if he was to have any hope of salvaging the book.

When the Duke arrived in New York on 6 December, he was greeted by a line of photographers and reporters – and his wife. One journalist with an eye for detail informed his readers that they threw their arms around each other and kissed seven times. With this public display, rumours of an estrangement were effectively checked.

Two months later, the Duchess entered hospital for an operation. Details were not disclosed for several years, but she had cancer of the womb, and had to undergo a hysterectomy. The Duke was so worried that even Queen Mary was moved at his distress. She wrote to sympathize with him and asked him to send her 'a short account of what has really happened.'

With such distractions, the Duke was in no frame of mind

to concentrate on the book more than fitfully, and Murphy completed it with only sporadic assistance from his employer.

On 3 May 1951, King George VI opened the Festival of Britain from the steps of St Paul's. It was intended to mark the centenary of Prince Albert's Great Exhibition, and also as a symbol of prestige to show how far Britain had come from the ordeal of the war. Austerity was still the order of the day, and an economic crisis did not seem far away, but at least the nation had an excuse to try and throw off the shackles of the grey post-war world.

On 24 May, the King attended a ceremony at Westminster Abbey to install the Duke of Gloucester as Grand Master of the Order of the Bath. Everyone remarked how ill he looked. Although running a temperature, he insisted on going through with the ceremony, and that evening he retired to bed with all the symptoms of influenza. The doctors diagnosed a small area of 'catarrhal inflammation' on the left lung, which he was told was pneumonitis – 'it is not pneumonia though if left it might become it.'[9] They did not tell him that they suspected he had lung cancer.

During June and July, he convalesced at Royal Lodge and then at Sandringham. The only semi-public engagement he undertook was opening a community centre, the York Club at Windsor, on 7 July. That he was still under strain was evident when he and the Queen attended the confirmation of their niece, Princess Alexandra of Kent, in a chapel at Royal Lodge. Just before the choirboys entered and the service began, his voice was heard raised in lively argument with the Queen. 'They're off again,' groaned Alexandra, 'Why can't they wait till I've been done?' In August he moved to Balmoral, feeling fitter and stronger. Unfortunately, a spell of cold weather gave him a chill and a sore throat, yet he insisted on going out shooting, though he no longer strode up the hills with the light, long gait of previous years. Instead his step was laboured, punctuated by frequent rests to cough and lean on his crummock. After dinner he would retire to bed early.

Princess Margaret was celebrating her twenty-first birthday and had invited a few friends of her age to stay. Soon after going to bed one evening the King rang for his equerry, Peter Townsend, with whom Princess Margaret's name was soon to be inextricably linked. Townsend entered his room to find 'a lonely, forlorn figure' standing there, with a 'glaring, distressed look' in his eyes. Raising his husky voice above the noise of music and dancing that came from below, he almost shouted. 'Won't those bloody people ever go to bed?'[10]

Cutting short his holiday, he left for London on 15 September. On the day after his return he was examined by doctors, and they confirmed that he was suffering from a malignant growth. The bulletins were worded cautiously.

The King was told that his illness was caused by a blockage of one of the bronchial tubes which necessitated the removal of his left lung. To him, it was a relief that the ill-health which had plagued him all summer might be relieved permanently. 'If it's going to help me to get well again I don't mind but the very idea of the surgeon's knife again is hell,' he confided to a friend. On 23 September the operation took place at Buckingham Palace. It was fraught with danger, for a coronary thrombosis might occur at any moment while it was taking place, and after preliminary examination, Mr Clement Price Thomas found that certain nerves of the larynx would have to be sacrificed. It was possible that he might never speak again above a whisper.

Though the operation went satisfactorily, Churchill's physician, Lord Moran, recognized that the King could scarcely live more than a year.

Ironically, this breakdown in the King's health coincided with the launching of his brother's long-threatened book, *A King's Story*, in Britain, five months after its American publication. Reviews in the United States had been very favourable, but in Britain (where eighty thousand copies were sold in the first month), the critical reception was mixed. It was impossible for anyone who had had any part in the abdication drama not to feel deeply for the King, whose ill-health and low spirits could hardly be improved by the spectacle of his elder brother publicly re-opening old wounds for financial gain.

Journalists praised its general style, and its less controversial contents, such as the Duke's account of his boyhood and early family life. In the *Manchester Guardian* Roger Fulford commented that it was 'marked throughout by firmness and generosity', and in the Economist it was called 'most dignified, objective and historically valuable'. Others echoed the views of Wilson Harris, who commented in the *Spectator* that 'on the Duke's resolve to drag every detail of this unhappy affair to light again when it had been well forgotten some judgement is called for. It must be unreservedly averse.'[11]

As was to be expected, the Duke's recollection of events during the year of 1936 was written completely from his point of view – so much so, that some of those involved were astonished and angry to read a description which bore no relation to their own memories. Many felt that he had been particularly unfair to Stanley Baldwin, who had treated his sovereign with unfailing tact and sympathy throughout the crisis. Only consideration for the ailing King, and a desire not to make things even worse, restrained them from making any public protest.

The Windsors stayed briefly in London, at a house in Upper Brook Street. On the eve of his operation, the King charitably gave instructions to the Master of the Household to deliver three brace of grouse as a present to the Duke. His gratitude at the gift was tempered when he agreed to cancel an invitation to address the annual dinner of the Book Publishers' Representatives' Association to coincide with the launch of his book, out of respect and concern for the King's ill-health, only to be told later that the King's daughters were seen at Ascot races that same afternoon.

That autumn, Attlee dissolved Parliament. A second post-war election in February 1950 had produced a slender Labour majority of eight seats, and his second administration had been under constant threat from the opposition. When the votes were counted after the polls on 25 October 1951, the result was a majority of seventeen seats for the Conservatives. At seventy-six, Churchill was back at Downing Street. Sadly, King and Prime Minister were now shadows of their former selves. The King did not receive the outgoing members of Attlee's Cabinet, a formality which he would never have foregone had he been in better health; and he did not discuss the new appointments with Churchill, increasingly deaf, bent and aged.

The Duke of Windsor had looked gloomily on the political complexion of the kingdom that had been his but briefly. Though claiming, shortly after the announcement of the general election results in 1945, that tradition prevented any political comment on his part, he was soon writing to friends about the 'crazy and dangerous socialists', and in particular what he saw as their concerted attack on any form of wealth, their far-reaching nationalization programme, their continuation of wartime rationing for its own sake, and above all the apathy of the people towards all rules and regulations imposed on them.[12] In November 1951, he welcomed cautiously the Conservatives' return to power, after 'six years of Socialist misrule based on class hatred.'[13]

On 21 December, the King recorded his Christmas broadcast at Buckingham Palace in easy stages of a sentence or two at a time. He was reluctant to do so, regarding it part of his duty to broadcast live, but the Queen knew that in his post-operative state he had to be spared the ordeal. When it was transmitted on Christmas Day, his listeners were moved by the effort and courage that went into every word he spoke.

They spent the festive season at Sandringham, and he seemed in good form. The family gathering embraced all ages, from Queen Mary in her eighty-fifth year, to the King's second grandchild Princess Anne, sixteen months. He began shooting again and took a great interest once more in the affairs of the estate.

On 29 January 1952, soon after returning to Buckingham Palace, he was examined again, and the doctors pronounced themselves pleased with his progress. The following evening, the family went to see *South Pacific* at Drury Lane Theatre. It was partly to celebrate the King's recovery, and partly as a farewell to Princess Elizabeth and the Duke of Edinburgh, leaving next day for a five-month tour of Africa, Australia and New Zealand.

On the morning of 31 January, the King and Queen, the Duke and Duchess of Gloucester, and Princess Margaret went to see them off at Heathrow Airport. As the King stood waving, his eyes straining for a last glimpse of his elder daughter, the cameras caught his gaunt, hollowed-out features as he stood hatless in the biting wind. Pictures in the press and on television and cinema screens shocked the country.

It was with guarded optimism that Lady Hyde wrote to Lady Astor two days later that 'The King will not be dining out at all until the summer, as though he is wonderfully well, his voice is still very croaky, especially at the end of the day.'[14]

By this time the family had returned to Sandringham. On 5 February the weather was mild for the time of year, and the King enjoyed a good day's shooting. He returned to the house for tea, and then went to see Prince Charles and Princess Anne in the nursery. The Queen and Princess Margaret had gone for an afternoon cruise on the Norfolk Broads, and returned to the house much later. That evening the King did a crossword, then walked to the kennels to check the paw of his golden retriever, injured by a thorn. On his return they listened to the BBC radio news to hear about Elizabeth and Philip relaxing at a game sanctuary, Treetops, in Kenya. He retired to bed at 10.30 in a ground floor bedroom which saved him the strain of climbing stairs. At midnight, a watchman in the garden noticed him fixing the latch of his window.

At 7.15 on the morning of 6 February, his valet, James MacDonald, came to wake him. It was too late. Sometime during the small hours, the coronary which had threatened him for so long, claimed his life peacefully as he slept.

Moments later the Queen's equerry, Commander Sir Harold Campbell, asked to see her urgently. It was such an unusual request and at so early an hour that she guessed it was bad news. She asked for a vigil to be kept at the door of her husband's room, saying that 'the King must not be left.'

At 9.30 that morning, Queen Mary was working in her sitting-room at Marlborough House, when her Woman of the Bedchamber, Lady Cynthia Colville, asked to see her. Looking steadily at Lady Cynthia, she asked calmly, 'Is it the King?' Like Queen Elizabeth, she had been prepared for the fact that his death could come at any time.

The Duke of Gloucester was similarly shocked, as he told his brother-in-law Sir Geoffrey Hawkins' 'he was just getting back to his old self again.'[15]

Both the King's post-war Prime Ministers were deeply affected. Only once, Labour member of Parliament Michael Foot later recorded, did he ever see Attlee emotionally affected in public. When he spoke of King George VI's death, tears were in his eyes and voice. Churchill was shattered; his secretary Jock Colville found him later that day in his study, sitting alone with tears in his eyes, looking straight in front of him, reading neither his official papers nor the newspapers. 'It was only a week ago when I saw the King at the airfield when the Princess left,' he told Lord Moran. 'He was gay and even jaunty, and drank a glass of champagne. I think he knew he had not long to live. It was a perfect ending. He had shot nine hares and a pigeon a hundred feet up, and then he dined with five friends and went out in the night. What more could any of us ask?'[16]

The King's elder daughter, now Queen Elizabeth II, wrote to Lady Astor on 2 March in replying to a letter of sympathy that 'My father was indeed beloved by his people, who feel they have lost a friend as well as their King.'[17]

12

'This wretched business of growing older'

King George VI's death left three survivors from the nursery at York Cottage. The eldest, the Duke of Windsor, was still in France. Both the Princess Royal, a widow for nearly five years, and the Duke of Gloucester, continued to maintain a relatively conspicuous profile in public at home. The latter was among the select group at the young Queen Elizabeth II's 'very sad homecoming' as she stepped off the plane at Heathrow Airport on 7 February.

The Windsors were staying at Waldorf Towers, New York, when they were informed by telephone that same day of the King's death. At a hasty press conference later that day on the deck of the Cunard liner, ironically named Queen Mary, the Duke read a prepared statement, announcing that the voyage he embarked on that night was 'indeed sad – and it is all the sadder for me because I am undertaking it alone.'[1] Officials at Buckingham Palace had let it be known that there was no question of the Duchess accompanying him.

Arriving at Southampton on 13 February, the Duke of Windsor drove to Marlborough House, where he stayed with his mother throughout the visit. In the afternoon he went to Buckingham Palace for tea with the widowed Queen Elizabeth – their first meeting since the abdication – and Queen Elizabeth the II. Polite conversation between the Duke and his sister-in-law masked fifteen years of bitterness and resentment on both sides.[2] That evening the Duke accompanied Queen Mary and

195

the Princess Royal to Westminster Hall, where they stood in silent homage for quarter of an hour before the purple-draped catafalque containing the King's coffin as it lay in state.

As the funeral cortege moved through the streets of London on 15 February, four royal Dukes – those of Windsor, Gloucester, Edinburgh and the young Duke of Kent – walked behind the coffin. 'Windsor jaunty' noted 'Chips' Chanon; 'what must have been his thoughts and regrets?' Queen Mary watched from her window at Marlborough House. 'Here *he* is,' she whispered to Lady Airlie in a broken voice, dry-eyed, as the coffin came past..

The King was buried beside his ancestors at St George's Chapel, Windsor. Jaunty he may have looked in the earlier procession, but those who saw the Duke of Windsor as he watched the widowed Queen noticed eyes that looked haunted by guilt.

The Windsors hoped that a new reign might bring about a change for the better in the official British attitude to their standing. They were soon disabused. As they already enjoyed tax-free status in France, they were eager to know if they could do so in Britain, so they could return at last to Fort Belvedere. As only the sovereign was traditionally exempt from taxation, the answer was a firm no. The Duke of Windsor still hankered after an official job – such as the post of a Governor-General or Ambassador abroad. The Queen consulted Churchill, who advised against it. Finally, would the sovereign receive the Duchess of Windsor, and recognize her at last as a Royal Highness? The Duke was optimistic in supposing that his niece would go against the wishes of her late father, her mother, and her grandmother, and in any case the Donahue liaison was still too recent in public memory. Again the answer was negative.

Shocked at being informed that the allowance he had received from the Palace, a personal favour granted by King George VI, ceased with the latter's death, the Duke returned to France with bitterness in his heart. His female relatives were dismissed angrily as 'these ice-veined bitches'. Even his mother, for whom the death of a third son appeared to those around her as the loss of one son too many, did not escape his venom, 'Mama as hard as nails but fading. When Queens fail they make less sense than others in the same state.'[3]

Soon afterwards the Fort, echo of a past that so many wished to forget, was sold on a Crown lease to the Queen's cousin, the Hon. Gerald Lascelles. He lived there till 1976, when he sold the property to the Sultan of Dubai.

During the first few months of his neice's reign, the Duke of Gloucester maintained a full schedule of duties. In April and May 1952, he visited regiments in Northumberland, Ireland and Germany, and in July he paid his first visit to the Channel Islands. On Jersey he and the Duchess attended the centenary celebrations of Victoria College, visited the headquarters of the Order of St John, and inspected a herd of Jersey cattle. On Guernsey he demonstrated his interest in the cattle and expressed concern at an outbreak of foot and mouth disease on the island, especially to another guest at the state banquet, who had just lost his entire herd of Guernseys.

Before returning to England, the Gloucesters paid a brief visit to Alderney. Observing the Duke from a distance, the novelist T.H. White compared him irreverently to 'an anxious porker which had escaped from the Cavalry Club.' The remark was not meant unkindly; His Royal Highness, he noted, was 'a kind, good Englishman, and a King's son to boot.'[4]

Yet too often the Duke was irked at the tedium of state visits and other duties demanded by his position. 'What a bloody big marrow,' he announced when opening a fruit and flower show, 'glad I don't have to eat it.' When the memoirs of his second cousin Prince Marie Louise were being discussed, he joked, 'I am thinking of writing my own. And do you know what I shall call them? *Forty years of boredom.*'[5]

A story was told to illustrate the problems he had with making small talk. On a visit to Africa in the 1930s he and his entourage were entertained one evening at Cairo with the spectacle of a belly dancer. After the show, he was introduced to the perspiring girl, clad in a thong and little else. To the amusement of his sniggering escorts, all he could ask her was a hesitant 'Ever been to Tidworth then?'[6]

In later life, as his obituary in *The Times* would remark, the Duke shone in the mess, the hunting field, the covert, and the big game reserves. By nature he was a countryman, reluctantly drawn to laying foundation stones, making speeches, or being the centre of attention in other ways.[7]

In his undemonstrative way, he was devoted to his two sons. As one of his equerries would later recall, he was determined that his children should not be as afraid of their father as he had been of his.[8] He wanted them to feel that they could always talk to him about their problems. At Barnwell, and at the House of Farr in Scotland, where they went every year for shooting, this royal gentleman farmer could get to know his sons better and lead as normal a family life as possible. To his elder son, William, the Duke was basically a gentleman farmer at heart.

Early in the new year of 1953, Queen Mary's health began to fail. At eighty-five, she knew the end could not be far off. She let it be known that her death and subsequent court mourning should not be allowed to interfere with the festivities for her granddaughter's Coronation.

The Windsors were in New York at the time, and the Princess Royal had been in the Caribbean. She paused in New York for one night between planes to join her brother so they could travel back to England, and only then did she meet her American sister-in-law for the first time since the abdication. Only a brief comment by Princess Mary's son, the Earl of Harewood, gave any clue as to how the meeting went. His mother, he said, told him she had found Wallis 'charming'. The Duke thought his sister had 'become more human with age'.

On arrival in England, the Duke of Windsor stayed at his former home, York House, with the Duke and Duchess of Gloucester. By the evening of 24 March, the Queen's end was evidently near. The Duke was summoned urgently to Marlborough House, reaching her room five minutes too late. Only his sister was there, 'and none of the rest of the family showed up that night.' When he returned to York House for a few minutes afterwards, he found brother Harry, with a glass of Scotch in his hand 'and feeling no pain* . . . I guess it was emotion!'

Much as he had loved his mother, the Duke's sadness 'was mixed with incredulity that any mother could have been so hard and cruel towards her eldest son for so many years . . . I'm afraid the fluids in her veins have always been as icy cold as they now are in death.'[9]

At her funeral he looked unhappy, 'very nervous and fidgety'. Perhaps he would have been unhappier still had he known that his wife and Jimmy Donahue were about to spend an evening dining and dancing. The incident did not escape the notice of the Queen or her mother, and it strengthened their conviction that the Duchess was still totally unacceptable as a member of the family.

Mary, Princess Royal, the Duke of Windsor wrote to his wife, was 'quite sweet and human on the whole and Harry and Alice have been friendly hosts here. But of course they don't talk our language and never will.'[10]

No invitation was extended to the Duke and Duchess for the Coronation of Queen Elizabeth II on 2 June. He had prepared a statement for the press which he showed Churchill, explaining that it would be contrary to precedent for any sovereign or former sovereign to attend. Churchill confirmed that this was the case, and agreed that it would provide a dignified reply to anyone enquiring whether they would be there.

They watched the ceremony on television at the house of American friends in Paris, and later the Duke told Princess Arthur of Connaught that he found it very moving, and that 'Lilibet conducted herself superbly throughout the long and trying ceremony.'[11] American friends who had detected in his attitude an apparent indifference towards the royal family were surprised to find that he still took such intense interest, and

---

* A private expression of the Duke of Windsor, meaning 'the worse for drink'.

that his protestations that he did not 'give a damn' about the new regime were unfounded.

A couple of months later, the Duke and Duchess went for a cruise around the Gulf of Genoa, aboard Jimmy Donahue's yacht. Though the latter's friendship had come close to wrecking the marriage, the Duke appeared to hold no grudge against him. Before long, though, Donahue fell from favour. One day at their hotel suite in Baden-Baden he lost his temper, and kicked the Duchess on the shin. In a rare display of self-assertiveness, the Duke ordered him never to darken their doors again.*

When it was suggested to the Duke that he should employ his talents in further writing, he was delighted. What had begun as a long article on the constitutional role of the British monarchy resulted in articles for the *Sunday Express* and *Women's Home Companion*, and a slim volume, *The Crown and the People 1902–1953*, published in September. It was largely a series of recollections of the two Coronations in which he had taken part, plus uncontroversial and well-reasoned if not particularly original reflections on the nature of the monarchy and its future. He paid tribute to the contributions made by his parents and brother, who had been a faithful reflection of his father. Had his own reign run its course, 'it is possible that its mood and texture would have followed more that of Edward VII.'[12]

In November, shortly after the Queen and the Duke of Edinburgh's departure on a six-month Commonwealth tour, the Windsors arrived in London, accompanied by thirty-five pieces of luggage – 'just an ordinary wardrobe for a week's stay', their secretary remarked lightly. While there, they made their first visit to a theatre in the city for seventeen years, to see Agatha Christie's *Witness for the Prosecution* at the Winter Garden Theatre. The management had been asked to keep their arrival a secret, but to reach their box they had to walk through the stalls. Everyone in the theatre soon knew

* Donahue was found dead in bed by his mother in December 1966, aged fifty-one. The official cause of death was given as 'acute alcoholic and barbiturate intoxification.'

they were there, and the entire audience rose and applauded. Looking surprised and very moved, the Windsors walked to the front of the box to acknowledge the ovation. After they left the theatre, cheering crowds surrounded their car. The press and photographers made much of the incident next day.

Cameramen were also present at a rather less dignified public appearance on New Year's Eve, where the Windsors were snapped celebrating at the El Morocco Club, New York, with paper crowns on their heads. Though obviously enjoying themselves, there was something sadly symbolic about the party headgear, worn by a couple who had indeed become tinsel figures.

To the outside world, they gave every appearance of mutual devotion. Only their household and closest friends knew that what his family had feared still held true. The Duchess retained her domination of him, and when bored she still found his dog-like devotion to her intensely irritating. Their private secretary, John Utter, revealed after his retirement in 1975 that their life was essentially one of entertainment, empty of everything else. They were a wretched, egocentric couple, and though the Duke did not generally touch a drop of alcohol before seven in the evening, after that the sound of their drunken bickering was unbearable. Despite everything, 'he was certainly sincerely in love with her.'

A couple of years later, the Duchess of Windsor followed her husband's example and published her memoirs. Again Murphy was engaged as ghostwriter, but he so irritated her by his scepticism about her version of events, that in exasperation she fired him. Two more ghostwriters were brought in, but they were equally unable to accept her distortion of events, and she had to beg Murphy to return. The resulting work, *The heart has its reasons*, was published in February 1956, but met with little enthusiasm from reviewers. Murphy had remained steadfastly unconvinced by her persistent abuse of her sister-in-law, whom he judged 'an admirable woman and a very proper Queen.'[13]

Though she insisted that it no longer mattered to her, the Duchess of Windsor was still angry that the style of HRH was withheld from her. After retiring from the House of Commons, Sir Walter Monckton was created Viscount Monckton of Brenchley, and he and his wife visited the Windsors at Paris. Although he had done so much for them in the past, she reproached him bitterly for having got himself a title, but not one for her. He and his wife were so upset that they left immediately.

When James Pope-Hennessy was commissioned to write the official life of Queen Mary later that year, he visited the Windsors to obtain the Duke's impressions of his mother. Their Paris home, Le Moulin de la Tuilerie, struck him as 'intensely American', and far exceeded in luxury and provision of creature-comforts Queen Elizabeth's house at London; the Queen Mother, he thought, was leading a lodging-house existence compared to this.

They were still bitter about what they derided as their 'treatment' by the royal family. In particular, the Duchess's expression when speaking of the Queen Mother, was 'very unpleasant to behold' and almost 'akin to frenzy'.[14] The Duke still spoke with some affection of his mother, comparing her favourably to his father's sisters, who were grossly inferior in intellect and education, and could just read and write – that was all. In particular the spinster Princess Victoria, he recalled, was 'a bitch of the first order'. The Duchess, who had aspired for so long to be accepted as 'royal' herself, told Pope-Hennessy that there were only three royal royalties left in the world – 'The Dook [sic], his brother Gloucester, and his sister.'[15]

Kenneth Rose, later the author of a biography of King George V, commented that 'perhaps the most memorable remark' ever made to him was when the Duke of Windsor told him: 'I served my country well for seventeen years, and all I got was a kick on the ass.'[16] In 1960, the Duke published another book. Despite the title *A family album*, it was somewhat short on entertaining anecdotes and dwelt mainly on clothes worn or not worn by the royal family. *The Times* reviewer complained that 'much of this smells of the lamp in the sense that it reads as though it had been quarried out of dress manuals.'[17]

The next year, a contract was drawn up for a biography of King George III, to be written yet again with help from Charles

Murphy. Provisionally titled *My Hanoverian ancestors*, the Duke entered on the idea with great enthusiasm but quickly lost interest.

The Princess Royal continued her supportive role as a royal representative. She enjoyed travelling abroad, and in 1957 she undertook an unofficial tour of Nigeria, including the inauguration of two legislatures on behalf of the Queen, opening new universities, factories and hospitals. Three years later, she made a three-month tour of the West Indies and British Honduras, and in 1962 she was present at ceremonies marking the independence of Trinidad and Tobago. Two years later she was at Lusaka, representing the Queen at Zambia's independence ceremonies. In the autumn of 1964 she made a private visit to Newfoundland, in her capacity as Commander-in-Chief of the Royal Newfoundland Regiment, for the fiftieth anniversary celebrations of their reformation at the start of the Great War.

Earlier that same year, the Queen had delegated various duties to other members of the royal family, as she was expecting her fourth child, Prince Edward, born on 10 March.* She asked the Princess Royal to distribute the Royal Maundy on her behalf, no mean honour, as before then the Queen Mother was the only woman to have acted as deputy on such an occasion. An Abbey official who sought to instruct her in the ceremonial was assured, 'I've been reading it up to refresh my memory.'

In public, the Princess Royal cut an assertive figure. Privately, though, she showed a very different face to the world. Though the people of Yorkshire who had seen her regularly during her married life said she had never really looked happy, in widowhood she appeared a forlorn, unobtrusive figure. Her gardener Geoffrey Hall thought she was often a very lonely woman. At Harewood she rarely missed her daily walk, or

---

* The Queen's second son, Prince Andrew, had been born on 19 February 1960.

what the other gardeners would call her 'rabbit run', a distance of nearly two miles, half-circling the lake and returning to Harewood House. It would follow a distinct pattern; in the afternoon she would be accompanied by a lady-in-waiting, but in the evening alone with only her dogs. Sometimes she seemed to crave for company, and when Mr Hall worked on summer evenings she would come and chat to him, discussing the tasks in hand or talking about new plantings by the lake.

Despite her interest in gardening, she was diffident about voicing her own personal opinions. Perhaps occasionally, remarked her gardener, one would find out from the lady-in-waiting 'that a certain coloured flower was not suitable in the House, or a new variety of vegetable did not relish the palate,'[18] but never did he hear her say definitely that anything was good or bad.

The Windsors were not invited to subsequent family weddings, such as that of Princess Margaret in 1960, the Duke of Kent a year later, or Princess Alexandra in 1963. Speculation was mounting in the press as to whether there would be any further contact between the royal family and the ageing ex-King.

However, on his seventieth birthday in 1964, he received a telegram of congratulation from the Queen. Later that year he was admitted to hospital in Houston, Texas, for heart surgery, and on his arrival he found the room brightly decorated with flowers sent by the Queen, Princess Margaret and the Princess Royal.

The year of 1965 opened with concern over the failing health of Churchill. Knighted by the Queen on his eightieth birthday in November 1954, he had resigned as Prime Minister a few months later due to increasing age and infirmity. Although he sat in the House of Commons until the dissolution of parliament in September 1964, he was a shadow of his former self. On 24 January 1965 he died at the age of ninety.

After attending the funeral at St Paul's on 30 January, the Duke and Duchess of Gloucester joined the Queen's lunch party at Buckingham Palace. Though warned by his doctors not to drive if he could avoid doing so, in view of his failing health and circulation problems, the Duke insisted on taking the wheel of his Rolls-Royce on their journey back to Barnwell, with the chauffeur William Prater beside him and the Duchess in the back. Not far from home, the Duke lost control of the car. They swerved off the road, crossed a footpath and a four-foot ditch, crashed through a hedge, and ended upside down in a field. The Duke was thrown clear, shocked but almost unhurt. Fortunately the next vehicle to come past was a bus with a team of Mansfield miners, many of whom were members of the St John's Ambulance Brigade. They administered first aid until an ambulance arrived to take them to Bedford Hospital, where the extent of the damage was revealed. Prater had sustained rib injuries, and the Duchess had a broken arm and nose, and cracked knee and facial wounds, requiring fifty-seven stitches.

The Duke was treated for shock, but sent home next day. At first to those around him he seemed to take it lightly, and when he tried to visit his wife's bedside, she was too angry to see him. Whether he had dozed off, suffered a minor stroke, or whether his attention had wandered, nobody was to know; but he was never quite the same again.

A few weeks earlier he had accepted an invitation for himself and the Duchess to visit Australia again for ceremonies at Canberra marking the fiftieth anniversary of the Anzac landings. In view of his failing health, he accepted only on condition that the expedition would be fairly leisurely and informal. After the accident, the visit was in doubt. In the end, it was postponed by only a week, and they left from London airport on 15 March, calling first at San Francisco where they stayed with J. Wallace Sterling, Chancellor of Stanford University, where Prince William had recently been a student.

While the Duke and Duchess were abroad, the health of his surviving brother and sister was causing concern to the family at home.

After a medical examination, the Duke of Windsor's doctors recommended an operation to repair the detached retina of his left eye. This surgery, it was felt, would be best performed at the London Clinic. As the Duke and Duchess arrived in London on 23 February 1965, the press wondered if this would at last bring about the first official public recognition of the latter by the British sovereign. Their advancing age and the Duke's impaired vision brought them sympathy from a generation too young to remember clearly the events of 1936.

The Queen's advisers knew that the court had been criticized on humanitarian grounds, and that the time was right for a reconciliation. Even Monckton's widow, who had been so insulted by the Duchess a few years previously, magnanimously contacted Buckingham Palace to say that the Duke of Windsor would be greatly touched and cheered if Her Majesty could visit him while he was at the clinic. With some hesitation, the Queen consulted her mother, who had arrived back from a visit to Jamaica on 27 February. Evidently the Queen Mother acknowledged that some kind of *rapproachement* was expedient by now. On 15 March the Queen called upon her uncle and aunt at the clinic, after the Duke had undergone three operations. It was the first time she had come face to face with the Duchess since that spring day of 1936, when the then King and Mrs Simpson had paid that fateful visit to Royal Lodge.

The meeting lasted twenty-five minutes with the Duke, clad in pyjamas and dressing gown, and his eye heavily bandaged, seated between his niece and his wife. Also present was the Queen's private secretary, Sir Michael Adeane. The ward was festooned with flowers, including one striking arrangement, signed personally 'to David' by his sister-in-law.

The Queen had also been told of another request that the Duke wished to make. In 1957 he had bought a plot in Green Mount Cemetery, Baltimore, where many of Wallis's relations were buried. Now, fearing that he had not long to live, he felt unhappy at the idea of being buried on foreign soil. He wanted to be laid to rest at Windsor with the rest of the family, at the private burial ground at Frogmore, near his favourite brother the Duke of Kent. And naturally, he wanted Wallis to be laid to rest beside him when the time came, and further to have a private funeral service at St George's Chapel, Windsor.

It was a request to which the Queen could hardly accede at once. She knew how much it would mean to her uncle and aunt, but weighed against this was the reaction of her mother, and what her father would have thought. Promising to give the matter careful consideration, she visited them again a few days later and told them that their request was granted. Touched, the Duke gave orders for his plot at Baltimore to be sold.

Another visitor to the bedside was the Princess Royal, who arrived on the evening of 17 March, bringing a bouquet of flowers. She stayed for forty-five minutes, meeting her sister-in-law for the second time in twenty-eight years. Although she had suffered from colds that winter she left, apparently in perfect health and spirits. Only a few days earlier she had flown to Stockholm to represent the Queen at the funeral of Queen Louise of Sweden.

The Princess Royal also nursed her own private grief caused by the shadow of divorce, for her elder son's marriage had fallen apart. The Earl and Countess Harewood had had three sons, but since then he had fallen in love with an Australian-born divorcee, Patricia Tuckwell. He was living with her, but only after she had borne him a son in 1964 did the Countess agree to a divorce.

From her mother, the Princess Royal had learnt the art of mastering her feelings. She never spoke to others in the family about the painful matter. Only once did mother and son discuss the subject. After listening pensively to all he had to say in complete silence, her only comment at his mention of divorce was, 'What will people say?'

How much she brooded on the disgrace of it all, nobody would know. For some time she had been suffering from mild heart trouble, and told her eldest son that she was considering a move nearer Sandringham, in order to cut down on her travelling. Yet the doctors were reasonably satisfied with her health, while warning her not to exert herself too much. The end was to come quite suddenly. On 28 March, she was taking an after-lunch stroll at Harewood with the Earl, and his sons James and Jeremy. Suddenly she stumbled, complaining of dizziness. The Earl helped her to a seat and asked her what was wrong. 'I don't really know,' she answered faintly. He supported her while the boys ran to the house for help. By the time a car arrived quarter of an hour later, she had passed away peacefully in the arms of her son.

'An active, unobtrusive, and personal life,' *The Times* headed its obituary for the Princess Royal next day. It paid her tributes which she would have greatly appreciated, remarking on 'her natural reserve,' and how 'she overcame this and served the nation especially in Yorkshire where she was dearly loved with a constant and rare fidelity.'[19]

Ironically, BBC Television followed the news bulletin announcing her death with a satirical programme, *Not so much a programme*, which included among other items an operatic portrayal of the abdication with footage of the Duke and Duchess of Windsor. After protests were made at this lapse of taste, the Director-General of the BBC, Sir Hugh Greene, regretted what he defined as 'an error of judgement'.

Meanwhile at Harewood the estate staff were engaged in preparations for the funeral, which took place there on 1 April. Bowing to medical advice, the Duke of Windsor did not make the journey to Yorkshire, but he and the Duchess attended a memorial service at Westminster Abbey, their first official public engagement since the abdication. They entered by a side door to avoid danger from jostling crowds outside and from camera flashlights, the Duke in dark glasses looking very frail with the Duchess guiding him. As they entered, the congregation rose to its feet spontaneously as a mark of respect.

The Duke of Gloucester, in Australia, missed the opportunity to pay his last respects to his sister. The tour which he had asked to be 'leisurely and informal' proved quite arduous, with a round of civic welcomes, state receptions and several similar engagements, many of which he would quite happily have foregone.

On 25 April, Anzac Day, they attended a military ceremony at the Australian War Memorial. Shortly before this was due to take place, the Duke had suddenly seized up. When he tried to stand his legs failed him, and he appeared unaware of what was going on a round him. The Duchess and his valet, Alfred Amos, got him to his feet and he took a few paces in the garden. Realizing that any delay would upset the schedule of the parade, he told his chauffeur to make up for lost time, and they sped towards the ceremony, narrowly missing a woman pushing a pram. The shock of another lucky escape on the road cleared the Duke's brain, and when they reached the venue he seemed to be his normal self again. None the less it was fortunate that the parade was his last official function in Australia, as they were due to fly out the following day; it was clear this time that he had had a minor stroke.

The Duke's health would evidently soon put an end to such representative missions. Later that year, a visit to Malaysia was planned, where he was to give moral support to the local rulers and British forces who still maintained a considerable military presence in the area.

On 5 January 1966, the evening before they were due to leave, the Duke and Duchess received Field-Marshal Sir Richard Hull, Chief of Defence Staff, at York House. He briefed the Duke on the Far-Eastern situation, and after he had left, it was agreed that they would need to make an early start next day. Suddenly the Duke looked completely baffled; he had apparently lost the thread of their earlier conversation, and seemed unaware of plans for the visit. Seriously alarmed, the Duchess summoned their doctor. Though he had evidently suffered another minor stroke, it was decided that they should go ahead with the programme as far as possible.

Two days later they landed in Singapore. The British Commander-in-Chief, Air Chief Marshal Sir John Grandy, was shocked at the change in his friend, whom he had last seen a year or so previously. Coming down the steps of the plane, he looked 'pale and rather slow, self-possessed, but clearly not fit.'[20] All the same, their two-week Malaysian mission passed off satisfactorily, with dinners, a polo match at the Selangor Turf Club, military displays, and a demonstration by tank landing craft.

For the sake of the Duke's health, they went to Jamaica in February. When he returned home in March, people realized that he was clearly not well. The times when his mind seemed not to function were becoming more frequent, and deafness impaired his conversation.

The Duke of Windsor was especially concerned at reports of his brother's failing health. 'I'm afraid it's this wretched business of growing older,' he wrote to him in February 1967, 'for which there are absolutely no compensations.'[21] The following month, when the Gloucesters paused in New York on their way back to England from Jamaica, the Duke of Windsor went out to Kennedy Airport specially to see them during their wait between planes.

In view of Queen Mary's disapproval of the Windsors' marriage, it was ironic that the celebration of her life should be the catalyst for a public *rapprochement*. A plaque on the side of Marlborough House was to be unveiled to commemorate the centenary of her birth.

After the royal family's visits to him at the London Clinic two years earlier, it was difficult to imagine such a ceremony taking place without the elder of the Queen's two surviving children present – and to invite the Duke of Windsor, but not his wife, would be unthinkable. Adding further weight to the case for the Windsors were the shock waves from the Harewood divorce. Lady Harewood had been granted a decree nisi in April, which became absolute in July, on the grounds of her husband's adultery.

The unveiling was to have been held on 26 May, the date of the centenary, but was postponed for a fortnight because of the Windsor's long-standing engagements. On the afternoon of 5 June, they arrived at Southampton on the liner *United States*, on which they had celebrated their thirtieth wedding anniversary two days before. As they came hand in hand down the gangplank to be welcomed by Lord Mountbatten, a crowd of dockers cheered, yelling, 'Good old Teddy.'

To journalists' questions, the Duke was gracious but guarded in his replies. He expressed the hope that 'the very private nature of our visit will be respected.' When a television interviewer boldly asked about 'disagreements with the royal family,' he interrupted that 'we know nothing at all about them,' a reply which brought a look of regret to the Duchess's face.

They spent the night at Broadlands, Romsey, Lord Mountbatten's home. Next day, a crowd assembled outside Claridge's to watch them enter. At a shout of, 'Welcome home, Sir,' the Duke raised his trilby in acknowledgement. The Windsors lunched with the Gloucesters at York House, where the Duke was concerned to see his younger brother supporting himself with a walking stick.

At the unveiling, there was a tangible sense of anticipation. How would the sisters-in-law react? Every lady present curtsied to the Queen Mother as she walked towards the guests, except the Duchess of Windsor. They shook hands, and were seen to make conversation for several minutes, the Queen Mother moving her head from side to side, while the Duchess's replies verged on the monosyllabic.

Their *tete-a-tete* was curtailed by the arrival of the Queen and Prince Philip. The Queen looked severe, well aware of the momentous encounter which had just taken place before her arrival. When she walked past, the Duke bowed his head deeply and the Duchess curtsied. As she did so, she looked at the Queen Mother as if to say that she would curtsey to her daughter, but never to her.

After the ceremony, most of the royal family departed for Epsom to attend the Derby. The Windsors went to a small private family lunch hosted by the Duchess of Kent at Kensington Palace, before flying back to Paris in the afternoon.

The surviving participants of the abdication crisis were growing old, but the next death was an unexpected one. In July 1968 the Duchess of Kent entered hospital for investigation of a muscular weakness in her left leg which had troubled her for some time. A medical examination revealed that she was suffering from an inoperable brain tumour. On 27 August she died in her sleep at Kensington Palace, aged sixty-one.

The Windsors were invited to the funeral on 30 August, but

the Duchess stayed away 'out of tact'. At St George's Chapel, the Duke and the Queen Mother were among those who followed the coffin to its final resting place in the private burial ground at Frogmore. While there, the Duke chose the site where he wished his wife and himself to be buried, a few yards from the graves of the Kents. It was as if he had a premonition that he would be the next to go. As he was driven back to Heathrow Airport, perhaps he sensed that he had seen British soil for the very last time.

Age was indeed taking its toll. As he had told his last remaining brother the previous year, there were no compensations for growing old. That summer the Duke of Gloucester had suffered another stroke, followed by partial recovery and then a second attack. By the time of Marina's death, he was confined to a wheelchair, virtually deprived of the power of speech.

Despite his own failing infirmities, the Duke of Windsor was growing old with serenity, as suggested by a television interview recorded in October 1969 between the Duke and Duchess and journalist Kenneth Harris. Screened on 13 January 1970 by BBC Television, it attracted over eleven million viewers. At the end, Harris asked the Duke if he had any regrets about not having remained King. After a pause, he answered that he would have liked to remain on the throne, but only on his own conditions. 'So I do not have any regrets. But I take a great interest in my country – my country which is Britain – your land and mine. I wish it well.'

In retrospect, the interview was a graceful *Adieu* to the land of his birth. A year later his voice became increasingly hoarse, sometimes shrinking to a mere whisper. The doctors diagnosed a small tumour in his throat. A biopsy was performed in November 1971, and the growth was discovered to be malignant and inoperable. Daily cobalt therapy was prescribed, but the treatment exhausted him, and when he and the Duchess attended a gala evening at the Paris Lido on 15 December, wearing dark glasses and a red carnation in the buttonhole of his dinner jacket, even hardened press photographers were shocked at his shrunken appearance. Soon after Christmas, the therapy was discontinued. It had failed to reduce the tumour and had weakened him so much that it was considered dangerous to continue.

In February, he was operated on for a double hernia at the American Hospital in Paris. The operation was successful, but at the same time the tumour was examined again and not found to be in remission. The Duke's nurse, Oonagh Stanley, was told that nothing could be done but to make his remaining few months as comfortable as possible.

Within forty-eight hours of the operation, the Duke had recovered enough for the Duchess to visit him twice a day. Though the hospital was only a few minutes' drive from their home, he fretted over the inconvenience of her having to make even such a short journey as this. He was anxious about her health; she had been suffering from arteriosclerosis for about three years, as well as sudden personality changes and lapses of memory. To a friend, he admitted sadly that his wife was literally losing her mind.

At the end of February, he discharged himself from hospital, declaring that he wanted to die in his own bed. Like the doctors, he suspected that it was only a matter of time.

Physically frail, his mind was still as active as ever. Since his great-nephew Charles, Prince of Wales, had paid him a visit in the autumn of 1970 while staying at the British Embassy in Paris, both men had engaged in occasional correspondence. The Duke of Windsor was fascinated to see how his young relative was faring as heir to the throne and bearer of the title which had been his half a century earlier. Moreover, he pondered on the irony that over the years some things had hardly changed. A letter to Prince Charles, dated 8 February 1972, commented on the similarity between problems faced by the Conservative government of Edward Heath, and the problems that bedevilled MacDonald and Baldwin in the 1920s. 'The insoluble Ulster crisis' was the most tragic, and he recalled how many responsible politicians had expressed the view that partition would never work. Unemployment, strikes and the effects of inflation also had 'much to do with the present troubles and I am sure you must be as concerned as I was forty years ago over the tragic plight of thousands of men thrown out of work by the closing of pits, ship yards and other industries.'[22]

On 15 May, the Queen and Prince Philip were due to begin a state visit to France. If the Duke was to die before that date, it would have to be cancelled because of court mourning; should he die while the visit was in progress, it would need to be curtailed. The Duke's physician, Jean Thin, was told by the British Ambassador in Paris, Sir Christopher Soames, that nothing could be allowed to interfere with a carefully planned schedule of official meetings designed to improve the atmosphere for Great Britain's imminent membership of the European Economic Community. There would be no problems if the Duke was to die before or after the visit, but should he expire while the tour was in progress it would be politically disastrous. Could Dr Thin do anything to reassure him about the timing of the Duke's end?[23]

Astonished, the doctor replied that he could give no such assurances. His patient was so weak that he could die at any moment. By the end of April, his coughing spasms had worsened, his fevers were more frequent, and he weighed less than seven stone. On 10 May he had a minor heart attack and was close to death. All the same, he was determined to see 'his family' one last time.

On the morning of 18 May, the day they were due to visit, he was so weak that he was given a blood transfusion. Against the doctor's advice, he insisted that they should not see him in his pyjamas or dressing gown; he wished to be up and properly dressed when he received them.

When the Queen and Prince Philip and the Prince of Wales arrived at the house, the Duchess entertained them to tea in the drawing-room. She apologized for the Duke not being strong enough to come downstairs, but he greatly looked forward to receiving them in his sitting-room adjoining the bedroom on the first floor. This was the only reference made to his condition.

As the Duchess led the Queen to his room, the gaunt, emaciated figure in a wheelchair made a great effort to stand up, as he bowed slightly and kissed her on both cheeks. Seeing how much the effort had drained him, the Queen insisted he must sit down again. Prince Philip and the Prince of Wales followed a moment later, but after a few minutes of conversation, the Duke's throat began to convulse and he started coughing. He motioned to the nurse to wheel him away, and his guests stood up. He was pleased to have met them one last time, but wanted to avoid any formal goodbyes.

Though he had managed to leave his bed every morning, by 25 May he was too weak to do so. Two days later his temperature soared, and the Duchess struggled to maintain her self-control as she sat beside him, knowing that the end could not be far away. When she left the room for a moment, he asked the nurse, 'Am I dying?' 'You're quite intelligent enough to decide that for yourself,' was her reply. When the Duchess wanted to stay up all night, he begged her to go and get some rest, as he would soon be asleep himself. He drifted gently into unconsciousness, and at 2.20 a.m. on 28 May 1972, as the nurse was monitoring his pulse, his heart ceased to beat altogether.

The Duke's funeral took place at Windsor on 5 June. After weeks of strain and anxiety, the Duchess suffered a nervous collapse. Heavily sedated at the funeral, she seemed confused, bewildered and apprehensive. Members of the family were startled as she asked them where the Duke was, as if she expected him to be joining them. Later she told Edward Heath that he ought to come to Paris, as she and the Duke would both love to see him there. After asking several more times where he had gone to, the Queen Mother gently led her to a chair. 'I know how you feel,' she said, 'I've been through it myself.'

The Duchess returned alone to Paris, a solitary, confused figure in black. Her mental and physical condition swiftly deteriorated; increasingly housebound, within a few years she was confined to her room, a ghost of the woman she had once been, until death finally released her from a twilight existence on 24 April 1986.

The last surviving child of King George V wept as he sat in his wheelchair at Barnwell Manor, watching his brother's funeral on television. Incapable of speech, virtually paralyzed, his understanding of what went on around him was limited. He found solace in his television, and particularly enjoyed *Dad's Army*, the British Home Guard comedy series starring Arthur Lowe and John Le Mesurier. Though unable to attend the wedding at Barnwell Church of his younger son Prince Richard and Miss Birgitte van Deurs on 8 July 1972, he joined them for the reception at the Manor afterwards.

His elder son Prince William, who remained a bachelor, carried within him the seeds of a tragedy which had blighted the lives of previous generations of the royal family before them. During adolescence he had suffered severe discomfort from a recurring blistery rash, and in 1970 several physicians examined him, diagnosing variegate porphyria in relative remission, a milder form of the condition which King George III had endured for so many years. A theory that the Duke also had porphyria remains unproven.[24]

William became the first member of the royal family to pilot a racing aeroplane, but it was destined to end all too soon. On 28 August 1972, he and his co-pilot, Commander Vyrell Mitchell, were killed when competing in a race from a private airfield in Staffordshire, where their plane took off and hit a tree almost at once. Ironically, it was thirty years to the week that his uncle the Duke of Kent had also met his death in a flying accident during the war.

The Duke of Gloucester lingered on in a void for almost two more years. Unlike King George VI, and the Princess Royal, he was denied the dignity of a sudden death. It was tragic that this once most active of princes should be doomed to spent his declining days in such a state.

On the evening of 9 June 1974, it was noticed that his strength was ebbing, and in the early hours of the following morning, he slipped quietly away. That same day, 10 June, was the Duke of Edinburgh's birthday, and flags were raised all over the contry in salute. When news bulletins announced

216

the death of his uncle later that morning, they were lowered to half-mast. Four days later, close to his son, and the Duke of Windsor, the last surviving prince from the nursery at York House, Sandringham, was laid to rest at Frogmore.

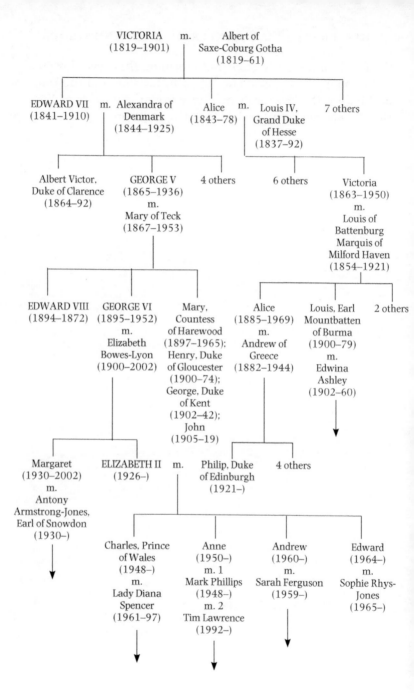

King George V's Children and Grandchildren

1. Edward Albert Christian George Andrew Patrick David, born 23 June 1894 at White Lodge, Richmond; created Prince of Wales, 23 June 1910; ascended throne as KING EDWARD VIII, 20 January 1936; abdicated 11 December 1936; created Duke of Windsor, 8 March 1937; married Mrs Wallis Simpson (nee Warfield) (1896–1986), 3 June 1937; died 28 May 1972 at Paris, without issue.

2. Albert Frederick Arthur George, born 14 December 1895 at York Cottage, Sandringham; created Duke of York, Earl of Inverness, and Baron Killarney, 5 June 1930; married Lady Elizabeth Bowes-Lyon (1900–2002), daughter of 14th Earl of Strathmore, 26 April 1923; ascended throne as KING GEORGE VI, 11 December 1936; crowned 12 May 1937 at Westminster Abbey; died 6 February 1952 at Sandringham. Issue:
   (1) H.M. Queen Elizabeth II (1926–)
   (2) Margaret (1930–2002)

3. Victoria Alexandra Alice Mary, born 25 April 1897 at York Cottage; married Viscount Lascelles, later 6th Earl of Harewood (1882–1947), 28 February 1922; declared Princess Royal, 1 January 1932; died 28 March 1965 at Harewood House, Yorks. Issue:
   (1) George, 7th Earl of Harewood (1923–2011)
   (2) Hon. Gerald Lascelles (1924–98)

4. Henry William Frederick Albert, born 31 March 1900 at York Cottage; created Duke of Gloucester, Earl of Ulster and Baron Culloden, 31 March 1928; married Lady Alice

Montagu-Douglas-Scott (1901–2004), daughter of 7th Duke of Buccleuch; died 10 June 1974 at Barnwell Manor, Northants. Issue:

(1) William (1941–72)

(2) Richard, Duke of Gloucester (1944–)

5. George Edward Alexander Edmund, born 20 December 1902 at York Cottage; created Duke of Kent, Earl of St Andrews and Baron Downpatrick, 12 October 1934; married Princess Marina of Greece and Denmark (1906–68), 29 November 1934; killed on active service over north-west Scotland, 25 August 1942. Issue:

(1) Edward, Duke of Kent (1935–)

(2) Alexandra, Hon. Mrs Angus Ogilvy (1936–)

(3) Michael (1942–)

6. John Charles Francis, born 12 July 1905 at York Cottage; died 18 January 1919 at Wood Farm, Sandringham.

Reference Notes

FOREWORD
1. *The Times* 16.4.1981
2. *Times Literary Supplement* 11.4.1980

PROLOGUE
1. Pope-Hennessy, *Queen Mary* 209

CHAPTER 1
1. Windsor, Duke of *King's Story* 1
2. Victoria, Queen, *Beloved and darling child* 168
3. ibid. 184
4. Donaldson 10–11
5. Wheeler-Bennett 18
6. Frankland 4
7. Rose, *George V* 55
8. Windsor, Duke of, *King's Story* 24–5
9. Pope-Hennessy, *Queen Mary* 392
10. ibid. 392
11. Windsor, Duke of 19
12. Alice, Countess of Athlone 78
13. *Daily Mail* 25.1.2003
14. Wheeler-Bennett 28
15. Carey 29
16. Windsor, Duke of, *King's Story* 19
17. Wakeford 208
18. Pope-Hennessy, *Queen Mary* 409
19. Wheeler-Bennett 32
20. ibid. 33

21. ibid. 39
22. ibid. 41
23. Frankland 11
24. ibid. 12
25. ibid. 13

CHAPTER 2
1. Windsor, Duke of, *King's Story* 68
2. ibid. 69–70
3. Esher Vol. III 7
4. Windsor, Duke of, *King's Story* 57
5. Morgan 153
6. Wheeler-Bennett 45
7. ibid. 47
8. Frankland 21
9. Bradford 45
10. Nicolson, George V 147
11. Windsor, Duke of, King's Story 79
12. Nicolson, *George V* 206
13. Windsor, Duke of, *King's Story* 79
14. Rose, *George V* 310
15. Frankland 26
16. ibid. 27
17. Ziegler, *Edward VIII* 32
18. as 14
19. Mackenzie 101
20. Ziegler, *Edward VIII* 35
21. ibid. 41
22. ibid. 45
23. Windsor, Duke of, *King's Story* 105

CHAPTER 3

1. Ziegler, *Edward VIII* 49
2. Windsor, Duke of, *King's Story* 108
3. Wheeler-Bennett 79
4. Frankland 35
5. Ziegler, *Edward VIII* 80
6. Wakeford 209–10
7. Wheeler-Bennett 89
8. Ziegler, *Edward VIII* 64
9. Wheeler-Bennett 90
10. ibid. 97
11. ibid. 109
12. ibid. 117
13. Pope-Hennessy, *Queen Mary* 511
14. Windsor, Duke of, *Letters from a Prince* 128
15. Battiscombe 280
16. Grieg 152
17. Pope-Hennessy, *Queen Mary* 512
18. Wheeler-Bennett 159
19. Windsor, Duke of, *King's Story* 129

CHAPTER 4

1. Frankland 52
2. Wheeler-Bennett 140
3. Ziegler, *Edward VIII* 100
4. ibid. 99
5. Donaldson 72
6. Windsor, Duke of, *King's Story* 144
7. Ziegler, *Edward VIII* 118
8. ibid. 122
9. Windsor, Duke of, *Letters from a Prince* 289
10. ibid. 140
11. ibid. 231
12. Ziegler, *Edward VIII* 171
13. Pope-Hennessy, *Queen Mary* 522

14. Harewood 27
15. Wheeler-Bennett 213
16. Bradford 112
17. Ziegler, *Edward VIII* 172
18. Rose, *Kings, Queens and Courtiers* 132
19. Ziegler, *Diana Cooper* 126–7
20. *The Times* 11.6.1974
21. Frankland 63
22. Trzebinski 134–5

CHAPTER 5

1. Windsor, Duke of, *King's Story* 223
2. ibid. 224
3. Clark 289–90
4. Pope-Hennessy, *Queen Mary* 391
5. Wheeler-Bennett 215
6. Trzebinski 137
7. Thornton 397
8. Ziegler, *Edward VIII* 201
9. ibid. 201
10. Bradford 135
11. Ziegler, *Diana Cooper* 174–5
12. Windsor, Duchess of 190–1
13. Vanderbilt 298
14. Donaldson 297
15. Van der Kiste 169
16. Bradford 141
17. Windsor, Duchess of 205
18. Astor Papers MS 1416/1/4/5 18.11.1934
19. Gore 427
20. Bradford 143–4
21. Rose, *George V* 392
22. Alice, Duchess of Gloucester 104
23. Windsor, Duke of, *King's Story* 260
24. ibid. 261

CHAPTER 6

1. Astor Papers MS 1416/1/4/15 23.1.1936
2. Ziegler, *Edward VIII* 242
3. *The Times* 22.1.1936
4. Windsor, Duke of, *King's Story* 278
5. ibid. 292
6. Ziegler, *Edward VIII* 206
7. Thornton 110–11
8. ibid. 112–13
9. Ziegler, *Edward VIII* 288
10. ibid. 290
11. ibid. 289

CHAPTER 7

1. Windsor, Duke of, *King's Story* 335
2. Donaldson 250
3. Ziegler, *Edward VIII* 324–5
4. Donaldson 253
5. Wheeler-Bennett 283
6. Nicolson, *Diaries 1930–39* 280
7. Ziegler, Edward VIII 310
8. Wheeler-Bennett 285
9. ibid. 309; Lacey 129
10. Morrah 62
11. Airlie 202
12. Windsor, Duke of, *King's Story* 397
13. Ziegler, *Edward VIII* 333
14. Windsor, Duke of, *King's Story* 414
15. ibid. 415

CHAPTER 8

1. Wheeler-Bennett 293–4
2. Donaldson 310
3. James 188–9
4. Lockhart 407
5. Nicolson, Diaries 1930–39 298
6. Donaldson 311

7. Ziegler, *Edward VIII* 340
8. ibid. 343
9. Van der Kiste 176
10. Bloch, *Duke of Windsor's war* 18
11. Time 22.3.1937
12. Wheeler-Bennett 313
13. Donaldson 323
14. ibid. 325–6
15. Ziegler, *Edward VIII* 361
16. *Times Literary Supplement* 4.1.1980
17. Ziegler, *Edward VIII* 380
18. Bryan & Murphy 354
19. Ziegler, *Edward VIII* 393
20. Wheeler-Bennett 315
21. Frankland 144
22. Thornton 178
23. *The Times* 11.11.1989
24. Alice, Duchess of Gloucester 117
25. *Daily Telegraph* 30.1.2003
26. Nicolson, *Diaries 1930–39* 405
27. Wheeler-Bennett 405
28. Windsor, Duchess of 329–30

CHAPTER 9

1. Ziegler, *Mountbatten* 125
2. Bloch, *Secret file of the Duke of Windsor* 144
3. Wheeler-Bennett 417
4. Moran 97
5. Ziegler, *Edward VIII* 425
6. Bloch, *Duke of Windsor's war* 93
7. Thornton 208
8. Wheeler-Bennett 468
9. Nicolson, *Diaries 1939–45* 100
10. *The Times* 11.6.1974
11. Wheeler-Bennett 534
12. ibid. 536–7
13. ibid. 538
14. Frankland 172
15. Astor Papers MS 1416/1/4/5 12.9.1940

16. Astor Papers MS 1416/1/4/5
    23.2.1942
17. Wheeler-Bennett 548
18. Ziegler, *Edward VIII* 484
19. Warwick, *George VI and
    Elizabeth* 151

CHAPTER 10
1. Wheeler-Bennett 551
2. ibid. 553
3. ibid. 578
4. Frankland 175
5. ibid. 177
6. Astor Papers MS 1416/1/4/8
   12.7.1944
7. Wheeler-Bennett 625
8. ibid. 626
9. ibid. 627

CHAPTER 11
1. Wheeler-Bennett 637
2. ibid. 654
3. Ziegler, *Diana Cooper* 242
4. Alsop 55
5. Ziegler, *Edward VIII* 237–8
6. Wheeler-Bennett 753
7. ibid. 754
8. Aronson, *Royal family at war*
   111–2
9. Bradford 452
10. Townsend 190
11. *Spectator* 28.9.1951
12. Ziegler, Edward VIII 498
13. ibid. 516
14. Astor Papers MS 1416/1/4/10
    2.2.1952

15. Frankland 237
16. Moran 372
17. Astor Papers MS 1416/1/4/10
    2.3.1952

CHAPTER 12
1. Thornton 256
2. ibid. 257
3. Bloch, *Secret file of the Duke of
   Windsor* 265
4. Frankland 248
5. Rose, *Kings, Queens and
   Courtiers* 132
6. Morrow 68
7. *The Times* 11.6.1974
8. Aronson 218
9. Bloch, *Secret file* 277
10. ibid. 279
11. Ziegler, *Edward VIII* 540
12. Windsor, Duke of, *Crown and
    People* 41
13. Thornton 275
14. Pope-Hennessy, *Lonely business*
    211
15. ibid. 216
16. Rose, *Kings, Queens and Courtiers*
    79
17. *The Times* 13.10.1960
18. Hall 55
19. *The Times* 29.3.1965
20. Frankland 289
21. ibid. 292
22. Bloch, *Secret file* 300
23. ibid. 301
24. Röhl, Warren, Hunt, 215,
    218

Bibliography

I MANUSCRIPTS

Astor Papers, Reading University

II BOOKS

Airlie, Mabell, *Thatched with gold*. Hutchinson, 1962

Alice, Princess, Countess of Athlone, *For my grandchildren: some reminiscences of Her Royal Highness Princess Alice*. Evans Bros, 1966

Alice, Princess, Duchess of Gloucester, *The memoirs of Princess Alice, Duchess of Gloucester*. Collins, 1983

Alsop, Susan Mary, *To Marietta from Paris, 1945–1960*. Weidenfeld & Nicolson, 1976

Aronson, Theo, *Royal family: years of transition*. John Murray, 1983

—— *The Royal family at war*, John Murray, 1993

Battiscombe, Georgina, *Queen Alexandra*. Constable, 1969

Bloch, Michael, *The Duke of Windsor's war*. Weidenfeld & Nicolson, 1982

—— *The secret file of the Duke of Windsor*. Bantam, 1988

Bradford, Sarah, *George VI*. Weidenfeld & Nicolson, 1989

Bryan III, James, & Murphy, Charles, *The Windsor story*. Granada, 1979

Carey, M.C., *Princess Mary*. Nisbet, 1922

Cathcart, Helen, *Anne, the Princess Royal: a Princess for our times*. W.H. Allen, 1988

Clark, Alan (ed.), *A good innings: the private papers of Viscount Lee of Fareham*. John Murray, 1974

Donaldson, Frances, *Edward VIII*. Weidenfeld & Nicolson, 1974

Dupuch, Etienne, *Tribune story*. Ernest Benn, 1967

Esher, Viscount, *The journals and letters of Reginald, Viscount Esher, 3 vols*. Nicholson & Watson, 1934

Frankland, Noble, *Prince Henry, Duke of Gloucester*. Weidenfeld & Nicolson, 1980

Gore, John, *King George V: a personal memoir*. John Murray, 1941

Grieg, Geordie, *Louis and the Prince: a story of politics, intrigue and royal Friendship*, Hodder & Stoughton, 1999

Hall, Geoffrey, *Fifty years gardening at Harewood*. EP, 1978

Harewood, Earl of, *The tongs and the bones: memoirs of Lord Harewood*, Weidenfeld & Nicoloson, 1981

Hibbert, Christopher, *The court of St James's: the monarch at work from Victoria to Elizabeth II*. Weidenfeld & Nicolson, 1979

Hough, Richard, *Born royal: the lives and loves of the young Windsors (1894–1937)*. Andre Deutsch, 1988

Howarth, Patrick, *King George VI*. Hutchinson, 1987

James, Robert Rhodes, *Victor Cazalet: a portrait*. Hamish Hamilton, 1976

King, Stella, *Princess Marina, her life and times*. Cassell, 1969

Lacey, Robert, *Majesty: Elizabeth II and the house of Windsor*. Hutchinson, 1977

Lockhart, J.G., *Cosmo Gordon Lang*. Hodder & Stoughton, 1949

Longford, Elizabeth, *The royal house of Windsor*. Weidenfeld & Nicolson, 1974

Mackenzie, Compton, *Windsor tapestry*. Rich & Cowan, 1938

Middlemas, Keith, *The life and times of George VI*. Weidenfeld & Nicolson, 1974

Moran, Lord, *Winston Churchill: the struggle for survival 1940–1965*. Constable, 1966

Morgan, Kenneth O. (ed.), *Lloyd George family letters 1885–1936*. University of Wales Press/Oxford University Press, 1973

Morrah, Dermot, *Princess Elizabeth, Duchess of Edinburgh*. Odhams, 1950

Morrow, Ann, *The Queen Mother*. Granada, 1984

Nicolson, Harold, *Diaries and letters 1930–1939*, (ed.) Nigel Nicolson. Collins, 1966

—— *Diaries and letters 1939–1945*, (ed.) Nigel Nicolson. Collins, 1967

—— *King George V, his life and reign*. Constable, 1952

Pope-Hennessy, James, *A lonely business: a self-portrait of James Pope-Hennessy*. Weidenfeld & Nicolson, 1981

—— *Queen Mary, 1867–1953*. Allen & Unwin, 1959

Röhl, John C.G., Warren, Martin & Hunt, David, *Purple secret: genes, 'madness' and the royal houses of Europe*, Bantam, 1998

Rose, Kenneth, *King George V*. Weidenfeld & Nicolson, 1985

Thornton, Michael, *Royal feud: the Queen Mother and the Duchess of Windsor*. Michael Joseph, 1985

Townsend, Peter, *Time and chance: an autobiography*. Collins, 1978

Trzebinski, Errol, *The lives of Beryl Markham: Out of Africa's hidden free spirit and Denys Finch Hatton's last great love*, Heinemann, 1993

Van der Kiste, John, *Edward VII's children*. Sutton, 1989

Vanderbilt, Gloria, and Furness, Thelma, Viscountess, *Double exposure*. Frederick Muller, 1959

Victoria, Queen, and Victoria, Consort of Frederick III, German Emperor,

Beloved and darling child: last letters between Queen Victoria and her eldest daughter 1886–1901, (ed.) Agatha Ramm. Sutton, 1990

Wakeford, Geoffrey, *The Princess Royal*. Robert Hale, 1973

Warwick, Christopher, *George and Marina, Duke and Duchess of Kent*. Weidenfeld & Nicolson, 1988

—— *King George VI and Queen Elizabeth: a portrait*. Sidgwick & Jackson, 1985

Wheeler-Bennett, John W., *King George VI: his life and reign*. Macmillan, 1958

Whiting, Audrey, *The Kents*. Hutchinson, 1985

Windsor, Duke of, formerly King Edward VIII, *The crown and the people, 1902–1953*. Cassell, 1953

—— *A King's story: the memoirs of HRH the Duke of Windsor*. Cassell, 1951

—— *Letters from a Prince: Edward, Prince of Wales to Mrs Freda Dudley Ward, March 1918–January 1921*, (ed.) Rupert Godfrey. Little, Brown, 1998

Windsor, Duchess of, *The heart has its reasons*. Michael Joseph, 1956

Zeigler, Philip, *Diana Cooper*. Hamish Hamilton, 1981

—— *Mountbatten: the official biography*, Collins, 1985

—— *Edward VIII: the official biography*. Collins, 1990

III PERIODICALS

Daily Mail
Daily Telegraph
Royalty Digest
Spectator
Time
The Times
Times Literary Supplement

BIBLIOGRAPHY

Index

Abbreviations: A, GVI – Albert, Duke of York, later George VI (according to context); E – Edward VIII; G – George, Duke of Kent; H – Henry, Duke of Gloucester. Nicknames are only given if used in text.

INDEX